FUTURE PERFECT

FUTURE
PERFECT

P R E S E N T
E M P O W E R M E N T

A Road Map for Success
in the 21st Century

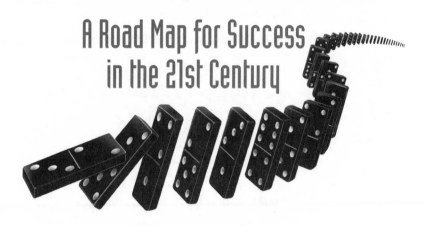

WILLIAM B. WILLIAMS

PATRIOT'S
PUBLISHING

Patriot's Publishing
P.O. Box 4307
Lisle, IL 60532

Cover illustration and
book design by Tilman Reitzle

Photo credits appear on page 380.

Printed in the United States of America

1 3 5 7 9 10 8 6 4 2

Publisher's Cataloging-in-Publication Data

Williams, William B.,
Future perfect: present empowerment /
by William B. Williams.—Lisle, IL :
Patriot's Pub. Co., c1995
p.   cm.
ISBN: 0–9645641–0-6
1. Forecasting. 2. History—Philosophy
I. Title.
CB 161.W55   1995
901 dc20   95-67587

DEDICATION

---

to Jonathan (Jo) E. Fremd (d. 1965)
Master at Lake Forest Academy (1944–1965)

As long as one of us students is still alive,
you have not left us yet, Jo.

ACKNOWLEDGMENTS

The number of skills and, therefore, people who must contribute to make a first-class book is truly astounding. For the sake of brevity, I will only be able to list those who helped with this project and their skills.

Pamela Jean (Cute, little, sweet Pammy) Peterson—
    Manuscript computer entry
Henry D. Williams—brother and prime mover
David Thalberg—Planned Television Arts
Jerrold Jenkins—overall planning and coordination consultant
Dan Poynter—marketing consultant
John Kremer—marketing consultant
Carolyn Porter—One-on-One Consulting
Agincourt Press—
    David Rubel
    Sarah Weir
    Tilman Reitzle, the world's greatest book designer
Howard J. Rubenstein Associates, Inc.—
    Howard Rubenstein, public relations
    Mary Ann Bohrer
    Joanne Derby
    Laura Klein
Denhard & Stewart, Inc.—
    Jeff Stewart, advertising
    Caroline Barnett
    Lee Wiggins—copywriter
Sensible Solutions—Judith Appelbaum, testimonial consultant
    Florence Janovic
Nancy Shore—fact checking
Alice Albert—photo research
David Plakke—photographer
Ingram Book Co.—book wholesalers
    Wanda Smith, publisher relations
    Keith Owens, purchasing
    Shannon Smith, advertising
The Newman Group—Mary Mayotte, media consultants
RLS Associates, Inc.—Robert L. Smith, Jr., distribution
Publishers Design Service—Mark Dressler, book consultants
Design and Production Service—Ed Sturmer, consultant
The Clan
Darlene (Ms. Hassenboodle) Hass—I do not suppose that authors very often have the opportunity to have a person with an I.Q. over 145 enter their manuscripts in a computer. I have had such a pleasure and have met perfection.
Jennifer (Yennifernian) Dickey—Without Jennifer, this project might not have gotten much beyond a manuscript. The woman is incomparable and indescribable.
And others yet to come.

CONTENTS

CAUTION: *The reader of this book is about to embark on an intellectual journey of great magnitude. Due to its unusual nature, **this book cannot be skimmed**. To understand it, the reader must necessarily read this book word-for-word, front to back. Additionally, it should be read within a period of no more than four or five days. To do otherwise will leave the reader unenlightened.*

APOLOGIA

Every expert in every field upon which this work alights will correctly decry the brevity of this treatment. The importance of the work lies in its very breadth rather than in its depth. In fact, the precise purpose of the work is to display the whole rather than plumb the depths of any one area of knowledge. To drive every nail in every coffin would result in a work of preposterous length. Many single sentences in the following work have had or could have had entire books written about them. The author is more than content to leave to the experts in their respective fields an in-depth explanation of their field to the general reader. For the inevitable case of error or misinterpretation that of necessity must creep into a work so broad, the author alone is fully responsible. When error is discovered in the work, please be so kind as to inform the author so future printings can be corrected.

The Gauntlet Tossed Down

WHEN I WAS FOURTEEN YEARS OLD, I had the fortunate experience of attending one of America's finest prep schools. It was a demanding environment, not only intellectually but also on one's time. The entire day, from 6:00 A.M. wake-up to lights-out at 10:00 P.M., was fully programmed. There was rarely any free time; but when there was, quite often several of us would meet in someone's room and have discussions the likes of which I have not encountered since. The topics of these discussions ranged over all that is important to young, fresh boys, but the discussions in which I took particular delight concerned the fundamental questions of the universe: How and when did everything begin? How does one live the best possible life? What is the purpose of Life? In short, what is going on around here?

Of course, the answers were not forthcoming, but it was exciting as we let our minds soar in unfettered freedom against those mighty questions. Some of those minds belonged to future National Merit Scholarship winners, summa cum laude graduates of Harvard, and one mind that taught itself ancient Greek in study hall for lack of other challenges. During these discussions, my thinking evolved to the point that I knew I wanted to live the "best" possible life, but I did not know what "best" meant. Does "best" mean living like a country squire or living like Mother Teresa helping the poor? I did not know. It is impossible to determine what is ultimately "best" without knowing what the ultimate goals and rules of life are.

In my own mind I thought life to be somewhat like a game of Monopoly that is already in progress when we sit down to play. We dimly and slowly become conscious that we are players when we are babies and first realize that our wiggling toes belong to us. Meanwhile, the token that represents our body has already been chosen for us by the genes we received from our parents. Many decisions in the game have already been decided for us by our parents—where we live, what our socioeconomic level is, who our neighbors are, etc. Slowly at first, but gradually as we grow, we take control of our own game. We have to decide: Do we buy Boardwalk? Should I trade for a Monopoly? What do I want my career to be? Whom shall I marry? What type of lifestyle do I want to live?

On what basis do we make these decisions? In Monopoly it is easy because every game comes with a rule book. A reading of the rule book gives each player a complete and intimate knowledge of the purposes and goals of the game. It explains precisely how to win and the penalties for error. With these clear goals in mind, correct decision-making becomes very easy. We know that if we land on Boardwalk, we should buy it. However, with life we have no rule book. We do not know what the ultimate purposes and goals are. If we do not know what the rules are, how can we be sure that we are making the best possible decisions? We cannot. Therefore, we need the rule book. We need to answer the most profound questions of existence before we can do our "best" in the game of life.

As we became older I noticed that we young boys asked ourselves these profound questions less and less. The discussions turned to dating, after-shave lotions, and colleges, but I had become intrigued by these profound questions. I kept them in the back of my mind and went away with them to university. I soon discovered that the only relationship between my fundamental questions of the universe and the university was a semantic one.

I was coming to the conclusion that not only did no one seem to know what was going on around here in a profound sense, but that, preposterously, no one was interested. I had one last hope. The wisest and intellectually most courageous man I have ever known was a professor at my old prep school. I returned to ask him the ultimate questions of the universe. When I found him, he was with several ex-students and had to leave shortly for a faculty dinner. Our brief talk was amiable, but clearly it was not the appropriate moment for my questions. I left. When I returned months later, he was dead.

I know now that if my wise professor had held any of the keys to the questions of the universe, he would not have told me. The incredible adventure of the mind on which I was to embark for the next twenty-five years of my life was reward enough, but when the answers began to materialize, I was astounded. Not only did the most profound questions of the universe have verifiable answers, but unbelievably the future became quite easy to predict as well.

I invite the reader to accompany me on a profound intellectual journey of immense scope that will take us to the beginning of time and to the end of time—To the edges of the universe and inside the human brain. We will even find out what truly makes human beings human. By the end of our journey, we will be able to answer for ourselves the most profound questions. We will be able to verifiably understand what the true position of humankind is and what really has gone on, is going on, and will go on around here. We will learn the most fundamental and most important knowledge (database), which will be of immense value throughout the life of the reader. We will be able to verifiably determine the fundamental laws of the universe in any and all areas in which we are interested. We will be among the first humans to ever provably and verifiably know in the most profound sense what reality is. Armed with a simple logic, we will be able to control our own lives and have our goals and dreams come true. All questions can be answered.

For instance, the classic question "Which came first, the chicken or the egg?" has been a model throughout western civilization since Roman times of a question that cannot be answered. No amount of thinking about this question will render us an answer. An intellect like Albert Einstein's could think about this problem for a hundred years and never arrive at a satisfactory answer. However, the question becomes easily solvable when we become aware of two facts:

1. Reptiles have been laying eggs since they first inhabited the Earth 360 million years ago.

2. Birds, in our case chickens, evolved from reptiles 160 million years ago and inherited their egg-laying method of reproduction.

Presto! The answer: The egg came well before the chicken.

A person without those two facts, even with the intellect of an Einstein, could never resolve the question. Having the abundance of facts available to our generation is what will enable us to solve whatever problems we choose. That is why these problems are solvable for the first time in the history of the world.

If you felt the answer to the chicken and the egg question was unimportant, may I suggest to you that the question was unimportant. If we ask important questions, we will derive important answers.

Before we leave for our journey of the mind, we need to make a stop at the armory. We cannot go unarmed on our quest. We need to learn an extremely powerful system of logic, the Black Box Technique. For if we go with blank baby eyes we will come back with blank baby answers. Also, we must leave some baggage behind at the armory, for we cannot go with our preconceived notions from this society. We can take only the inherent power of our minds.

Now please follow me to the armory.

CHAPTER ONE

The Black Box Technique

CAUTION: *Slow reading zone ahead. It may be advisable to slow down one's normal reading rate and possibly re-read certain paragraphs to thoroughly acquaint oneself with the concepts presented. The concepts presented in this chapter are not difficult but merely require persistent and sustained attention by the reader. Normal speed can be resumed in Chapter Two.*

1. The Truth-Meter

IF WE ARE TO GO ON A QUEST FOR "TRUTH," we will have to take along a method for recognizing truth when we find it. Truth, reality, the answers to the most profound questions in the universe—call it what you will—are actually different ways of saying "facts." We are searching for the facts concerning Reality. Facts can be placed in two categories:

1. Those that we witness *first-hand*. For instance, we see a car accident. We observe it and accept it as the "truth."

2. All other facts from all other sources are the second kind that we learn about *second-hand*.

For example, let us imagine that a person tells us there has been a car accident. Do we have a fact or not? Let us say we do not choose to accept it as a fact because we have insufficient evidence. Then a policeman runs up to us and says there has been a terrible accident, phone for an ambulance. Now we are fairly certain there has been an accident. When we see an ambulance pass by with injured people and tow trucks towing cars we become certain that the truth is that there was indeed an accident. Some people would have accepted the car accident as the "truth," when it was first reported to them. Some people would have accepted it as the "truth" after the policeman told them, and some not until after they saw the accident victims. Therefore, we know three things about truth:

1. For an individual to accept second-hand information as the "truth," he or she must be presented with a sufficient amount of evidence for him or her to accept it.

2. The amount of evidence required to convince an individual of the "truth" varies from individual to individual.

3. Truth is not an "either-or" condition. All of us have beliefs which we "kind of" believe to be true, but which we are not absolutely sure are true. Therefore, each of us has various levels of confidence that something is true.

An example: If I hold an ordinary water glass six feet above a concrete floor and then release it, the water glass will fall to the floor and break. I could cite this event as an example of the "truth" of gravity at work. However, another person could assert that the truth is that all water glasses are controlled by hobgoblins on the planet Mars. I cannot disprove that there are hobgoblins on Mars controlling water glasses. I cannot take the person to Mars and show the person first-hand that there are no hobgoblins. All I can do is offer a preponderance of evidence to show that gravity is the agent at work. More than this, unfortunately, is not in the power of any author. If the other person has little or no evidence, then gravity is to be tentatively accepted as the truth. A preponderance of evidence is the test used by every civil court in this land to determine truth.

Additionally, we have a weapon of logic that can tell us under what conditions to absolutely accept truth. Two of the greatest intellects ever produced in the human species, Aristotle (384–322 B.C.) and Sir Isaac Newton (1642–1727), arrived at the same conclusion separated by almost 2,000 years of history.

Aristotle: "Predicting an event and the proving that it occurs is the highest form of proof."

Sir Isaac Newton: "The true test of a Scientific Principle is if it can be predicted."

When an event is predicted and then occurs, we can rely upon it as the truth. For example, let us say an eclipse of the sun has been predicted. If the precise time is predicted in advance and the eclipse actually occurs at the predicted moment, then the person who made the prediction must know what he is talking about. It is the highest level of proof, and we should rely upon it. If we are presented with merely a preponderance of evidence, we can tentatively pencil it in, but when an event is predicted and occurs, then we are to accept it as fact. Therefore, if an event is predicted and then occurs, we can be confident that we have discovered fact. The minimum that we can accept as the truth is a preponderance of evidence. Between two or more candidates for truth we can tentatively accept as true the one that has a preponderance of evidence.[1] The evidence must also be able to pass our test for truth.

Equally important is to know what not to accept as true. If a candidate for truth has substantially less evidence that can pass our test for truth, or no supporting evidence at all, then that candidate for truth is an opinion. Opinions are like noses: everybody has one. Opinions are not to be accepted as the truth. Opinions, therefore, cannot be relied upon to render us correct results if used in our developing system of logic.

---

1. We will find out what to do later in this chapter if no candidates for the truth have a preponderance of evidence.

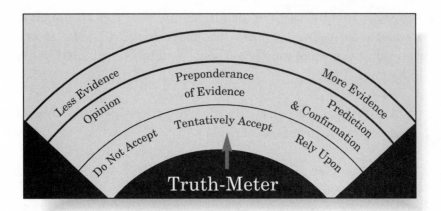

The complete truth, when we find it, must be able to tell us not only what is going on around here, but also what has gone on in the past and what will go on in the future. Therefore, we will need tools of logic for dealing with the past, present, and future.

2. Cause and Effect

Random Events—Definition: Events that have no causes.

If we heard that our next-door neighbor, George, was barbecuing in his backyard and at 6:00 P.M. was struck in the head and killed by a meteorite,[2] we might be tempted to conclude, "It was one chance in a billion, a freak, random accident." We would be wrong. It would not be a random event. If we had known of the existence of the meteoroid, its precise course and speed and all other facts pertaining to it, it would have been relatively simple to determine through mathematics that it would fall near George's house at 6:00 P.M. days, weeks or even

---

2. Meteor: The luminous phenomenon observed when a meteoroid is heated by its entry into the Earth's atmosphere. Meteorite: That part of a relatively large meteoroid that survives passage through the atmosphere and falls to the surface of a planet or moon as a mass of metal or stone. Meteoroid: Any of the many small, solid bodies traveling through outer space.

months prior to George's "random" event. If we also knew that George normally barbecues in his backyard at 6:00 P.M., we could have told George well in advance that he had an excellent probability of being killed by a meteorite. By the time the meteor entered Earth's atmosphere, it would have been a certainty. We could have yelled out the window to George that he was about to be killed, but since we lacked the facts about the meteoroid we concluded it was a random event. ***No event is a random event.***

What we call a random event is merely an event about whose causes we have insufficient information to predict the event in advance. It is a case of our being unaware of the precise causes of the event, not that the event did not have causes. Let us examine the case of an event that epitomizes randomness—the next number to come up on a roulette wheel. The very existence of the game depends on the next number's being random. In reality, the next number is not random, but is 100 percent predictable. If we could precisely measure the causes of the event—acceleration of the roulette ball, its coefficient of friction, the precise speed of the wheel, the friction of the wheel on its pivot point, and the many more small forces (causes) involved—we could determine precisely into which slot the ball is going to fall (the effect). Casinos do not let us measure these forces (causes), so we lack the facts required and call the event random. I cannot think of one event that is truly random because I cannot think of any event that does not have causes, and I challenge the reader to think of one.[3]

If there is no event that does not have causes, then all events must have causes. If all events are the result of causes

---

3. Particle physicists and quantum mechanics have a principle known as Heisenberg's Uncertainty Principle that, just like the casino, prevents us from obtaining the data and therefore from making an accurate prediction in some quantum-level applications. However, nothing in the principle states that an electron, for example, was not caused by something and that the electron will not cause an effect in the future, which is the point under discussion.

then by definition all events are effects. If all events are effects, then the events that caused the effects—which by definition are the causes—are also effects. Further, by definition, if all events are effects and if all effects have causes, then all events are cause-and-effect relationships. At this point I believe an example would be most helpful.

If I set two dominoes on a table and knock one over so that it falls and knocks the second domino down, clearly the first domino was the cause and the second domino's fall was the effect. If I set the two dominoes back up and place a third domino in line, then when I knock the first domino over, the second domino falls and strikes the third, knocking it over also. From the previous example, we know that the first domino was the cause and the second domino was the effect, but when the second domino struck the third domino, the second domino changed from an effect and became a cause and the third domino's fall became the effect. Therefore, an effect becomes a cause, depending upon the time frame from which it is viewed. In other words, had we been able to stop time when the second domino was falling we would have observed a simple cause-and-effect relationship. However, by stopping time after the third domino fell down we have two causes and one effect. Therefore, effects are converted into causes by the passage of time.[4]

By placing a continuing number of dominoes in sequence on the table, we create a model of simple events interacting over time. If we look upon whichever dominoes are currently colliding as the present, then the past would be the dominoes that have already fallen, and the future would be the dominoes that have yet to fall. In this case, the cause-and-effect relationship

---

4. The fact that effects are turned into causes by the passage of time was first recognized by John Stuart Mill (1806–1873), the son of a Scottish philosopher. John Stuart Mill is generally considered the smartest person who ever lived. *The Guinness Book of World Records* reported that his I.Q. is estimated to have been over 200. He studied ancient Greek at three years old.

between dominoes is known with 100 percent certainty. Then we can predict the future with 100 percent certainty—the next domino will fall down, and the next, and the next. We can predict the future as long as there are dominoes (events) and as long as we know the cause-and-effect relationships (laws) that govern these events.

Clearly our weaponry is taking a quantum leap in terms of power. The future, which appears to be the most difficult of the past, present, and future to determine, does not appear so formidable. However, we still need a weapon for determining facts that have occurred in the past about which we have little or no knowledge. Let us return to our long line of erect dominoes on the table and observe them as we knock the first one down again. Let us watch the chain reaction for a while and then turn our eyes away from the dominoes for a few moments, during which time we know nothing of the events occurring on the table. Then we look back at the table and observe the final few collisions between the dominoes. If we call the time period when we looked back at the dominoes and witnessed the final few collisions as the present, then from that reference point we have a period of time in history when we turned our heads from the table, in which we do not know what happened. However, we do know precisely what occurred to the dominoes preceding our gap in knowledge, because in this case we witnessed it ourselves. In other cases we could accept second-hand information (history books, for instance) as to what had occurred, if the second-hand information had passed our test for truth. Either way, we know precisely what occurred prior to our gap in knowledge. If we view the period of time in the past, when we knew with 100 percent accuracy what occurred as the artificial present, then we can use the same technique that we used to predict the future to in fact predict the past. We predict what the effects must be of the causes currently occurring in the artificial present. At any time that we have 100 percent knowledge of an event in the past, present, or future and 100 percent knowledge of the cause-and-effect relationships (laws) governing that event, we can predict with 100 percent accuracy what the subsequent events were or will be.

Our weapons grow even more powerful, but we have only used them on dominoes, which are extremely simple in their cause-and-effect relationships. How will they work on events that are more complex and on events of which we do not have 100 percent knowledge either of the event or the cause-and-effect relationship (law)?

3. Occam's Razor

In 14th-century England lived a very wise man by the name of William of Occam (c.1285–c.1349), a Franciscan monk. He postulated a little-known tool of logic called Occam's razor. It states "It is vain to do with more what can be done with fewer." In modern English, "No more things should be presumed to exist than are absolutely necessary." For our purposes: When an event is unknown, the simplest answer that fits the other known facts is to be tentatively accepted as the truth. A thinker no less illustrious than Bertrand Russell (1872–1970) has stated, "I have myself found this a most fruitful principle in logical analysis."

4. The Black Box Technique

The most powerful weapon in our arsenal is the Black Box Technique. The Black Box Technique can be deployed when we have no candidates for the truth that our truth-meter permits us to accept. With the Black Box Technique we will be able to determine with varying degrees of confidence what is occurring in events of which we have no direct knowledge. In the case of the dominoes, it can be visualized as a tunnel or open-ended Black Box—hence the name—through which the line of dominoes passes. We have no idea what is in the Black Box or of the cause-and-effect relationships (laws) that occur inside of it. All we know is that a line of falling dominoes enters the box and then a while later, the dominoes on the other side of the box begin to fall.

This case is very different from the case wherein we turned our head from the dominoes because in that case we knew there were dominoes in the sequence, and therefore all we had to do was predict the cause-and-effect relationship (law). In this case of the Black Box we do not know what is in the box and therefore cannot know what the cause-and-effect relationships (laws) might be.

If we apply Occam's razor to our domino problem, we can hypothesize that there are dominoes within the Black Box identical to the ones outside. If it is true that there are identical dominoes in the Black Box, then we know that identical cause-and-effect relationships (laws) must be governing what is occurring inside the Black Box. Then by formulating tests for the presence or absence both of identical dominoes and of these cause-and-effect relationships (laws), we can attempt to compile a preponderance of evidence that will satisfy our test for truth. For instance, if we time how long it takes for one domino to knock down another and then we time whatever it is that goes on inside the Black Box, we can divide the first time into the second. If the answer is a whole number, say 5, then we have not only discovered evidence indicating the presence of identical dominoes, but also if there are identical dominoes in the Black Box, there must be five of them. These two facts alone are, in my opinion, insufficient to pass our test for truth. Let us proceed by testing for the presence of five identical dominoes. If there are five dominoes in the Black Box, then the Black Box must be a certain physical length for our cause-and-effect relationship to operate. The Black Box can then be measured to determine if it is the predicted length. If it is, then we have additional evidence for our truth-meter, and, continuing this process, at some point our conditions for truth will be met. If either of these tests had rendered us an answer incompatible with identical dominoes' being in the Black Box, we would then know that identical dominoes could not be in the Black Box. We would then return to Occam's razor and hypothesize the next simplest answer that explains what is in the Black Box—perhaps dominoes that are not identical to the ones in view. We would then formulate new tests to determine the presence of those dominoes and/or cause-and-effect relationships (laws). We could continue this process until we arrived at the "truth" or we failed to find the "truth" due to a lack of facts for which to test prior to achieving our needed preponderance of evidence. Therefore, we can fail to find the "truth" only when we have an insufficient amount of fact concerning the event in question. Fortunately, we live in the "age of facts"—the information age. Within the life span of the elderly residents of this age, humanity's accumulation of facts has become many times the number of facts available to any previous human seekers of truth. This superabundance of fact, combined with the Black Box Technique, is an incredibly powerful weapon that will permit us to attain comprehensions of reality that were impossible to previous generations.

We now have a weapon that, interestingly enough, enables us to know things about which we do not know anything. But what about complexity?

5. Complexity—Our Ally

What about when events become complex? Complex events can be our allies. A complex event by definition has a large number of smaller events occurring within and around that event. The more events there are occurring, the more opportunities we have to use the Black Box and, therefore, the greater the likelihood of success. If we view the unknown event as a castle into which we must break to find out what is going on, the more complex the castle is, with more roads leading up to it, and more gates by which to enter, the more opportunities we have to gain entry. In other words, the fact that an event is complex usually means that there are more angles to it, and therefore the potential to derive "more" information about it is greater.

Let us investigate the condition of an unknown event with a higher level of complexity. Imagine that we walk onto the factory floor of a manufacturing company and are shown a curtain behind which we have no knowledge of what is occurring. What we want to find out is precisely what is occurring behind the curtain and, if possible, the color of whatever is there. An apparently impossible task. First, let us determine what occurs immediately before and after the unknown event. Prior to the unknown event, raw yellow plastic periodically is placed behind the curtain. At the other end of the curtain, yellow plastic bowls periodically emerge. If we Black Box the unknown events behind the curtain, then by using Occam's razor, the simplest explanation that fits the facts, we can accept the premise that whatever is behind the curtain transforms raw plastic into plastic bowls. Furthermore, insofar as we are in a factory, we can also tentatively hypothesize that the agent causing the transformation is a machine or machines. We can test for the presence of machinery by inspecting a bowl for "telltale" tool marks. Let us say we find the tool marks. We now know that behind the curtain there is machinery transforming raw plastic into bowls. Perhaps you and I, being unknowledgeable about the conversion of raw plastic into bowls, could be no more precise about the machinery behind the curtain. However, if we had the sum total of the world's knowledge of converting raw plastic into bowls with us, perhaps in the form of the world's foremost expert in the field, then we could, thanks to the expert's knowledge of cause-and-effect relationships (laws) about plastic, determine the method of manufacture—extrusion, injection molding, pressing, whatever. If we had even more precise knowledge of the conditions before and after the unknown event behind the curtain, such as identifying the change in location of individual molecules of plastic, our expert could tell us the precise amount of heat involved in the process. If our expert knows the temperature at which the plastic was formed, he can then derive the amount of pressure used. If our expert knows the temperature and pressure used, he can then derive the amount of time the plastic was exposed to the temperature and pressure. By now, our expert could not only tell us precisely what is going on behind the curtain, but could also give us a list of the manufacturers and model numbers of the machines that could possibly be behind the curtain. The Black Box has done its job, but there is more.

Let us Black Box the machine itself. If there is uniqueness among plastics-forming machines, we could test for it and determine which machine is behind the curtain. By looking up the model of the machine in the machinery manufacturer's catalog, we could determine what color the machinery manufacturer paints that particular model. We would then not only know precisely what occurs behind the curtain but also have a high probability of knowing what color it is.

As we analyze what we have just done, three points become apparent. First, the more precise knowledge we have concerning the cause-and-effect relationships (laws) and the more precise knowledge we have concerning the events before and after the unknown event, then the more information we can derive about the unknown event. Second, the more complex an unknown event is, the greater our opportunities are for deriving information about that event. Third, if we view the event or events prior to the unknown event as the past and the event or events following the unknown event as the future and the unknown event itself as the present, then in our example, the expert derived the present from knowing the past and the future. Moreover, if we were to change the position of the Black Box (the unknown event) to either the future or the past, our expert would still be able to solve it. For instance, if we told the expert precisely what the raw material was (the past) and precisely how the machine operates (the present), then quite clearly he could tell us precisely what the finished product would be (the future). Additionally, if we had no idea what the raw material was (the past) but if we told the expert precisely how the machine operates (the present) and precisely what the finished product would be (the future), then he could tell us precisely what the raw material must be (the past). Therefore, if we know precisely the events occurring at any two of the three periods of time concerning an unknown event, and if we know precisely the cause-and-effect relationship (laws) governing the unknown event, that unknown event can be precisely determined regardless of whether it occurred in the past, present, or future. The Black Box is a very powerful weapon, indeed.

6. Einsteinian Thought Experiment

An additional weapon of logic that we will find extremely valuable is one of the techniques used by Albert Einstein (1879–1955) to create his famous theories of General and Special Relativity. He called the technique a Thought Experiment (in German, a *Gedanken* experiment). An Einsteinian Thought Experiment allows us to use our imagination to mentally travel to any place in the universe at any point in time—past, present, or future—and mentally conduct any experiment that we choose. We can even be a participant in our imaginary experiment if we so choose, or merely be an observer.

Einstein used thought experiments extensively. In one of his thought experiments, he imagined a man in an elevator in outer space, who was therefore weightless. Einstein imagined what would happen if the elevator suddenly descended very rapidly. The result would be that the roof of the elevator would slam into the man's head. Then Einstein imagined how the man in the elevator would analyze what had just happened to him. The man in the elevator would have no way of knowing whether the elevator descended very rapidly or if he himself had accelerated upward very rapidly. Hence, what happened is relative to the perspective of the observer. Einstein, through the use of thought experiments, was able to change his relative perspective. In so doing he gained such enormous insight into reality that he is generally regarded, along with John Stuart Mill, as one of the greatest intellectuals of the past two centuries. Not bad for a simple technique that in essence is merely sophisticated daydreaming!

So far, we have discussed how to determine a totally unknown event when the previous and subsequent events are precisely known. What happens when we do not have absolute precision? The less precise our information, the less precise we can be about what is in the Black Box. It is as if we were attempting to peer into the Black Box through a microscope. As our information becomes less and less precise, we slowly go out of focus until, at some extremely low level of precision, the image goes out of focus entirely. However, in real-world conditions, we usually have some facts about what is in the Black Box that more than make up for our lack of precision. Also, we very rarely need to know with absolute precision what is in the Black Box. For example, it is not very informative to attempt to discover how many times during his life Genghis Khan blew his nose.

7. Trends: Sir Isaac Newton's First Law of Motion (modified)

"A body in motion tends to stay in motion unless acted upon by an outside force (cause)." If, in the course of accurately determining the past and the present, we discover a trend, say an increasing murder rate, then when we predict the future, we must predict the continuation of that trend unless we can identify rather specific cause-and-effect relationships that will halt and/or reverse the trend. In other words, if a trend is demonstrated to be occurring, then the burden of proof is on the predictor of the future to identify the specific cause-and-effect relationships that will modify that trend. Failure to do so means that the trend should be predicted to continue. To put it in more Newtonian terms: "A trend in motion tends to stay in motion unless acted upon by an outside force (cause)."

8. Anomalous Data

When we are Black Boxing an unknown event and we review what data we *do* have, not only about the unknown event but also about what occurred before and after the unknown event, we should actively seek anomalies in our data. We should be very aware of any information that is unexpected, does not seem to fit with the rest of the information, is irregular or abnormal. We should focus on the anomaly and attempt to determine what caused it using our Black Box Technique. Very often, resolving the anomaly or anomalies will either give us great insight into the original problem or solve it outright. An example would be if an archaeologist found a fossilized skeleton of a 50,000 year-old Neanderthal man with a wrist watch on it. Needless to say, focus on what caused the wrist watch to be there.

9. Subtraction

Up to this point, we have used our Black Box Technique on very simple problems. Let us, with the aid of an Einsteinian Thought Experiment, use the Black Box Technique on a more complex problem. Let us imagine that all knowledge about the year 1953 is completely destroyed. All the information in libraries, every human being's memory, old newsreels, everything about 1953 has vanished. We have no direct knowledge about 1953. However, we have all the knowledge about 1952 and 1954 still existing. We want to know what happened in 1953. All events that occurred in 1953 are in our Black Box. However, just as with the falling line of dominoes, we know precisely what occurred prior to the Black Box (1952), and we know precisely what occurred after the Black Box (1954). We can determine what occurred in 1953 about any subject in which we are interested by noting its condition at the end of 1952 and comparing it to (subtracting it from) its condition at the beginning of 1954. Any and all changes in its condition must have occurred in 1953. For example, at the end of 1952 the Korean War was being fought. At the beginning of 1954, there was no war in Korea. Therefore, the Korean War must have ended in 1953.

Another example: If we want to know how many television sets were sold in the United States in 1953, we can subtract the number of households with televisions in 1952 from the number in 1954. This will give us an excellent approximation of the number of television sets sold in 1953.

We are literally *subtracting* or noting the difference between a later period and an earlier period. The difference between the two must have been what occurred during the interim period.

If we use the Black Box Technique in conjunction with our Truth-Meter, Occam's razor, Einsteinian Thought Experiments, Complexity, Newtonian Trends, Anomalies, and Subtraction, then our knowledge that everything operates by cause-and-effect relationship, and the incredible amount of information available to our generation, means that very little can remain unknown to us.

Just as we have used the Black Box Technique on 1953, we can use the Black Box Technique on the Ice Age, the beginnings of life on Earth, or the beginning of time. We can use it on any period of time to determine what has happened, what is happening, or what will happen. Wow!

The Seven Steps of the Black Box Technique

So far we have only applied the Black Box Technique to determine what has occurred in single unknown events at one specified period of time. The Black Box Technique becomes even more powerful when applied systematically against more difficult and more complex real-world problems such as those we face in our daily lives. It can and will profoundly improve the individual life of everyone who employs it. The proper use of this technique can make the reader's dreams and goals come true. Please note that the author makes no promise that the proper use of the Seven Steps of the Black Box Technique will make the reader happy, but that the reader's goals and dreams will be made to occur. Happiness is an emotional state that will be discussed later. The advantage granted to *individuals* by this technique is so great that we must discuss its application to our daily lives—in our daily decision-making, career choices, choices in marriage partners, decisions about any problems we face. This all-important technique may also be applied to larger-scale systems, businesses, governments, and even entire societies, as we shall see later. All we have to do is perform the following seven easy steps.

Step No. 1: Determine the Accurate Past and Present

First, as we have learned, predicting the future accurately requires that we accurately know the past and the present. We can decide what is factual about the past and present by using the Truth-Meter. Any unknown events can be Black Boxed.

Step No. 2: Predict the Real Future

Then by viewing the accurate present events as causes, think what their effects will be and you have just predicted the future. We can use our knowledge of cause-and-effect relationships (laws) that we acquired a) by experience with similar cause-and-effect relationships (laws) in our lives; b) in closely reviewing the cause-and-effect relationships (laws) that we discover when we accurately determine the past and present; c) by performing an Einsteinian Thought Experiment to derive unknown cause and effect relationships (laws). If anything remains unknown, either events or cause-and-effect relationships (laws), it can be filled in by cautiously using Occam's razor: The simplest explanation that fits the other known evidence is to be tentatively accepted as the truth. We must bear in mind that the principle of Newtonian Trends requires us to predict that trends must continue into the future unless we can clearly identify the causes that will alter or end them.

If you want to go farther into the future, view the effects that you have just created as causes and think what their effects will be, and on and on until you have predicted the future as far as need be. How accurate your view of the past and present is, and how accurate your knowledge of cause-and-effect relationships (laws) is, will determine how accurate your prediction is. As you get farther into the future, your accuracy may decrease due to the intervention of unforeseen causes. That means we did not understand the past and present as fully as we should have. Accuracy in predicting the future is a skill that can be developed. Practice is essential. Begin with cause-and-effect relationships (laws) with which you are familiar. If you are a student, predict what your grades will be at the end of next semester. If you are a homemaker, predict how each family member will react when you serve your family some food they have never had before. At work, predict how your boss will act when you perform some act above and beyond your normal duties. Most important, become a wide-awake observer of the cause-and-effect relationships (laws) happening around you. As we discovered earlier, everything is both a cause *and* an effect. If something unusual occurs, attempt to determine the causes. It seems that as we humans age and settle into the fixed routines and patterns of life, we cease being curious. We stop asking, "Why?" Do not do that. Never stop asking, "Why?" And very, very important, when you learn one fact, you really learn three facts. A) You learn the fact itself; and with your knowledge of cause-and-effect relationships (laws), you learn b) what must have caused that fact; and c) you know what that fact will cause (the effect).

Under certain circumstances, it may be advisable to predict more than one real future. For example, let us say a young man may or may not be drafted into the armed services by a draft lottery. The young man has two possible alternative futures with a realistically high probability of occurring. The young man would be wise to predict both real futures and apply the following steps to both. Then, whichever occurs, the young man will be able to achieve the best future.

This technique may be applied by everyone, not only to everyday life situations but also to the entire future as well. It will no doubt be of interest to most of us what our working careers will be, how our marriages will turn out, how our children will turn out, etc. As we predict farther into the future, the effects of what the society (in our case the United States of America) in general will be experiencing at that time must be taken into account.

Step No. 3: Predict the Idealized Future

Next we need to determine how we would ideally but *realistically* like the future to turn out. This idealized future then becomes our goal. Three words of caution about goal-setting: 1) Perform an Einsteinian Thought Experiment and have your mind take you into the future and view the world around you from the perspective of having achieved your goals. 2) Set your goals very high and very carefully. This is an extremely powerful technique and you will probably achieve your goals, but if your goals are improperly set, you will derive unintended results. An example: Let us say one of our goals is to own a 200-mile-per-hour, $200,000 Italian sports car. Part of the reality of owning a car like that is continuous fear of theft; of leaving it unattended; of turning it over to the valet parking lot attendant; of the nervous breakdown that will inevitably occur when someone inevitably runs into it. All that for some illusory social prestige. Be sure that your goals are what you intend. 3) If your idealized, but realistic, future involves the modification of another human being's habitual behavior (such as wife-beating, alcoholism, etc.) or personality, whether relative or friend, my advice is to alter your idealized future either to acceptance of that person's current behavior, or, if that is too disruptive to the achievement of your goals, to the removal of that person from your future. My experience is, that the amount of effort and energy expended is so large, and the probability of success so low, in modifying habitual, individual, human behavior, particularly of adults, that it is not worth it. It is far easier, for instance, to become a multimillionaire than to modify someone else's behavior.

Now we have five sets of facts: a) the accurate past, b) the accurate present, c) the real future that we predicted when we worked the cause-and-effect relationships (laws) forward in time, d) the series of causes and effects that will cause the real future, and e) the idealized future.

Step No. 4: Determine the Causes of the Idealized Future

Next, we need to determine what the series of causes and effects will have to be in order to achieve our idealized future. To accomplish this, we begin with our known effect (the idealized future) and work the cause-and-effect relationships (laws) backward in time from the idealized future toward the present. We know what the effect is, the idealized future. We also know what the past and present are. Therefore, we have a gap in time from the present to our idealized future that we can Black Box, except that we will work the cause-and-effect relationships (laws) backward in time from the future. We know the effect, the idealized future, so we want to determine the cause that will cause that effect. Then view that cause as an effect and determine what must be the cause of that effect and so on until we arrive back at the present. We can also work the cause-and-effect relationships (laws) forward from the present exactly as in step #2 above, and exactly as we did to find out what was behind the curtain on the factory floor. Then we will have an additional piece of information—the series of causes and effects that will have to occur in order for our idealized future to actually happen.

Step No. 5: Determine the Difference Between the Two Sets of Causes and Effects

Now we have two sets of causes and effects: a) one that results in the real future, and b) one that results in the idealized future. Next, we compare the two sets of causes and effects. We note where the differences are in the two sets. The differences between the two are what we must focus upon. Our task is to make the idealized future the one that actually occurs. We know what makes things happen—cause and effect. If we want our idealized effects to occur, we must change the causes from those that produce the real future to those that will produce our idealized future.

Step No. 6: The Plan

The actions necessary to substitute our desired causes for the undesired causes become our plan. We substitute those causes that bring the *desired* effect for those causes that would otherwise bring the *undesired* effect.

Step No. 7: Sacrifice

Then as long as we are willing to sacrifice to enact our plan, presto, the future turns out as we desire it. However, this ability to sacrifice to carry out the plan is essential. The very word "decadence" connotes the inability to sacrifice today for tomorrow. If you cannot sacrifice today then you give up control over tomorrow, your future.

I invite the reader to apply the Seven Steps of the Black Box Technique to his or her own life. The results over time can be incredible as the future unrolls and brings you what you want.

I took an informal survey among various young adults I have met. I asked them on what basis they made decisions about their lives. Sadly, the number one answer was trial and error, which, by definition, meant they will have lives filled with a great deal of error. Although "the Seven Steps of the Black Box Technique" is an effective technique at any age, it is most advantageously employed by high school and college-age people before training and career paths have been chosen. Particularly if the plan chosen is a flexible one that can support a later redefinition of goals.

It has already been shown that everything operates by cause and effect, so when you start controlling the cause-and-effect relationships in your life, you start controlling **the fundamental force that operates everything**. More powerful than that, I do not know how to tell you to be.

The Plan for the Quest

Now let us plan our quest. In the initial paragraphs of this chapter, the reader will recall that we devised a line of falling dominoes to represent a model of simple events occurring over time. Let us mentally change the line of dominoes for a strip of motion picture film. Each frame of the film causes the picture in the next frame of the film to occur and was caused by the picture in the frame that immediately preceded it. If we want the strip of motion picture film to represent all the events of the past, present, and future, then the present is one frame of the film showing the events occurring everywhere in the universe at this point in time. Everything that ever occurred in the past would be contained in chronological sequence on the frames of the film to one side of the present, and everything that will occur in the future is in chronological sequence on the frames in the other direction. Since we do not know how long events have been occurring or how long events will continue to occur, we do not, at this point in the analysis, know how long the strip of film is. However, we do know that we are currently living in the present frame. If we let each frame of the film represent not 1/24th of a second, as in a normal motion picture, but a lifetime of say seventy years, then our task becomes clear. With intimate first-hand knowledge of only one frame—one lifetime—we must deduce the plot of an extremely complex motion picture—the past, the present, and the future. It would be similar to viewing a still photograph of one frame showing the burning of Atlanta and attempting to deduce the entire plot of *Gone With the Wind.*

Fortunately, we have an absolutely staggering abundance of second-hand information not only from individuals who have lived before us but also, and more important, from an avalanche of data cascading upon us from every corner of contemporary society. The difficulty lies not in obtaining a sufficient quantity of data, but in discriminating between fact and fiction. However, we have already learned how to discern fact from fiction—the Truth-Meter.

Armed with our Truth-Meter, we can search for that fact that occurred the longest time ago. Or, to put it another way, we need to find the first fact that ever happened that can pass our test for truth. Or, to put it a third way, we need to look at a frame from the movie as close to the beginning as possible. However, we must be absolutely positive that it is a factual frame from the movie. For if we accepted a fictitious event instead of a real one as our starting point, then when we apply the Black Box Technique we will derive meaningless fiction in place of reality. It would be as if we mistook a scene from a Three Stooges short for the first scene in *Gone With the Wind.*

Trying to Black Box the Three Stooges scene and a real scene would result in gross distortion.

Then we will have seen two frames from the movie:

1. The earliest frame that can pass our test for truth, and,
2. The frame in which we are currently living.

With these two points separated in time we could then utilize the Black Box Technique (as we did in the example of determining what was behind the curtain in the factory) to determine what events occurred in between the two known points in time. As these two events, by definition, will be separated by all the time that is known to have passed, we would not expect our Black Box Technique to render us detailed results. However, if we can find other points in time (frames) between the beginning and the present that can also pass our test for truth, then the Black Box Technique will have to be applied only between events that are relatively close in time. It will be like stringing a telephone line between telephone poles. We can then expect excellent results from the Black Box Technique. The Black Box will fill in the unknown frames.

For the purposes of this book, the vast scope of the material to be covered prevents us from a lengthy treatment of every point, but it does not prevent us from a profound treatment. Important facts that, to the author's knowledge, are first revealed in this book will be identified by footnote. There are several reasons for this. 1) To emphasize the power of the system of logic. 2) If discoveries of this book are not brought to the attention of the reader, then the book is subject to criticism for inaccurately reporting what is currently generally accepted to be reality; and 3) the reader would not be able to discern generally accepted reality from new information. Then when conclusions are drawn based upon the discoveries of this book, the reader would have no basis for evaluating the validity of the conclusions. However, the author cannot possibly be certain that no one has ever previously discovered the facts purported to be discovered in this book.

We will continue this process of constructing our movie of reality from the first provable point in time until the beginning of the Modern Era (roughly A.D. 1500). It will take us a substantial amount of this book (approximately 100 pages) to determine what has occurred prior to the Modern Era, but do not skip it. It is not only extremely interesting, but it will be impossible to understand the rest of this book if it is not read all the way through. It will also give the reader an incredibly important comprehension of reality and a database with which the Black Box Technique works very well. If, while we assemble our film of reality, we bear in mind that every event we investigate is not merely an event isolated in time, but also is an event caused by the events that preceded it, and which will in turn cause the events that follow it, we should be able to observe the cause-and-effect relationships (laws) that shape the past and hence our universe, our planet, our society, and even our own lives. We should be able to identify important cause-and-effect relationships that operate repeatedly or that cause important events to occur. Another name for these cause-and-effect relationships is the Fundamental Laws of the Universe. Eureka! Pay dirt! We will have discovered essential parts of the rulebook, not for the Monopoly game mentioned in the Introduction, but the grandest game of all—our own lives. Then we will continue assembling our film of reality from roughly A.D. 1500 to the present by narrowing our focus to what is now the United States. For if we maintain a global perspective, this book will become far too long. This will complete the first step of the application of the Seven Steps of the Black Box Technique: *Step No. 1: Determine the Accurate Past and Present.*

After we have determined what has occurred from the most remote provable point in time to the present, and after we have discovered many Fundamental Laws of the Universe (cause-and-effect relationships), we will view the present as a cause and predict the effect, the future (*Step No. 2: Predict the Real Future*). We will have done exactly as the expert did in the plastics factory when he knew the past (the raw plastic) and the present (the bowl-forming machine), and could therefore easily predict what the real future would be (yellow plastic bowls).

Then we will be in an excellent position to continue to apply the Seven Steps of the Black Box Technique to the United States and take *Step No.3: Predict the Idealized Future.* Then with our knowledge of part of the past, the present, the real future, and the idealized future, it should not be very difficult to Black Box that part of the past, if any, prior to the first provable event. Then we will know what has occurred since the inception of time and what will occur until the end of time. In addition, if the differences between the real future and the idealized future of the United States are too large, we can apply steps No. 4 through No. 7 of the Black Box Technique to ensure that the idealized future actually occurs. In effect our quest will enable us to apply the Seven Steps of the Black Box Technique to the United States of America. Not only will we discover astounding realities about our society that stump our current leaders, but we will also be able to predict an idealized but realistic future for our society that could be made to occur during this generation. We have much to accomplish.

Now that we are armed with these extremely powerful but simple weapons, we are ready to slay dragons of enormous dimensions. One final thought: After we have derived events from the beginning of time until the end of time, how will we be absolutely sure that we have understood reality sufficiently well to have derived them correctly?

In the early 1960s, during the embryonic days of the computer, the U.S. Air Force was seeking designs for a new aircraft. Many aircraft companies submitted design proposals, but the design with the most impressive specifications came from the one company that used a computer to design its aircraft. Inherent in designing a new aircraft is the presumption that the designer knows the laws that govern objects in flight sufficiently well that the aircraft, when built, will fly to specifications. The Air Force, quite correctly, wanted to know, "How can we be absolutely sure that your computer knows the laws governing objects in flight sufficiently well to design a superior aircraft?" Clearly, building the aircraft would be too expensive a test. It would be far easier to test the computer's knowledge of the laws governing objects in flight. Therefore, the Air Force tested the aircraft company's computer by programming into it the design of a bumblebee and requesting the computer to derive the bumblebee's flight characteristics. The computer said that the bumblebee would never fly. Obviously, the computer did not know all of the laws governing objects in flight. However, after further computer testing, the aircraft that the computer designed was built and flew to specifications.

The computer knew enough of the laws governing objects in flight to design a superior aircraft, but it demonstrably did not know all of the laws. Therefore, the computer did not know the complete reality, the truth if you will, concerning these laws of nature. How will we, in our quest for the truth, determine whether we have derived the truth in its totality or merely a fraction of it?

We will know that we have derived the truth in its totality when everything becomes explicable. We will know that we have derived the truth in its totality when we have a comprehensive and cohesive understanding of reality in which everything fits. We will know that we have derived the truth when we have no flightless bumblebees.

Now that we have armed ourselves, let us kick in some doors and slay some dragons.

Step No. 1:
Determine the Accurate Past and Present

Congratulations! You have successfully completed the most difficult part of this book. The remainder will flow more like the story-line of our theoretical movie. For if we were to maintain a conscious and rigorous use of the Black Box Technique, pounding every nail in every coffin, this book would (1) become a textbook in logic, which is not its purpose, (2) become preposterously long, (3) exhaust the reader, (4) exhaust the author, and (5) not be readable by the general reader. However, we will follow closely the Seven Steps of the Black Box Technique and where useful demonstrate its applications.

CHAPTER TWO
Take No Prisoners

From the First Known Event to 4.6 Billion Years Ago

WE ARE ARMED WITH TWO WEAPONS:

1. The Truth-Meter to act as our shield against accepting fiction as fact.

2. The Black Box and associated techniques that will act as our sword to enable us to determine what occurred either in between, before, or after factual events.

All we need is any factual event that happened as long ago as possible that can pass our test for truth. It is critical that the event that we accept as our initial starting point be absolutely and positively an actual happening. We must rigorously apply the preponderance-of-evidence test by obtaining a significantly large amount of verifiable evidence such that we are convinced that the event in fact occurred. Now let us begin our quest.

Since the ancient fact we seek happened long before anyone currently on the planet was alive, we will have to rely upon second-hand information in our search for the earliest possible event.

In our society, there are primarily three different systems of thought that purport to know what is going on around here in a fundamental sense: New Age Philosophy, Religion, and Science. Let us conduct an Einsteinian Thought Experiment. Let us imagine that we are in a hallway facing three doors: One marked "New Age," one marked "Religion," and one marked "Science." Behind each door is a person at a desk (similar to an information desk at a library) who knows everything there is to know about the subject marked on the door. Instead of all the facts being kept in books on the shelves, all the facts are in the person's head. The person will gladly and honestly answer any questions we care to ask about the subject marked on the door. Let us enter the door marked New Age and initiate our quest for the oldest provable event.

Us: Knock, Knock.

New Age Expert: Come in.

Us: Good day. We want to know what the oldest event was, when it happened, and what proof or evidence you have for it.

New Age Expert: According to which sect of New Age Philosophy?

Us: Are there different sects and therefore different explanations of the oldest event?

New Age Expert: New Age Philosophy is a catchall phrase for an eclectic variety of intermingled belief systems. Some of the beliefs are very old, like the belief in astrology, and some are very new, like the belief in UFOs. In addition, there is typically belief in an extraterrestrial force or power that can be used by or work through "special" individuals who are attuned to receiving the messages or energy.

The New Age Philosophies are not consistent or cohesive enough to present us with an explanation of the earliest known event. It might be useful to view the New Age Philosophies as a belief system in an embryonic stage. If enough people come to believe in one cohesive philosophy it may even turn into a religion one day.

Us: But the most common threads are astrology, UFOs, and extraterrestrial forces, right?

New Age Expert: Right.

Us: Tell us about astrology, then.

New Age Expert: Astrology was invented around 1300 B.C. by the Babylonians. They thought that the position of the stars and planets when one is born influences one's life. The constellation in which the sun rises on the morning of a person's birth determines his sign of the Zodiac. Persons born on a given date can then look up their signs in almost any newspaper and read an astrologer's advice on how to conduct their lives.

Us: Does it work?

New Age Expert: No. The Earth has a wobble in its rotation called precession. In the 3,300 years since the Babylonians assigned the signs of the Zodiac to specific dates of birth, precession has caused the Earth to tilt sufficiently that the sun no longer rises in the assigned constellations on the assigned dates. Therefore, people are no longer the sign they think they are, and moreover, everyone is reading the wrong astrological advice. Second, the astrological advice given is not consistent. On any given day an East Coast newspaper may give advice for a particular sign, whereas a West Coast newspaper will give exactly contradictory advice for the same sign.

Us: Aha! The next time I read a newspaper with an astrology chart in it that purports to print "All the news that's fit to print," I will think to myself "All the news that's fit to print and some that's not." But what about UFOs?

NEW AGE EXPERT: UFOs, or Unidentified Flying Objects, are purported to be extraterrestrial spaceships. In the 1950s people who believed in UFOs thought they came from Mars. As the U.S. space program progressed, the people who believed in UFOs changed the UFOs' home to star systems outside of our solar system. The distances the UFOs would have to travel to reach Earth became immense. It takes light traveling at 5.88 trillion miles per year, hundreds and even thousands of years to reach us from the stars we see in the sky. Our scientists tell us that it is impossible to travel faster than the speed of light. Therefore, there are only two possibilities. The first is that if there are UFOs, they must travel at sub-light speeds, which means that it is very difficult for them to reach us. It must take a major effort for their civilization to reach us. After the expenditure of time and effort required to reach us, what do they accomplish? They supposedly burn some cows and kidnap some rural people. It does not make sense.

The second possibility is that the aliens' technology is so superior to ours that it is easy for them to come here. If that is the case, then the aliens would hardly need the famous stick-figures of Earth animals in the Nazca desert of Peru to direct them to a suitable landing spot after successfully navigating trillions and trillions of miles of space. Once again, it does not make sense.

Either way, if only one percent of the reported UFO sightings were accurate, then Earth would have to be a major cross-

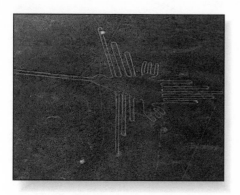

The Nazca lines, Peru — a hummingbird

roads in space. It just does not make sense.

Us: Well, what about extraterrestrial forces that communicate with "special" people?

NEW AGE EXPERT: As far as evidence is concerned, there is only the word of individual "special" people. The only force known to function at the immense distances involved is gravity. The amount of gravity exerted by one's house cat is more powerful than the gravity received from a distant star. Therefore, it is virtually impossible that gravity from a star can be sensed by anyone, let alone convey a message.

In addition, if one analyzes the people who claim to be able to receive messages from an extraterrestrial power, they typically are at a phase in their lives when the acceptance of reality would bring great pain. For example, an aging movie star faced with the loss of her beauty and the realization of her mortality; or a middle-aged person facing the prospect of a bleak old age; or a person in need of affection who seeks to be "special" to compensate for the lack of attention.

Us: Thank you very much for your help.

Let us enter the door marked Religion and continue our quest for the oldest provable event.

Us: Knock, Knock.

RELIGIOUS EXPERT: Come in.

Us: Good day. We want to know what the oldest event was, when it happened, and what proof or evidence you have for it.

RELIGIOUS EXPERT: According to what religion?

Us: Well, since this is the United States, let us discuss the ones with the most adherents.

RELIGIOUS EXPERT: In the Jewish, Christian, and Islamic religions, the earliest event as written in the book of Genesis is the same—Creation. God created the heavens and the Earth. In 1648, this event was computed by Irishman James Ussher, Archbishop of Armagh, Northern Ireland, to have occurred in 4004 B.C. Englishman John Lightfoot (1602–1675), vice-chancellor of Cambridge University, added that it was October 23 at 9:00 A.M.

Us: What is your evidence that Creation occurred?

RELIGIOUS EXPERT: The story of Creation was written and rewritten over a long period of time, but was in its Old Testament form by 300 B.C. It was written by persons unknown.

Us: Is there any physical evidence that supports the story of Creation as presented in Genesis?

RELIGIOUS EXPERT: No. None.[5] Asking religious experts about "provable" events is meaningless, anyway, since religion deals almost by definition with precisely those things that are beyond proof.

Us: Thank you very much for your help.

---

5. The reader is strongly cautioned against leaping to invalid conclusions based on the above, such as that the Bible does not contain truth, or that God does not exist. The above passage only addresses the very narrow question of what physical evidence exists that can be used in our preponderance-of-evidence test to support the story of Creation as reported in Genesis. An analysis of the existence of God is presented at the appropriate place later in this text.

Now that we have Religion's version of the first event and its supporting evidence, let us knock on Science's door and hear what it has to say.

Us: Knock, knock.

SCIENCE EXPERT: Come in

Us: Good day. We want to know what the oldest event was, when it happened, and what proof or evidence you have for it.

SCIENCE EXPERT: According to Science, the earliest known event occurred about 15 billion years ago when the totality of everything that exists, all matter and energy, every atom, every molecule, every star you can see in the sky—everything in the universe, including space itself—was gathered together in one place. It exploded, and was so hot (100 billion degrees C) that at no time since, not even in science laboratories, has that temperature ever been reached. The surface of the sun, at 11,000 degrees F, is but a cool cinder in comparison. To help you think about this, imagine that everything in the universe consists of weapons-grade plutonium, is made into a gigantic bomb, and is detonated. There is an enormous explosion, but nothing is blown up because everything is the bomb itself. The actual explosion, called the Big Bang, which took place approximately 15 billion years ago, was many times more powerful than our imaginary explosion.

Us: We have been warned that it is very important that we do not accept fiction as fact. We are prepared to be extremely tough about the quality of your evidence. What is your evidence that the Big Bang actually occurred?

SCIENCE EXPERT: In 1965, two Bell Laboratories physicists, Drs. Arno Penzias and Robert Wilson, were analyzing the data from a large antenna that had been built for the communications satellite program. Their data showed low-intensity radiation coming from everywhere the antenna was pointed. This was unexpected. At first, the scientists had the antenna checked. Bird droppings were found and removed, but still the faint radiation persisted. Then the scientists had the critical components of the antenna disassembled,

Drs. Arno Penzias and Robert Wilson in front of their famous antenna

checked, and reassembled. Still the unknown radiation was present. In a quandary, the scientists consulted colleagues and friends about the puzzling radiation. One of their friends put them in touch with the work of Professor Robert Dicke of Princeton University, who had previously predicted that an echo of the Big Bang would still exist in the precise form found by Drs. Penzias and Wilson. Their annoying glitch turned out to be the remnant of the creation of the universe. For this great discovery, Drs. Penzias and Wilson won Nobel Prizes, and the Big Bang is accepted in science practically without dissent.

Us: Interesting. Do you have any other proof?

Science Expert: Yes. If you would like to see this residual radiation from the Big Bang for yourself, you can go to any television set, tune it to an unoccupied channel, turn the contrast down, and approximately five percent of the "snow" that you see on the screen will be from the background radiation left from the first known event in the universe—The Big Bang.

Us: Wow. Very impressive. Anything else?

Science Expert: Yes. Independent of Professor Robert Dicke's prediction of low-intensity background radiation surviving from the Big Bang, Dr. George Gamow made the same prediction in

1956, nine years prior to the Penzias-Wilson discovery. Therefore, we have more than one person predicting the existence of background radiation from the Big Bang, and we have more than one method of confirming the existence of the remnants of the Big Bang.

Us: Thank you very much for your help.

After listening to all three assertions about the first event and its supporting evidence, it is time for us to use our preponderance-of-evidence test to determine which version of events is to be accepted as the truth.

It is as if we are stewards at a racetrack who, not being permitted to bet on the horses, do not care which horse wins, only that the race be run fairly and impartially. We must be fair and impartial in our tasks as cosmic jurors. We must not use our emotions. It takes a great amount of intellectual discipline to seek fundamental truth.

It is apparent not only that the New Age Philosophies fail our preponderance-of-evidence test, but they lack any credible evidence whatsoever. Therefore, let us reject New Age Philosophy and proceed with the two remaining explanations.

On one side of the scale we place the religious evidence: a story written long ago by persons unknown with zero amount of physical evidence to support the story of Creation.

On the other side of the scale:

Cosmic background radiation from the Big Bang, continuously bathing the Earth and detectable by more than one billion antennae here on Earth. The existence of the remnant was independently predicted by two scientists and its presence confirmed and reconfirmed.

Verdict: The preponderance of evidence is clearly in favor of the Big Bang, particularly with the two independent predictions and numerous confirmations of the remnant's existence. There is more than twice as much evidence necessary to convince Aristotle and Newton that it is of the highest order of truth.

Therefore, the Truth-Meter requires us to accept the Big Bang as having happened. Let us apply our Black Box Technique. We know the Big Bang happened approximately 15 billion years ago. Therefore, we know our film strip of the past is at least 215 million frames, or lifetimes, long. Presumably we know what is going on in the present. Therefore, we should be able to deduce what occurred in between. However, using an event 15 billion years old and the present will probably render us a very generalized view. All the time that can be proved to have existed has elapsed between the two events that we are trying to Black Box. It would help us substantially if we knew other events that could pass our preponderance-of-evidence test that took place between the present and the Big Bang. Insofar as we have discovered a piece of truth from the scientific explanation of the first event, let us return to the door marked Science.

Us: Knock, knock.

SCIENCE EXPERT: Come in.

Us: Good day again. We would like to know what was the next event after the Big Bang and what is the evidence that it actually occurred?

SCIENCE EXPERT: After the Big Bang, the universe expanded and cooled.

Us: What is your evidence for this?

SCIENCE EXPERT: It is based upon sophisticated, high-level mathematical modeling.

Us: I am sorry, but speaking for myself and probably the majority of general readers, we must reject this type of evidence because we do not have the knowledge base to evaluate it. What is the next event that occurred that has a different type of evidence?

SCIENCE EXPERT: Twelve billion years ago the universe was made up of quasars (quasi-stellar radio sources). A quasar is an extremely powerful energy source emanating from a small area of space only a few times larger than our solar system. It is the farthest thing away from us that we know of in space except the cosmic background radiation from the Big Bang itself. However, science does not have a clear understanding of quasars. It is unknown how they formed, precisely what they are, and what happened to them. There are only about 600 known quasars. There are no quasars closer to us than 800 million light-years.

Us: (Aside to ourselves) If the Big Bang happened approximately 15 billion years ago, and the next known event happened 12 billion years ago, then the event in question is located 3 billion years after the beginning of the universe. An excellent location to use as one end of our Black Box Technique, with the other being the Big Bang. We should be able to derive the 3 billion years in between. However, let me strenuously warn again that the alleged event must pass our preponderance-of-evidence test.

Us: (To Science Expert) That is interesting, but we need evidence to prove the existence of the quasars and none of your fancy scientific mumbo-jumbo.

SCIENCE EXPERT: Will a photograph do?

Us: A photograph? Let me get this straight. You have a photograph of a quasar from 12 billion years ago?

SCIENCE EXPERT: That is absolutely correct.

Us: How?

SCIENCE EXPERT: When you take a photograph of a friend of yours in your home, the moment you press the button of the camera is virtually the same moment that light left the surface of your friend to speed across the room at, what else, the speed of light,[6] to enter the camera lens and be focused on to your film. Therefore, we tend to delude ourselves into thinking we are taking live pictures. In reality the light that sped across the room and into your camera actually did take some time, and crossed the living room in an infinitesimal fraction of a second. Therefore when you pressed the button of the camera you took a picture of an event that occurred an infinitesimal fraction of a second before. You were actually photographing the past. Now let us continue our thought experiment by having your friend back up not just to the next yard or the next street, but to the sun, 93 million miles away. Now, due to the increase in distance, you are photographing eight minutes into the past. It is true that when we watch a setting sun here on Earth, it has actually

A quasar 12 billion light-years away

already set eight minutes prior. If your friend were to back up even farther and wave to us from these aforementioned quasars, we would be photographing a scene that is 12 billion years old because the quasars are 12 billion light-years away.

US: Absolutely astounding! A photograph of what happened 80 percent of the way back to the first known event. Or, to look at it another way, the second event ever known to have occurred has been photographed. Clearly a photograph taken of a region of space 12 billion light-years away must show what conditions were like 12 billion years ago. Therefore, we will

---

6. The speed of light is approximately 186,282 miles per second in a vacuum (5.88 trillion miles per year). In the Earth's atmosphere, light travels slightly more slowly than in a vacuum.

accept the quasars as the truth. Now let us Black Box the 3 billion-year time span between the Big Bang and quasars just as
we did when we had to Black Box what was behind the curtain
in the factory. The Big Bang is the past, or the yellow plastic
pellets; and the 3 billion-year unknown period is the artificially
defined present or the part behind the curtain; and the quasars
are the future or the result—the little yellow bowls. We know
that the Big Bang caused whatever happened in the mysterious
missing 3 billion years, and that whatever happened during
those 3 billion years caused the quasars. Now, using Subtraction and Occam's razor—When an event is unknown, the
simplest answer that fits the known facts is to be tentatively
accepted—let us deduce what occurred in the unknown 3 billion years.

The temperature of the Big Bang was 100 billion degrees C.

The temperature of quasars is far less.

Therefore, during the unknown 3 billion years the universe
cooled.

The Big Bang occupied an infinitely small area in space.

Quasars are distributed over a rather wide range in deep
space.

Therefore, in the unknown 3 billion years the universe
expanded.

When we left the Big Bang it was exploding and expanding
at a very high rate. When we analyze the quasars we find
immense quantities of energy coming from small regions of
space. The amount of energy is so high from such a small area
of space that matter could not remain together in a cohesive
structure. Therefore, by definition, the quasars are exploding.

It is interesting to note that the first two events were both
explosions. At distances as great as 10 to 15 billion light-years,
our primitive sensors are not able to detect events with orders
of energy lower than massive explosions. However, if there had
been interim massive explosions between our two known explosions, our sensors probably would have picked them up, and

they have not. Therefore, having no evidence, we can reject there having been interim massive explosions.

Let us apply Occam's razor—the simplest explanation that fits the facts—to our meager data. Fifteen billion years ago a giant explosion, the Big Bang, spewed energy, part of which was later to become matter, over a vast region of space. It cooled and matter precipitated out. At some point, the force of the explosion spent itself so that the forces of gravity and electromagnetism were able to bring together matter in local neighborhoods and compress it. Then when they were compressed beyond a critical value, they exploded. These explosions we call quasars.

That is the simplest explanation that can explain how the Big Bang became quasars, and according to Occam's razor we should tentatively accept it until there is a preponderance of evidence to show otherwise.[7]

From 15 billion years ago to 12 billion years ago we have a very good idea of what our film is about. Now let us proceed with the same methodology to determine what happened between 12 billion years ago and the present. Let us see what our Science Expert says the next major provable event was.

Us: Pardon us, Mr. Science Expert. Would you please tell us what the next major provable event was?

Science Expert: The next major provable event of interest

---

7. A more profound Black Boxing of the early stages of our universe could be conducted that would render us a much more sophisticated picture of the events of the early universe. It would be a long and complex discussion that would take us to the leading edge of astrophysics and well beyond. However, it would not have any substantive effect on the rest of the book. In short, the juice is not worth the squeeze. Therefore, it is deleted for the sake of brevity. Presented here is a shortened version that is, of course, an over-simplification and, because we rejected much evidence, slightly in disagreement with some of the latest theories of science. For science's explanation of the early events of the universe, I refer the reader to the Bibliography at the back of the book.

to you occurred 4.6 billion years ago when the Earth, the sun, the other planets, and the rest of our solar system formed. The sun and its nine planets were formed in the aftermath of a gigantic explosion. The gigantic explosion was probably a massive star that blew up. Therefore, at least a portion of the matter in our solar system was once inside a star that exploded. Therefore, in the strictest scientific sense, we, the people of this planet, are made from stardust.

Us: That is truly amazing.

SCIENCE EXPERT: The Earth was a molten ball that cooled and became trapped in orbit around the sun.

Us: What is your evidence that this is what happened?

SCIENCE EXPERT: Here on Earth we have many examples of matter composed of very heavy atoms, such as gold, uranium, lead, etc. The only way these heavy elements can be made is in the final stages of the life cycle of a dying massive star. All stars begin life when a large ball of hydrogen is compressed by its own gravitational pull to the point where the hydrogen in the center of the ball is under so much pressure that the internal temperature rises to 20 million degrees F and is fused with another atom of hydrogen. The result is, in a two-step crushing, one atom of the heavier element, helium, and a bright burst of energy. The hydrogen keeps fusing into helium as long as the hydrogen lasts. Some 99 percent of a star's life is spent fusing hydrogen into helium. The final one percent of its life, if the star is large enough, is spent fusing the remaining matter into progressively heavier elements. Normal-size stars can produce elements as heavy as iron. However, very massive stars are needed to produce the heavy elements that exist here on Earth such as gold, lead, and uranium. A massive star ends its life by blowing up and spewing the heavy elements through space in an explosion called a supernova.

Additional evidence that the age of the solar system is 4.6 billion years comes from the age of rocks taken from the moon by our space program. It also is the same age as meteorites. We know this because the uranium contained in the rocks and meteorites is radioactive. This means that it is radiating part of itself away so that over time the uranium drops to a less dense but more stable state. It slowly becomes lead. The half-life of uranium is 4.6 billion years, which means that in 4.6 billion years, one-half of the uranium will have decayed to lead. In the next 4.6 billion years one-half of the remaining uranium will have changed itself to lead, and so on. Therefore, by measuring the ratio of uranium to lead a scientist can determine the age of the rock sample. The evidence appears to be very consistent in giving an age of 4.6 billion years for the creation of the solar system, including Earth. However, on the Earth itself no rocks have been discovered that are older than 4.1 billion years.

Our solar system is part of the Milky Way galaxy, which consists of at least 200 billion stars similar to our sun. Our galaxy is one of approximately 100 billion galaxies. It is a member of a local group of galaxies known uninterestingly enough as the "Local Group." The Local Group is a member of a large cluster of galaxies called the "Virgo Super-Cluster."

Let us use the Black Box Technique to determine what occurred between the quasars 12 billion years ago and the formation of our solar system 4.6 billion years ago. Because of the enormous amount of energy generated from such a small area in space, we presumed the quasars were exploding. As the force of the explosions dissipated, the forces of gravity and electromagnetism drew matter in local regions together. These collections of matter we call galaxies. A super-cluster of galaxies may be the remnants of one quasar. Within an individual galaxy, a large star went supernova and created the heavy elements that combined with a cloud of hydrogen gas to become our solar system. Hence, the creation of Earth.

CHAPTER THREE

...in Some Warm Pond

4.6 Billion Years Ago to 65 Million Years Ago

Life on Earth

SCIENCE EXPERT: The Earth's internal heat, combined with the heat from the sun, permits the Earth to maintain its surface temperature within the rather narrow range required to keep water in its liquid state. At 212 degrees F (100 degrees C) water boils and is driven off in the form of vapor. Below 32 F (0 degrees C) water is frozen and therefore cannot interact, mix, or otherwise become familiar with other chemicals. It is only water in its liquid state that can lap the shore forming alternating wet and dry bands; which can be sucked up into the trunk of towering trees, sent to the leaves to assist in photosynthesis; and be 65 percent of the human body.

Liquid water can form into large oceans on the surface of a thermally stable planet. These large oceans would have had local hot spots in them where volcanic action, which was much more prevalent on early Earth than it is now, would have boiled the water. The early Earth's atmosphere is thought to have contained water vapor, ammonia, methane, and hydrogen. Many energy sources would have been applied to this combination atmosphere and liquid water, ranging from the sun's energy, to the radioactive bombardment from inside the Earth itself, to lightning strikes. In 1952, Stanley Miller, a graduate student at the University of Chicago, was inspired by hearing a lecture about what the early conditions of the Earth were calculated to have been. He constructed a simple chemistry experiment that simulated the early Earth's environment. After only 24 hours he returned to his apparatus and recovered a large quantity of amino acids of several different kinds. Subsequently, the experiment has been repeated many times in many ways with different chemicals creating other amino acids. Amino acids are the building blocks of life.

Amino acids, linked together, form many kinds of protein: Two of the most important are structural protein, which makes up the structures of cells, and enzymes, which initiate, direct, and speed up innumerable chemical reactions that assist organisms in staying alive.

Stanley Miller and apparatus

There are 20 amino acids and five nucleotides which, as reported in *Red Giants and White Dwarfs* by Robert Jastrow, "are the same in every living creature on the face of the Earth, whether bacterium, mollusk, or man." The nucleotides were subsequently constructed in a lab in 1962 under circumstances similar to Dr. Stanley Miller's experiment. The nucleotides are arranged in various combinations to make many nucleic acids, but one of the nucleic acids is the all-important DNA. DNA is the molecule that permits every cell and therefore every plant and animal to reproduce and to permit its type to continue.

Us: (To ourselves) Let us Black Box how life started. Considering the ease with which Dr. Miller created amino acids in the laboratory, it is logical to assume the primordial ocean must have been a thick soup teeming with amino acids and nucleotides, especially around the many hot spots. If the reader has ever watched a lava lamp, or seen soup bones being boiled, then he knows that droplets of fat come to the surface and are smashed into one another by the roiling waters. They temporarily become one droplet. Their contents are mixed up by the buffeting of the boiling water. Then they cool, divide, and fall to the bottom of the pot with different amounts of chemicals arranged differently from when they went to the surface only moments before. That will give the reader some idea of what would have been going on shortly after the Earth cooled and reached a stable temperature that permitted liquid water to exist. Around the many hot spots in the primordial ocean, millions if not billions of organic blobs combined, exchanged, recombined, constructed, and divided amino acids and nucleotides each second. As the amino acids and nucleotides became mixed and fastened to one another, some of the chemical combinations or molecules were more stable than others and, therefore, lasted longer than others. These longer-lived globules had a distinct advantage over those globules that were shorter lived. They had a relatively long period of time to bump into other globules, combine with them, and achieve even higher states of complexity. After literally hundreds of millions of years, after trillions and trillions of combinations, some extremely complex characteristics had developed in the surviving globules.

They had a way to prevent themselves from 1) being torn apart by boiling water and 2) being ingested by other globules. Most probably protection was provided in the form of a membrane made of lipids (fat) around the globules. This membrane may have originally attached itself to appropriate large organic globules by naturally occurring surface tension.[8]

When a less advanced globule that had no membrane with which to protect itself bumped into the protected globule, they stuck together. Then, by means of a number of naturally occurring processes ("osmosis,"[9] diffusion, ingestion, etc.), the less advanced organic globules' amino acids and nucleotides could pass through the membrane. Once inside the membrane they would be free to mingle and react with the already present enzymes and nucleotides, forming novel combinations. We would call this act "eating" were it to take place in a living

8. There is also some evidence that shows that water droplets form a type of membrane when subjected to cooling lava.

9. Osmosis: The transference of a substance from an area of greater density to one of lesser density through a semi-permeable membrane.

thing. Those globules containing amino acids and nucleotides without a membrane became an easy source of chemicals for the globules with membranes. In a similar manner, dissolved gases could move through the membrane. Eventually after millions of years, the globules without membranes would have become extinct.

In order to continue to exist, the protected, eating globules would have to discard the used organic matter that, if retained, would only cause it to grow too large and be subject to being torn apart by physical forces. Due to the increased concentration and pressures inside the globule, excess molecules could have been forced back out through the membrane. At that point we have an organic globule with a membrane that eats and eliminates.

Surely many of the globules that became enveloped in a membrane contained quantities of the five nucleotides. With the large number of nucleotides safely tucked inside a membrane, with an almost infinite variety of enzymes that could mingle with them, the inevitability of reproduction by enzymes splitting a long chain of nucleic acid down the middle and attaching an identical nucleotide back on to where one just came off would be assured. The globule could then split in two, leaving two perfect copies of itself and hence reproducing itself. Imagine the advantage a globule that can make copies of itself has over a globule that cannot. Those globules that cannot evolve, no matter how numerous, are destined to die off as, over tens of millions of years, they are subject to the evolving globule's improving ability to eat them. They are bound to be ingested sooner or later, and once ingested that is it—they are gone forever. No more possibility of that unique globule's ever passing on its uniqueness to the future. The replicating globules would have continued to evolve and grow more complex while eating all the other organic globules present. It seems that the replicating globules continued to climb the ladder of evolution while pulling the ladder up after themselves by eating all the nonreplicating globules from which they came.

These primitive organic globules evolved to the point that they could replicate themselves very well—but not perfectly. Every so often, due to a number of causes, such as radioactivity, cosmic radiation, chemical reaction, etc., the nucleic acid's normal process was interrupted and the organic globule created an offspring with slightly different characteristics. Therefore, a self-replicating globule that makes mostly perfect copies of itself and sometimes imperfect copies (mutants) of itself over time is going to leave a population mostly of clones of itself but also replicas of itself with minor differences. When these minor differences improve the organic globule's chances of survival, they are, by definition, improvements. The improved organic globule, with its enhanced chance of survival and by making mostly faithful replicas of itself, will in a few short generations replace the organic globule from which it arose. Therefore, the harsh Law of the Survival of the Fittest is naturally inherent in a collection of interacting organic globules, and inexorably over time it drives those globules to evolve through a process which, at some point, lets us say, like Doctor Frankenstein, "Look, Igor! It's alive! It's alive!"

At precisely what point in time a replicating globule passed over an invisible line and became a "living" thing is a subjective opinion. In reality, there is no line, invisible or otherwise; only the one placed by human beings.[10] Life, rather than being created in an instant, was a natural process occurring over hundreds of millions of years. By 3.5 billion years ago, these complex globules had certainly become living things, because there are bacteria fossilized in rocks of that age.

Therefore, we have come upon an extremely important truth—the Law of the Survival of the Fittest applies not only to living things but also to organic globules. Life on Earth was inexorably *caused* by the Law of the Survival of the Fittest. Those organic globules with the "fittest" characteristics for sur-

---

10. Science defines life as having seven characteristics: 1) to eat, 2) to excrete, 3) to move, 4) to breathe, 5) to respond to stimuli, 6) to grow, and 7) to reproduce.

vival, did survive. Those that perished did not have the appropriate characteristics for survival. However, even a moment's reflection reveals that the Law of the Survival of the Fittest applies not only to living things but to all things. For example, if we build a house of brick and our neighbor builds one of papier mâché, the Law of the Survival of the Fittest will dictate that our house will survive and that our neighbor's will not. Like most "great truths," this one is disarmingly simple.

SCIENCE EXPERT: In fact, the second oldest known fossil from a living thing is a stromatolite. Stromatolites are lumps of calcium carbonate deposited by cyanobacteria. Cyanobacteria attach themselves to rocks in the tidal zone of the sea. Fossilized remains of stromatolites 3.3 billion years old may be found in the Precambrian rocks of the Medicine Bow Mountains in Wyoming. Modern stromatolites may be viewed in Shark Bay in Western Australia. Cyanobacteria are a type of the first known living cells, called prokaryotes (before a nucleus). They are characterized by having their DNA in a simple circle as opposed to the complex, double-

Stromatolites in Shark Bay, Western Australia

helix arrangement found in more advanced organisms. Cyanobacteria use photosynthesis to produce nutrients. A by-product of photosynthesis is the conversion of carbon dioxide into oxygen. We owe the cyanobacteria a large debt of gratitude because by 2 billion years ago they had converted the primitive atmosphere of Earth into an oxygen-based one, which permits complex organisms like ourselves to exist. The prokaryotes were the only living things on Earth until 1.5 billion years ago, when eukaryotes (true nucleus) evolved. Eukaryotic cells have a well-defined nucleus encapsulated by a double membrane that can contain a more complex, folded DNA molecule which

can hold much more hereditary information than the simple
circle of the prokaryotes. As animals become more complex,
their DNA molecule becomes bigger, until the largest naturally
occurring molecule in existence is the human DNA molecule
containing 10 billion atoms. *All* higher plants and animals are
made from eukaryotic cells. Many biologists consider the evolution of eukaryotes as the most important single advance in the
entire history of life on Earth.

Up until 750 million years ago, all living things had been
single-celled, but with an oxygen-based atmosphere and virtually unlimited ability to store hereditary information, the stage
was set for the rapid evolution of more complex organisms; 750
million years ago, multicellular creatures developed.

Us: Let us Black Box how multicellular organisms evolved.
Life evolved slowly. At first, as in the cyanobacteria, the
colonies of cells were undifferentiated. This means that each
cell performed all the functions necessary for life. However,
after the eukaryotes appeared, as the cells replicated themselves inexactly, differentiation began to occur. When the differentiation assisted the colony of cells to survive more efficiently,
a division of labor occurred. For instance, one cell might be able
to ingest organic globules, due to its different enzyme make-up,
which the other cells could not. However, the other cells might
be able to utilize extremely well the globules that the differentiated cell discarded. In effect the differentiated cell would be
performing the same task that a stomach performs in humans.
In a like manner, over millions of years and trillions of unsuccessful attempts, cells divided labor more and more and became
increasingly complex. Organisms that evolved characteristics
that could utilize the resources at hand more efficiently not
only survived but prospered and multiplied. Those that could
not failed and became extinct. All life is merely an increasingly
complex and interrelated division of labor by cells.

Worms appeared 700 million years ago.

Hard Bodies

Since the rest of the story of animal evolution is verifiable by the fossil record, we can dispense with the services of our Science Expert. 600 million years ago animals proliferated, and the fossil record teems with new species. Trilobites, brachiopods, and other hard-bodied animals flourished on the floor of the ocean.

The membrane that permitted the primordial organic globules to stay together had proved insufficient for billions of years. Almost three billion years of steady improvement in the ability of animals to penetrate the outer coverings of its fellow animals had brought about the development of the original hard body. The first hard-bodied creatures must have been able to eat with impunity their fill of their soft-bodied relatives. The population of hard-bodied creatures must have skyrocketed, as indeed the fossil record shows. At first, when the population of hard-bodied animals was small, it must have been very easy for the hard-bodied creatures to survive. The hard body is such an important advantage over soft-bodied life forms that it must have overcome what would normally have been disadvantages in comparison to the other hard-bodied animals. Therefore, most of the variant hard-bodied offspring, even the less fit, usually survived.

Trilobite

As a result, not only did the sheer number of hard-bodied organisms increase but a wide array of variant hard-bodied creatures began to appear almost immediately. The hard-bodied animals continued to increase in kind and quantity for 165 million years. These cumbersome and slow moving "tanks" roamed the ocean floor, conquerors of all the soft-bodied animals they stumbled upon.

The Rise of the Vertebrates

Fishes

By 500 million years ago a soft-bodied wormlike survivor had developed a primitive backbone. Its cells could utilize calcium found in sea water to build body parts. This creature resembled the still-living lancelet, "a small, translucent creature, lacking fins and jaws but possessing gills and most important, a primitive version of the backbone" (*Red Giants and White Dwarfs*, p. 158).

The backbone was used to great advantage, primarily by the fishes. With a backbone, spinal cord, internal skeleton, and attached musculature, the otherwise soft-bodied creatures could, among other things, make rapid getaways from clumsy, slow moving hard-bodied creatures. To graphically illustrate how important a backbone is to a fast getaway, let us use an Einsteinian Thought Experiment: Conceive of yourself without a backbone or bones of any sort, in a disheveled clump on your kitchen floor, when in through one door of the kitchen enters a pit bull terrier. Your friends with backbones yell, "Let's get out of here," and run for the other door. In view of your lack of rapid mobility, I believe that it is safe to assume that the pit bull will treat himself to whichever of your organic molecules he desires. Your friends, however, will be safe. It was as true in the Devonian Period, the age of fishes, as it is now. Do not underestimate the need for a fast getaway.

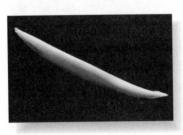

Lancelet

The fishes, armed with the defensive advantage of efficient mobility, multiplied in kind and quantity as the hard bodies did when they had the advantage. For the same reasons, the number of variants of the fishes increased explosively, and 435 million years ago, primitive fishes developed the jaw. The development of an offensive weapon, in the form of a hard jaw that could crush the hard body of a trilobite, combined with efficient mobility, caused a drastic decline in the trilobite population. The Law of the Survival of the Fittest had passed the advantage to the fishes.

A coastal, bottom-dwelling variant of the fishes had developed fins that could propel it on land. This particular fish could exploit land-based food sources first in the

Early jawed fish

tidal zones and later beyond. This creature was thought to have become extinct at least 40 million years ago, but in 1938 fishermen from the Comoro Islands were fishing in the Indian Ocean and pulled up a Coelacanth. It was dead due to the abrupt change in pressure. Several have been caught since. The Coelacanth and the lungfish, with primitive lungs for breathing

Coelacanth

air, were the bridge between an entirely aquatic life and part-time occupation of the land.

As Coelacanth variants called tetrapods (four feet) prospered in a virginal habitat, those variants with increasing lung capacity and with fins becoming more and more like legs were favored in the struggle for survival. Over time they needed to return to the ocean less and less frequently. Eventually some stopped returning entirely, and 375 million years ago the land-dwelling amphibian arrived, no doubt to exploit insect life, which had begun to populate the land more than 400 million years ago.

As we learn what other life forms dominated the planet in times earlier than our own, it would be wise to investigate a little more thoroughly what factors made these creatures the dominant life form and what conditions were like at that time. For these creatures successfully answered the very same questions that our contemporary human society must answer: How to survive, and how to continue surviving? Their answers to these questions will increase our knowledge of the range of the possible correct answers and also assist us by showing us the incorrect ones. Since both we and the animals are answering the same challenge, it is valid to compare and contrast the strategies employed by each. It is also valid for us to evaluate the animals' existence from the subjective viewpoint of our own.

One criterion humans use to evaluate human societies is the infant mortality rate. Clearly, if an infant of any species does not reach adulthood it does not have the ability to produce offspring and pass on its result of billions of years of refinement. From a subjective human viewpoint, a high early death rate is strongly unappealing because of the deaths of our children, brothers, sisters, etc.—a condition in which we would not like to live.

Also, it would be informative if we could administer some form of intelligence test to the various dominant species. Even rather rough estimates would be very valuable. We can do this by using Einsteinian Thought Experiments.

It is not very enlightening to us modern Americans that Darwin chose the word "fittest"[11] when he propounded his law of survival. The word "fittest" is not used much in modern English, and its meaning has become vague. If Darwin had used the phrase Survival of the Efficient, it would have been much more meaningful to us. Membrane-protected globules were more *efficient* at ingesting other globules without being ingested themselves. The hard-bodied could more *efficiently* obtain the

---

11. Darwin borrowed the phrase "survival of the fittest" from a brief essay, "The Theory of Population" written in 1852 by Herbert Spencer. Darwin originally used the phrase "natural selection."

organic molecules they needed without risking giving up their own, so they were far more *efficient*. The fishes were far more *efficient* due to mobility and speed. If Darwin had said Survival of the Efficient, he would have been much more informative. For that is what it really is. Therefore, let us change Darwin's Law of the Survival of the Fittest to the Law of the Survival of the Efficient.

Amphibians

(Land-dwelling animals that spend part of their lives in water)

Paracyclotosaurus

When most people think of amphibians, which is probably not very often, they think of frogs, toads, newts, salamanders, and other disagreeable, unimportant, little creatures. But it was not always so. Between 300 million years ago and 240 million years ago the amphibians were the kings of the land. *Paracyclotosaurus* was an amphibian the size and shape of a crocodile, and presumably fulfilled the same function. As with the animals before it, when some advantage permitted unrestrained access to a food resource, it multiplied explosively in kind and quantity.

I bet we can predict what happened next. Just as the other animals did before them when they had an advantage—they multiplied in kind and quantity until they became the dominant life form on Earth. We have witnessed the same event occur over and over again. I think we have witnessed enough to tentatively identify a law of the universe—"When a creature develops even a modest advantage over its fellow creatures, not only it but its variants increase until the available resources are fully exploited, including its fellow creatures." Clearly this is the case with modern humankind.

For an insight into the thinking ability of these early amphibians, let us analyze modern frogs. When I was about nine years old and did not know any better, I accompanied a group of older boys to a local frog pond. They had a BB gun with them and proceeded to shoot the frogs. The BB gun had a devastating effect on a creature as small as the frog. Many of the frogs were dismembered, maimed, and otherwise grotesquely mutilated. Their buddies, inches away, clearly able to view the carnage wrought upon their fellow frogs, continued unconcernedly about their business. They did not attempt to flee or hide. Clearly, the frogs were unable to make the intellectual jump from "my buddies are being horribly massacred" to "perhaps I will be next." Even on so basic a point as immediate survival, amphibians cannot understand cause-and-effect relationships. Amphibian intelligence must exist only in theory and not in reality.

The reason amphibians must spend part of their lives around water is that their skins are water permeable. Even the most advanced amphibian must return to water during its life. The desert-dwelling Australian water-holding frog even secretes a nonporous membrane with which it covers its body in an attempt to prolong water retention in order to remain alive longer without water, thereby increasing its chances of survival. Clearly, a variant of the rapidly expanding amphibian class with a watertight skin would be a highly successful creature. And it was. Only we do not call them amphibians when they have a watertight skin—we call them reptiles.

Reptiles

About 240 million years ago, the reptiles became the masters of the land. Some variants of the reptiles even returned to the oceans and became voracious predators of the fish from which they had evolved. One minor variant of the reptile was a warm-blooded, hairy, little creature. Rodentlike and nocturnal, this creature was to be subordinate to reptiles for 175 million years. We will pick up the story of this creature later.

Reptiles became enormously diverse—dinosaurs weighing tons and dwarf species weighing less than a pound. Variation proceeded upon variation until the reptiles filled most nooks and crannies of existence. The four orders of reptiles remaining today are merely a faint echo of the profusion of this great animal: 1) the turtles and tortoises; 2) the crocodiles, alligators and caimans; 3) the lizards and their descendants, the snakes; and 4) the tuatara.[12] Except for a few snakes, reptiles reproduce by laying eggs.

In an attempt to gain an understanding of what life must have been like during the age of the dinosaurs, and if possible to administer an intelligence test, a few years ago I journeyed to one of the most remote places on Earth, Komodo Island in the Indonesian Archipelago between Australia and Asia. The object of my quest was the Komodo dragon (*Varanus komodoensis*). Unevolved for 130 million years, it could truly be called the closest living creature to the gigantic carnivorous dinosaurs.[13]

Tuatara

Only 2,000 exist and only on Komodo Island and a couple of surrounding tiny islands. The largest of these creatures is 14 feet long and approximately 250 to 300 pounds. It has a three-foot tongue that flicks out like a snake's and senses the air. The powerful tail of the creature can be whipped around to break the legs of prey, thereby immobilizing them. The ripping and cutting teeth of the animal are coated with a green, bacterial slime so virulent that when the animal was first discovered by westerners in 1912 it was thought to be poisonous. If that were not enough, its six- to eight-inch claws can, in one swipe, disembowel a person.

---

12. The tuatara is a near-extinct, three-eyed-at-birth, cold-adapted reptile living in New Zealand and is closely related to dinosaurs.

13. Dinosaurs are differentiated from reptiles by the way their legs are attached to their bodies. Reptile legs are widely set out from the body, causing them to be slow. Dinosaur legs are close to the body, permitting rapid locomotion.

As an interesting aside, there are some who think the Komodo dragon gave rise to the notion of the fire-breathing dragons in Chinese mythology. Thousands of years ago, Chinese traders were known to sail near these remote islands. It does not take much imagination to visualize a local native attempting to describe the three-foot-long, red tongue of the beast in pantomime to a Chinese trader who mistakes the red tongue's description for red fire.

The Komodo dragon is born in a clutch of eggs, usually 28. After breaking its egg, the small creature is on its own. Not only does the baby dragon have the usual rigors of life with which to contend, it is also subject to being eaten by larger dragons. Most dragons do not survive to adulthood. Once past a critical size, about five to six feet, they are fairly impervious to damage except from the largest of the species. Then they stake out a ter-

Komodo Dragon and dead goat

ritory amongst one of the many systems of intermingled game trails. The trails are used by deer and wild pigs twice a day to go from the highlands down to the water. The dragon lies in ambush along one of the trails crossing its territory. If the dragon sees a hoof fall in front of it, the dragon lunges forward in a lightning quick move to firmly grasp the leg in its powerful jaws. The fate of the prey is sealed at that moment. The dragon waits for its victim to go into shock and become rigid, then in one rapid twisting move releases its hold on the leg, rolls over, and runs the top front row of its teeth, which are now inverted, along the soft underbelly of the victim. At least a portion of the intestines will usually hang to the ground. The poor frightened victim now realizes that it is no longer being held by the dreaded beast and runs off down the trail. However, with each step the victim takes, its hind legs pull more and more of its own bowel out, resulting in large amounts of blood being spread on the trail, and in very short order, the poor creature drags the entire length of its intestines behind it. After running as much as a mile the victim expires from loss of blood.

Then dragons from miles around smell the blood in the air with their flicking tongues and converge on the carcass. The dragon that killed the victim is not necessarily among the early arrivals on the scene. What ensues at the carcass site can only be likened to a shark feeding-frenzy carried out by land sharks. A hungry lion eats at the rate of about a pound and a half per minute. A Komodo dragon eats at a rate of about six pounds per minute. Entire hind quarters are literally ripped from the carcass and swallowed whole. It is an awesome sight to behold, for it is, to all intents and purposes, time travel back to 130 million years ago and watching a live dinosaur eat a meal. Our animal ancestors had to endure hundreds of millions of years of brutal existence to get us to the safe, sheltered, and cozy lives we lead today.

For all the ferocity of the dragon, it is a member of a class of abysmally stupid creatures. A fifteen-foot alligator has a brain the size of an almond. I Black Boxed reptile brain functions and concluded that the reptile brain can be that small because no thinking takes place. I assumed a reptile receives a stimulus that either triggers an instinctual response or does not. If this were true, I concluded that I should be able to observe a Komodo dragon from an extremely close distance— less than one of its body lengths away—as long as I did not appear to the dragon as something that would trigger an aggressive response. All I had to do was 1) not appear to be food and 2) not appear to be threatening. As far as number one is concerned, I may not be the best looking person in the world, but with only modest effort I thought I could dispel any putative claim to being a pig or any other prey of the dragon. As for number two, the heart of my strategy became not to scare a 14-foot, 250-pound, carnivorous reptile.

After a two-mile hike into the bush, we came to the spot where my guides said there should be dragons. And there were.

I had expected to test my logic on one lone Komodo dragon. What I encountered was 12 of them moving around in a field. I paused to consider how 11 additional dragons, on some of which I would not be able to keep an eye, would affect my plans. I came up with the following thinking: Komodo dragons are territorial. Therefore, that field belongs to only one of the dragons out there. The other dragons are there only because the owner allows it. They would not attack a suspected food source on the territory of a superior for fear of reprisal from that superior. Therefore, I reasoned that I would not be attacked by the other dragons unless I was first attacked by the dominant dragon. All I had to do would be to find the dominant dragon and not scare him or appear to be food. Finding him would be easy. One glance through the field showed me who it was. Naturally, it would be the biggest one.

I walked up to the dragon in a slow, steady gait. Not directly at it but obliquely in order to come alongside. I stopped and slowly waved my Chinese walking stick over my head. He was a true beauty in prime condition, around 14 feet long. The tail, which is about one-half the entire body length, was powered by muscles larger than an average man's waist. What a magnificent beast! His tongue kept flicking in and out, taking my molecules out of the air to see if they fit an instinctual code stored in its brain. After several moments it became apparent that the dragon had no pre-programmed instinctual reaction to a man waving a Chinese walking stick over his head. The dragon had no instinctual guidance because it was a new situation for him. A Komodo dragon is at a complete loss when he confronts a new situation, and neither attacks nor flees. Were I to attempt this with a thinking mammal, say a lion or a bear, the outcome would have been dramatically different. As it was, I received about as realistic an excursion to the age of dinosaurs as is possible these days. It must have been a cruel and brutal existence compared to our relatively kind society. Death could come at any time. Dinosaur infant mortality was no doubt well over 50 percent. Clearly, we are very lucky to be alive today.

The reptiles were so successful with their watertight skins that the variants produced variants that produced variants and so on for tens of millions of years. Some of the reptiles could fly, some were hairy, some could glide for long distances between trees. Eventually a group of characteristics came together that was so light and so delicate that at first it was overlooked by science. The fossil record of certain light-boned agile reptiles is so complete and changed so slowly that it was not originally apparent to its classi-fiers that the reptile had evolved into a bird. The fossils were misclas-sified. When the fossils were re-examined under a microscope the very faint impression of feathers could be clearly discerned. The

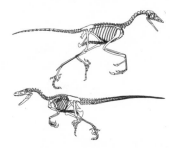

It is not easy to distinguish between the bone structure of Archaeopteryx, *a bird (above) and* Velociraptor, *a dinosaur (below) of* Jurassic Park *fame.*

change from reptile to bird was so smooth that the point where the reptile evolved into a bird is not a dramatic one. It is ex-tremely difficult to tell the reptile fossil from the bird fossil. Birds inherited egg-laying from their ancestors, the reptiles.

Birds

By 160 million years ago descendants of the reptiles, the birds, flew and dominated the air. With the advent of the birds we are now at the point in time where we can easily answer the chicken-and-egg question mentioned at the begin-ning of the book. It seems a childishly simple question to us now. However, the greatest intellects of history, Aristotle, da Vinci, and Newton, would not have been able to answer it. Only in the last 100 years has the question been answerable. We are gaining a profound understanding of reality. *Archaeopteryx* was the name of a bird so primitive that it had teeth, a lizardlike tail, and was one of the transitional animals between reptiles and birds. It may be related to a bird still living in South

Archaeopteryx—*note teeth, claws on wings, and tail*

America called a harridon.

"Rarer than hen's teeth" is an expression many of us use to describe an extremely unusual event, because no living birds have teeth. However, *Archaeopteryx* had teeth and also flew. The teeth were lost during evolution because they were just too heavy a burden with which to fly. A beak could be modified for the same purpose. Unfortunately for the bird, a large brain is also too heavy to carry around. In fact, we still use the phrase "dumb as a dodo" to describe less than exemplary human behavior. The dodo was made extinct in 1681. It lived on the remote island of Mauritius, in the Indian Ocean. Dutch sailors desiring fresh provisions for the journey to the East Indies found they could kill the dodo by walking up to it and slamming it on the head with a club in full view of other dodos. The remaining dodos neither fought nor fled and went about their business

Dodo bird

until they too were slammed in the head. Obviously, the thought process had not evolved very much from the frog, through the reptile, to the bird. Hence, the pejorative term "bird brain."

Bees

Bees are important to our analysis of life on Earth, because they demonstrate a remarkably advanced technique of survival—division of labor. A bee colony is divided into worker bees, drones, and a queen bee. The worker bees guard the hive, gather pollen, make honey, build and repair the hive, assist the queen bee, and take care of the young bees. They even have the ability to communicate. A worker bee who has found a source of pollen returns to the hive and performs a "dance" that informs the other bees where the pollen is. A human observer who knows the meaning of bee dances can easily understand the message and know exactly where the pollen is. It is a surprisingly advanced form of communication.

The worker bees also protect the hive and are responsible for stinging unwary human beings, amongst other things. The queen bee fulfills the reproductive role in bee society. The drones provide the queen with male reproductive services.

By dividing labor, the bees have achieved an advantage in the struggle for survival that no single bee could possibly attain. It is not possible for a single bee, no matter how industrious, to simultaneously find and produce food, guard the hive, and reproduce and care for the next generation. Therefore, to evaluate the advantages of bees in the struggle for survival of the efficient, it is inaccurate to analyze the traits of an individual bee. An individual bee cannot survive on its own. It is only enlightening when we analyze the entire bee society. When a group of animals divides labor, they become interdependent on one another. For instance, how well the worker bees guard the hive determines whether the drones live or die. The drones may be doing a great job, but if the worker bees guarding the hive are not efficient at their job, the beehive will be destroyed. To divide labor is to create a society. Therefore, in any group of animals that have divided labor, the entire society must be evaluated to determine success or failure in the struggle for the Survival of the Efficient. How efficiently do the various divisions of a society perform their tasks? How efficient is the coordination among divisions? These are the questions that must be answered to determine the advantages of a particular society in the struggle under the Law of the Survival of the Efficient.

CHAPTER FOUR

Bye, Bye Bronty; Hello, Bonzo

65 Million Years Ago to 125,000 Years Ago

Mammals

UNLIKE THE BIRDS, another creature was probably living by its wits. The hairy, rodentlike creature we mentioned as an early variant of the reptile was probably sneaking around at night eating insects, stealing eggs or young from reptile nests, and eating anything it could scavenge. The crea-

Megazostrodon

ture, called *Megazostrodon*, was warmblooded, which allowed it to be active at night when it was cool. The reptile is coldblooded and therefore sluggish in cool weather. A reptile needs to heat itself to about the same temperature as warmblooded creatures to be active—95 F versus 98.6 F for humans. Reptiles accomplish this by taking frequent sun baths. Hence, the obligatory scene in African safari movies of riverbanks lined with sunbathing crocodiles that slither ominously into the water upon being disturbed by the boat. Even with the advantage of being active at night, the hairy rodentlike ancestors of the mammals were not very successful.

In the normal course of evolution, over time, small, beneficial changes in the offspring of animals caused them to adjust more and more to a given environment. In this instance the Earth changed, which caused a not very successful advantage of the mammals—fur and warmbloodedness—to propel them to dominance. An asteroid struck the Earth about 64 million years ago, causing a crater 112 miles in diameter near the town of Chicxulub in the Yucatán Peninsula of Mexico. It raised a cloud of ash and dust which enveloped the Earth for years. The evidence for this is a thin layer of iridium in rock formations laid down at that time all over the Earth. Iridium is a very rare element on the surface of the Earth but is abundant in meteors. With the sunlight partially blocked from reaching the Earth, the sun baths became ineffectual. The reptiles became sluggish all the time. The warmblooded hairy mammals came down from the trees and out of their burrows in the ground. A warm cobra is no match for a mongoose. A cold cobra is merely dinner on the table. It must have been as if a giant dinner bell were rung world-wide calling the mammals to dinner. The reader should know extremely well by now what happened next. The mammals increased exponentially in both quantity and kind. By 45 million years ago all of the various orders of mammals had been promulgated. Bats were flying, horses were running around, and a wolflike creature had dived back into the ocean to become the whales, porpoises, and other marine mammals. The monkeys' ancestor was related to the mouse lemur. They were rodentlike insectivores and lived in trees.

Favored by an increased capacity for thinking, self-generated warmth, and a small number of well-protected young resulting in a high survival rate, the mammals rapidly supplanted the reptiles from thousands of ecological niches. Let us choose the male lion and his favorite prey, the wildebeest (or as he is otherwise known, the hairy-nosed gnu) for a close-up look at mammalian life.

Lion

The male African lion is renowned for having a soft, comfortable life while at the same time being so ferocious and powerful that he is called the King of Beasts. He is usually born with a litter of two or three. His first meals, being a mammal, are nutritious and easy to come by—milk from his mother. His days are spent in rest and in play with not only his litter mates but also the

The King of Beasts

cubs from previous litters. The play consists of chasing and jumping and fighting in preparation for adult life. It is not unusual for a cub to have an eye scratched out or to develop a permanent limp due to this rough play.

After the cub is weaned, mealtime becomes far more difficult. When the adult females of the pride go hunting, the cubs are left in the care of one or more adult females who act as nannies. When a kill is made, the nanny leads the cubs to it. It may be a couple of

miles to the kill site with the nanny riding herd on five to ten cubs. Often, by the time the cubs arrive, the prey has been completely devoured. When the cubs arrive while there is still food, it is not much better. Lions eat in order of dominance. The adult males eat first and as much as they want. Then the females, after which there is usually little left. The cubs, if they are to eat, must somehow squeeze themselves into the carcass around hungry, contentious beasts 10 to 20 times their size. While eating, the adults fight amongst themselves and think nothing of swatting a cub. This sends the cub head over heels for five or ten feet and leaves him obviously dazed. I invite you to compare this scene to your family's going out for Sunday dinner.

So far, a lion's childhood seems fairly difficult. However, those are the good times. Lion prides are territorial and therefore remain in one place all year round. The herds upon which they prey are migratory and follow good grass and abundant water. When the herds are in a given pride's territory, the lions feast. When the herds move on, the lions starve. Of course, the ones to suffer most in the annual drought and lean times are the cubs. There is no tendency, as there is in humans to feed the cubs first or save some for the young. Wild African dogs eat at the kill site and then return to the den and regurgitate food for their pups. No such advanced survival mechanisms exist for lion cubs. The cubs either make it or they do not. Most do not. Out of every five cubs born, only one will survive to adulthood.

As our male cub nears adulthood, life becomes easier, right? Wrong. When the adolescent cub shows signs of adulthood, the two adult males of the pride, allowing no competition, run the adolescent off. The manner in which this is accomplished leaves no doubt in the young male's mind that he would be hastily killed were he to return. The young male joins a loose group of bachelors where he survives by eating anything he can and hones his fighting skills against other males. After several years, if he matures into one of the largest, strongest, and toughest of the lions, he finds a buddy and they form a team. A variety of outcomes is possible at this juncture, but typically he and his buddy will begin to wander. One night his roars may be met by a young female with amorous intentions but whose pride is ruled by her own father. Therefore she seeks sex outside the pride. Lionesses are sexually mature at two years of age. The next day our young lion and his buddy may challenge the father and his teammate for control of the pride. After what may be a fierce fight, but rarely to the death, our lion may win and finally assume his position as head of the pride. His responsibilities are 1) to protect the pride from marauding male lions, of which he was one up until yesterday (the male lions routinely take turns patrolling the borders of their territories leaving scent markings to warn off intruders); 2) to settle disputes and maintain order among the females. Justice apparently plays no part in this, merely a desire for peace and quiet. The male lion's mane protects his neck from both claws and teeth. The female has no such protection and can be killed quickly by a male. However, the mane places the male at a distinct disadvantage in hunting, wherein sneaking up on game unobserved is of paramount importance; and, 3) to provide sexual services for the females, which is no mean feat as active lovemaking between lions may last a full twenty-four hours, at which time the male collapses into the bushes and his teammate may continue with the female. The female's responsibility to the male is basically to provide him with food and sex. Finally, our male lion is the King of the Beasts and lives happily ever after, right? Wrong. The average amount of time that a male lion remains the head of a pride is two years, after which he is thrown out by the females or new males. Two years out of a life span of 13–15 years.[14] It hardly seems worth it. After losing his pride, the lion usually becomes what is called a "rogue" lion. He wanders nomadically, feeding opportunistically. All things considered, the life of the King of the Beasts is definitely far more beastly than kingly. I would not trade places with him, would you?

Wildebeest (Hairy-Nosed Gnu)

The lion of the Serengeti plains of Africa dines most frequently on the wildebeest. The wildebeest looks like an old, shaggy carpet bag in search of a meal, and acts like a victim waiting for the crime. The nervous comedian Don Knotts appears overconfident compared to the wildebeest. Lions use wildebeest herds as we use supermarkets.

Usually, one calf is born in the spring of the year. The calf must learn to stand in a matter of moments and run within minutes of birth, or risk being lost to predators. Hundreds of thousands of calves are born each year out of a herd of over a million wildebeests.

---

14. Further evidence of how difficult life is in the wild is demonstrated by the lion's greatly increased life span in captivity—35 to 40 years.

The wildebeest grows up running and playing, strengthening its legs for the long migration ahead. It is always conscious of returning to its mother for the precious milk. The migration follows a route of several hundred miles, which the wildebeest has been using annually for thousands of years. There are many perils on the trip including swollen rivers, wild dog attacks at night, disease, leopard attacks at night, accidental injury, hyena attacks at night, not to mention lion attacks. The lion, as we learned earlier, is a territorial animal. As the wildebeests migrate they pass by the tens of thousands through various lions'

Wildebeests

territories. Where the grass is good the wildebeests stop to graze. The lionesses usually hunt for the pride every two days.

A typical hunting plan is for one line of the lionesses to chase the wildebeest herd up to a line of concealed lionesses, who at the last instant rise from concealment in the grass and bring down a wildebeest. This explains the old saying, "It's not the lion you see that will kill you, it's the one you don't see."

If we wanted to look at this from an economic viewpoint, we could say that the lions give grazing rights to the wildebeest in exchange for a few carcasses of raw meat. It is as if the lions charge a toll to the wildebeests, which they evidently do not mind paying because year after year they continue to pay it.

Thus, two, three, or even four wildebeests can be obtained in what may appear to be a simple trap to us but represents a monumentally advanced state of thinking, planning, and organization compared to the frogs, reptiles, or birds that we have studied so far. The lioness's plan involves close coordination and communication amongst eight or ten animals that do not have the power of speech. The lionesses must be taught to hunt. If you would like a test of how difficult this is, use an Einsteinian Thought Experiment to attempt to plan and carry out an organized hunt with eight or ten house cats. Being mammals, the lionesses have the mental ability to learn fairly complex tasks. They are not nearly as dependent on instinct as reptiles are. The plan itself involves the lionesses' ability to deceive the brain of the wildebeest. The wildebeest thinks he is fleeing danger when in fact he takes himself to the real danger. Definitely the lionesses show an increase in intellectual functioning of several orders of magnitude over the previous forms of life.

However, they have not progressed anywhere near as far as humans in intellectual thought. The lion and the wildebeest are fairly evenly matched in the grand game of survival. They have occupied the same lands for thousands of years. The wildebeest survives by virtue of masses of population. The lion survives by ferocity and intellect. The relatively few number of animals lost to the lions is insignificant to the long-term survival of the wildebeest. So the strategies for survival balance in the long run and both species would continue to survive and coexist, all other things being equal. However, let us do an Einsteinian Thought Experiment and replace the intelligence of the lion and the wildebeest with human intelligence and observe the results. Let us assume that we replace the mind of the lion with our very own minds. How would things be different? Well, first off this starving for part of the year is no good. I would have the pride dig a large pen out of the earth and then I would drive into the pen a sufficient number of wildebeests to keep my pride in meat for the year. In one flash of insight the lions could come to totally dominate the wildebeest as the neighboring Masai people totally dominate the cattle they raise. Why do the lions not do this? Their brains are not equipped to permit them to think in this way.

If the wildebeests were able to think like humans they could make a plan to rid themselves of the dreaded lion attacks. The plan could be very simple. As soon as a lion is spotted at close range, the entire herd should charge it and trample it to death. A few wildebeests might be killed initially, but some are being killed by the lions anyway. In a very short period of time, the lions would learn that attacking wildebeests results in certain death. It would become part of the survival strategy of lions not to attack wildebeests.

If only the wildebeests had the 1) intellectual power to overcome the emotional instinct to flee at the sight of a lion, plus 2) the intellectual power to realize that short-term sacrifices will result in permanent improvement of the life of the wildebeest. Given this increase in intellectual power, in one year the wildebeests could completely remove their name from the dinner menu of the King of the Beasts. Neither lions nor wildebeests have the ability to think in the future. No matter how long the claws, no matter how sharp the teeth, they are as nothing compared to human intellect.

Lemurs

Now let us return to the series of causes and effects that will result in the emergence of modern humans. Some 200 million years ago, the island of Madagascar broke off from the east coast of Africa and remained in virtual isolation until humankind arrived by boat across the Indian Ocean from Indonesia 2,000 years ago. The dinosaurs became extinct, leaving our ancestors, the lemurs, to evolve in isolation, which means hardly at all. The remote forested regions of Madagascar are like a life raft that has come down to us from the age of the dinosaurs. They retain, down to the present day, the characteristics that caused them to be able to survive alongside the dinosaurs. The nocturnal, tree-dwelling

Mouse lemur

lemurs have large eyes on the front of their faces resulting in binocular night vision. They retain grasping hands. Some lemurs are capable of incredible single leaps of up to 30 yards. However, in limited observations in the wild, the author has never witnessed an unbroken series of leaps by a lemur.

Monkeys

In Africa 38 million years ago, a descendant of the mouse lemur
had evolved into the monkeys. The extinction of the dinosaurs
permitted the monkeys to be active during the day. Hence, they
did not need the ability to see as well at night as the lemurs.
Daytime life in the trees equipped the monkeys with a complex
social structure, and, more important, a brain that could make
extremely rapid calculations. The
speed and agility of monkeys swinging
through trees necessitates an extremely high rate of signal processing, integrating, recognizing, decision-making,
and responding. Not much storage of
information (memory) is required,
hence a small brain suffices. However,
a high throughput rate is critical to
judge the distances between limbs,
what branches will or will not hold,
deciding when to move an arm or open
a hand at the absolutely incredible

Gibbon

speeds at which relatively small-brained monkeys can move
through trees. It demonstrates that in a compact space, a pow-
erhouse of processing can go on. I do not know of any animal
that has to make anywhere near the number of decisions per
second as a monkey or a gibbon ape, just to move around. A fall
to the ground is death or severe injury, which is the same thing
as death. In addition, the ability to make an unbroken series of
swings through trees demonstrates, however modestly, an
increased ability to think in the future by the monkeys compared to their ancestors, the lemurs.

The monkey became bigger and stronger and more apelike.
Two of the ancestors of modern primates were *Sivapithecus* and
Aegyptopithecus (literally "Egyptian ape"), a three-foot, apelike
creature that lived 28 million years ago.

Apelike Creatures

A pproximately 8 million years ago, two geologic incidents occurred that inexorably propelled the apelike creatures of Africa toward becoming human. The first event was the splitting open of the Rift Valley, which runs virtually the entire length of Africa, north to south. The Rift Valley made travel difficult between east and west Africa. The second geologic occurrence was the raising of a mountain range on the western side of the Rift Valley that further hampered travel but, more important, stopped the moisture-laden air of the Atlantic Ocean from reaching east Africa. The common ancestors of man and the chimpanzees were simultaneously separated and given increasingly different habitats. The chimpanzee ancestors to the west of the mountains enjoyed a relatively easy existence in lush rain forests, whereas our ancestors in east Africa quite literally had their hands full just trying to survive. The lack of rainfall caused the forests to shrink, depositing the apelike creatures unceremoniously on the grasslands, or "savannas." The apes were not adapted for life on the savanna. Therefore, times must have been extremely difficult. Those who changed their ways of living to adapt to the new environment were successful and survived. Those who could not adapt to the new environment were unsuccessful and failed to survive. The creatures who were to become the great apes (gorillas and chimpanzees) remained in the trees of west Africa .

The drying savanna, compared to the relative lushness of fruit and vegetable matter in a forest, must have caused great hunger and starvation. On the savanna was an exploitable, rich source of food, but it was not fruits and vegetables. All around, grazing on the savanna grasses, were endless herds of animals as far as the eye could see. If one were standing up, that is. There must have been a very severe natural selection in favor of those apelike creatures who spent the most time standing up. They would have the advantage of seeing threats and food from much farther away and therefore have a much better chance to survive. Those who could walk and run standing up would have an even better chance. It is easy to see that very rapidly the apelike creatures would have been forced to stand, walk, and run erect if they were to survive. That caused one of the most important and critical developments in the story of life on Earth. By standing, walking, and running in an erect manner, the apelike creature freed two limbs from taking an active role in locomotion. These two appendages came complete with a generalized grasping and manipulatory tool at the end of each, called a hand. These hands, freed of any function in locomotion, could be put to any use of which the owner could think.

The apelike creatures were severely disadvantaged due to the change in habitat from forest to savanna, where the coin of the realm had changed from fruits and vegetables to dead carcasses. The equipment with which the apelike creature had to survive was pitiful—relatively slow speed, insufficient teeth or claws to ward off predators or down game, no defense from attack by predators. In fact, no real way to either eat grass or down prey animals and no way to defend themselves against leopards and lions. The apelike creatures faced extinction if they could not find a good use for those hands.

Fortunately, some relative genius (or more likely a group of relative geniuses, as the idea was no doubt thought up and lost several times before it permanently took hold) got the idea of using the hands to carry objects as he traveled around. For a male, the most useful objects to carry would be a stick and a stone. For a female the natural object to carry was a child. The law of the Survival of the Efficient would have selected in favor of those mothers who could walk while nursing their children. Hence, the development of pendulous breasts in females. Suckling while walking can occur with a large flexible breast, but not very easily with a nipple almost flat against the chest. A newborn baby oftentimes must nurse up to six times per day for up to half an hour each time, for a total of three hours. If we perform an Einsteinian Thought Experiment by imagining ourselves observing a small band of perhaps twenty apelike creatures walking across the savanna, it becomes readily apparent that nursing while walking was extremely important for the survival of the group.[15] The entire group could remain together. The other available options would either greatly increase the risks of predation by lions or decrease the range of the group. If the females were left behind whenever they needed to nurse, their likelihood of being lost to lion attacks would increase dramatically in the absence of males and their sticks and stones. If some males were left behind to guard the females, then both groups' chances of death by lion attack would be increased. It is no easy task to drive off an attack by a pride of hungry lions with sticks and stones under the best of circumstances. Dividing the males would only make it more difficult. If the entire group stopped every time an infant needed to be fed, then the amount of territory from which the group could scavenge would dramatically decrease, and the chance of starvation would dramatically increase. If the females were left at the night's resting place, whether permanent or changeable, they and their infants would not only starve, but would be easy prey for a wide range of predators.

Therefore, nursing while walking would have been an extremely important survival strategy. The author also questions if the well-known calming effect that rocking has on human infants is due to its emulating the motion of walking. If this is true, then non-human infants should not be calmed by rocking. Then we should not be surprised if, were we to rock a tired puppy, the puppy might try to bite us for making it motion sick. If the reader actually attempts this experiment, please let the author know how it turns out.

---

15. The author believes the need to nurse while walking caused the development of larger breasts in human ancestor females than in apes. This is new knowledge in the field of anthropology and is first revealed in this book. If someone else has previously discovered this fact, the author apologizes and indeed welcomes it as further evidence of the correctness of the fact.

The apelike creatures' night resting place most probably would have remained in the trees. First, there would have been no pressure to change a strategy that had been successful. Second, sleeping on the ground on the savanna would have opened them to devastation by all the big cats armed with excellent night vision. For the apelike creatures to survive on the ground at night, it would have required them to develop night vision. Certainly far better night vision than we have. Therefore, lemurlike night vision would have been required to be re-introduced into human ancestors and then lost again. Occam's razor says otherwise. Therefore, nesting in trees probably continued for millions of years after human ancestors roamed the ground during the day. This would agree with the late date for the control of fire (400,000 B.C. or 1 million B.C., depending on which data are accepted). It would also be consistent with the large finds at Swartkrans, South Africa, of leopard predation on pre-humans. Leopards are the only big cats that routinely climb trees. This would also account for the vivid fear of falling in modern humans.

The time when our ancestors stopped nesting in trees and began sleeping on the ground at night was a true turning point in the evolution of humankind. We left behind in the trees any need to evolve further down the path of the apes (*pithecus*); in the strictest sense, we diverged from the line of the apes when human (*Homo*) ancestors began sleeping on the ground in open country.[16] All need for tree-dwelling skills was lost, and the need for a safe place to sleep on the ground began our ancestors on a journey that led to homes, cities, transportation systems, and us.

Hence, walking upright led to carrying, which led to the division of labor in human ancestors.[17] Then, for instance, when

---

16. The author suggests that the logical place for the dividing line between apes (*pithecus*) and humans (*Homo*) is when our ancestors came down to the ground to sleep at night.

a lion approached a group of scavenging apelike creatures, the lion was met by a barrage of stabbing sticks and flying rocks hurled by the males. They must have been proficient at throwing stones and sticks almost immediately because of their hand-eye coordination already developed for swinging through trees. The lion soon learned not to approach. In fact, over time the advantage may have shifted so far to the apelike creatures' favor that if the apelike creatures spotted lions at a kill the ape-like creatures, operating in a more or less coordinated manner, could drive them away as the diminutive Bushmen of the Kalahari Desert in Africa still do today. With a new arsenal of sticks and stones, the apelike creatures turned to scavenging other animals' kills, digging roots with a stick, opportunistic hunting, harvesting trees, in short eating everything edible that they could get their hands on. The apelike creatures must have become despised by the other animals as their small group wandered over the savanna throwing sticks and stones at every animal within range. Why not? For the first time, an attacker had a weapon that could be used at long range with no threat of injury to the attacker. The apelike creatures no doubt injured more animals than they killed. Over time they must have become feared and hated by the other animals. The apelike creatures slowly turned from victim to victor.

Carrying an object for a period of time prior to use involves thinking about the future, by definition. In the case of the ape-like creature, the thinking goes something like this: If I pick up this stone (now, in the *present*) and I go through the bother of

---

17. The author believes that the importance of carrying in causing the fundamental division of labor in human society is new knowledge in the field of anthropology and is first revealed in this book. If someone else has previously discovered that fact the author apologizes and indeed welcomes it as further evidence of the correctness of the fact. Monkey and chimpanzee mothers do not carry the baby, needing all four limbs for locomotion, but rather the baby clings to the mother's fur. Both male and female monkeys and apes, being vegetarians, have to spend approximately 60 percent of the day foraging for food. Of the higher animals, only carnivores, due to the high caloric content of meat, have the possibility of dividing labor in finding food.

carrying it with me during the day (*sacrificing* my short-term comfort), then (in the *future*) when I meet a lion or prey, I can throw it. The apelike creatures may not have consciously reasoned this specific pattern of logic but the brain had evolved to the point that they could, however dimly, think about the future.

Every act of invention must necessarily involve the future; because every act of invention begins as an idea in the present in the brain about how a change to be made in the future will alter the future.

Some examples:

1. If I combine this and this, then in the future I will have that.

2. If I cannot find a stone the right size to carry, then I can drop a bigger stone than I want to carry on a rock until it breaks, and then I can carry the right size stone.

3. I like the sharp edges on the stones I break myself. If I break all the stones myself I will in the future always have a sharp stone.

4. I notice that if I drop certain stones in a certain way I get a sharper edge. If I break all my stones that way in the future I will always have a sharper edge.

From the time the apelike creature came down from the trees to the stone-chipping *Homo habilis* of two million years ago, every invention has involved thinking about the future. Further examples:

1. If a steam engine drives a propeller, then a boat in the *future* will be able to travel where it wants regardless of wind and current (Robert Fulton's invention of the steamboat).

2. If society were organized in such a way that the people elected their leaders, then in the *future* the leaders will be responsive to the people's needs (Athens, Greece, 2,500 years ago).

3. If a chain reaction is induced in a fissionable material, an explosion will result and in the *future* we will win the war (physicists during World War II).

Even inventions that do not involve physical objects—such as inventions in social structure, economics, ad campaigns, and reorganization of our daily household chores—all result from an idea that involved thinking about the future.

When one person wanted to disparage another person's intelligence, he used to say, "Don't you know enough to come in out of the rain?" Not being smart enough to come in out of the rain is not regarded as a sign of low intelligence, but rather as a sign of no intelligence at all. Chimpanzees are man's closest living relatives. We share in common some 98 percent of our DNA. The two percent difference, however, amounts to some 20 million differences. One of these differences permits us to come in out of the rain, but not the chimpanzees. When it begins to rain in the tropical forest of central Africa, the chimpanzees react by ceasing doing whatever it was they were doing

Chimpanzees do not shelter from the rain and appear most disconsolate

and huddling themselves in a squatting position. They appear to do this without regard for what may or may not be over their heads. Standing under a tree affords little protection in a persistent tropical rain, as anyone who has tried it can attest. The chimpanzees appear most disconsolate.

They do not come in out of the rain because they lack the ability to think very far in the future. They do not have the brains (400 cc) that will permit them to think the following: "If I sacrifice to construct a hut from leaves (today) then when it rains (in the future), I will enter my hut and stay dry." If chimpanzees cannot think that many steps ahead, they can never build cities and do all the things necessary to create civilization. Chimpanzees, like their relatives, the monkeys, are excellent at observing behavior and then adopting it as their own. Monkey see, monkey do. Even the widely reported act of tool-making in chimpanzees (stripping the leaves from a stem to extract ants from an anthill) is for an immediate benefit. But to invent behavior for a future benefit is beyond the mental capacity of chimpanzees, because it involves thinking too far in the future.

Therefore, the most important difference between ourselves and the other animals is the human ability to think far into the future. A more complex form of this thought is when you are thinking in the future about not just one event but a series of events that take place over time. When you invent a series of events that will occur in the future you have created a plan. A goal is what the plan intends to accomplish. That is it—"bells and whistles." We have found the critical component of what makes us different from the other animals, what makes human beings human: what our advantage is in the competition for survival. It is an advantage so enormous that if we gave it to the gnu, the gnu could easily defeat the King of the Beasts in the struggle for survival. It is an advantage so large that it permits an otherwise fairly unremarkable animal, the human, to dominate the Earth: the

This diminutive humanoid has taken pre-planned shelter and appears to be enjoying the rain. The ability to think in the future, which permits planning and, therefore, permits preparation for the future, is what separates humankind from our closest living relative, the chimpanzee. However, the above photograph also demonstrates that human evolution has left some work undone, as the child is standing in a puddle.

ability to think in the future sufficiently well to set goals and make plans.

An additional ingredient is required to make the planning become reality—the social organization necessary to implement the plan. In the case of the apelike creatures, they came down from the trees with a social structure inherited from their tree-dwelling ancestors. They were already accustomed to living in groups, having a defined relationship with others of varying ages and, amongst other things, a hierarchy of authority. The apelike creatures over time were no doubt able to send small parties on quasi-organized scavenges much as chimpanzees do to patrol their borders or lionesses to hunt. Let us perform a small Einsteinian Thought Experiment. Let us assume that some genius apelike creature thought about the future and invented the city and the modern way we live. It would be to no avail. There is no way that a small group of perhaps 30 creatures, scratching a bare, scavenging existence, could learn the skills, devote the hours of labor, etc., to successfully construct a city life. Nor can they build the pyramids. Their social organization will not allow it.

Let me present an example from contemporary times. The Soviet Union and the Eastern European nations are restructuring their social organizations because their previous form of social organization was too inefficient to permit the fulfillment of those societies' plans.

Inherent in the process of setting goals and making plans that can only come to fruition in the future is the concept of sacrifice. By definition, sacrifice is the voluntary acceptance of unwanted burdens in the present in order to achieve an improvement upon completion of a plan at some time in the future. The completion of virtually every long-range plan entails sacrifice in the present. For example, when the frontiersmen built log cabins, they sacrificed their hard work today for the comfort of living in a house tomorrow; modern high school students who remain in school instead of quitting and taking a low-paying job sacrifice current rewards for a better future. Almost every act that results in a better future involves sacrifice in the present.

At a later time we will continue our discussion of these Four Critical Abilities, developed out of the struggle to survive, that make humans human:

1. The ability to *think in the future efficiently.*

2. The ability to invent a series of future actions, *to plan efficiently.*

3. *The social organization necessary to implement the plan efficiently.*

4. The ability to *sacrifice* to carry out the plan efficiently.[18]

These Four Critical Abilities are the human's advantage in the long, deadly struggle for survival. These Four Critical Abilities are the cause of the human mastery of the planet. These Four Critical Abilities place humankind in so superior a position to other animals that some humans deny that we are even related to animals. However, for now, let us return to our struggling ancestors.

R ecently, fossils of a new species, *Australopithecus ramidus,* (*Australo* = southern; *pithecus* = ape; *ramid* = root) were found in Ethiopia. The 4 to 4½ foot tall creature lived 4.4 million years ago. By 4 million years ago, an apelike creature, *Australopithecus afarensis* (Afar = a valley in Ethiopia), was walking upright. However, its small brain size of 450 cc, about one quarter the size of ours, meant the creature was more apelike than humanlike. The anthropologist Dr. Mary Leakey dis-

---

18. This book is the first work in which these attributes are recognized as the Four Critical Abilities that differentiate humankind from other creatures.

covered an 80- foot-long set of fossilized footprints of *Australopithecus afarensis* that date from
3.75 million years ago. It is estimated from the length of stride
that the hominids were approximately four feet tall. In 1974, Dr.
Donald C. Johanson found a 40
percent complete fossilized speci-
men of a hominid female in her mid-twenties, whom he named
Lucy. The fossils of the 3 ½ foot tall female date to 3.2 million
years old.

Australopithecus

B y two million years ago, *Homo habilis* ("Handy-Man") had
begun altering the stones he carried by chipping them
with other rocks. The apelike creatures had evolved into men -
not *Homo sapiens* of today, but an earlier type, which had a 750
cc brain cavity and was becoming smarter. They created tools
by chipping two rocks together to get a sharp point. The creation of a tool for future use is a giant step forward not only
because of the increased benefit of the tool but also for what it
demonstrates about the thinking of the animal who made it.

Homo habilis' larger brain size meant a more efficient adap-
tation to their environment. The scavenging-hunting parties
were more efficient. They were probably efficient enough to
allow the males to bring back surplus food, so the females no
longer needed to go scavenging with the males. They could
remain "at home" and exploit vegetarian food sources and raise
and protect the young without as much exposure to danger.
Thus began an elemental division of labor more profound than
is found elsewhere in the animal kingdom. The female had the
free time to assist the scavenging males in preparation to scavenge, to prepare a safe, comfortable place to sleep, to take better care of the young. A scavenger who had a female or females
assisting him chipping stones, sharpening sticks, or getting a
better night's rest was a better scavenger and more reliable

provider of food. The more the female helped and supported the scavenging male, the more reliable her food supply became, and therefore the more secure the female's existence became. The males and females began doing different jobs but in a coordinated, cohesive way that resulted in greater success in achieving their mutual plans and goals. Those scavengers who had no females assisting them fared worse than those with females. The females who had no one to bring them meat also suffered in comparison to those who did. The reader knows what happened next: Those with the advantage prospered and multiplied and those who did not, faced extinction.

Therefore, those who went into the field with females cooperating with them in preparation were better prepared than those who did not. In some cultures, like the traditional Yupik Eskimo (Inuit) culture of the Bering Sea in Alaska, prior to the introduction of modern equipment, a hunter might have had several women of several generations (daughters, wives, mothers-in-law, mothers, grandmothers) all working directly or indirectly to free his time specifically for hunting. The dangers inherent in hunting large animals in the Arctic typically caused a surplus of females. When the Eskimo hunted an animal, the situation was not one man against one animal, it was the product of two, three, or four humans against that animal. An enormous amount of skin chewing, sewing, mending, weapon making, weapon repairing, paddle making, etc., went into outfitting a first-class hunter and his boats, and sleds and dogs. By the simple expedient of dividing labor along sexual lines, the social organization permitted a more effective effort to be put forth in hunting. The lions also divide labor along sexual lines but do not combine these efforts to achieve one common goal. The bees are an excellent example of efficient division of labor. More efficient social organization permits increased labor to be applied to food gathering, making it in turn more efficient. The same advantages the hominids had at scavenging would have made them more successful at opportunistic hunting when they happened upon suitable live game. The change in social organization permitted two or more individuals to divide labor while still cooperating to achieve one mutually beneficial goal. This is a devastating advancement whose effects are still thundering down the corridors of time. In 1914, Henry Ford, recognizing the advantage of cooperative division of labor, invented the automobile assembly line. By merely recognizing and applying one of the fundamental advantages that humans have to an economic situation, Henry Ford instantaneously (on the time scales in which we have been thinking) obliterated his competition. He became one of the wealthiest men in the world. To compare it to the biological events we have been observing, it is as if Henry Ford had created the hard-bodied animal in a soft-bodied world. Since Mr. Ford's successful application of a rather simple and basic advantage of our human ancestors to a modern economic situation resulted in such an enormous advantage so recently, it might be seriously interesting to keep our eyes on the advantages that humans enjoy.

To further cooperate and coordinate their activities, particularly scavenging and opportunistic hunting activities, humans slowly developed language. As long as two people know the same language, even if they have just met, they can begin cooperating immediately. The advantage conveyed by the rapid transmittal of a thought or plan to all members of a scavenging party increases the likelihood of success in opportunistic hunting. Therefore, a slow change from scavenging to hunting was underway. Although we modern people have a tendency to look disparagingly on scavengers, in actuality it can be a fairly advanced method of providing oneself with sustenance. When it reaches the stage of routinely chasing lions off their kill, have not the scavengers mastered the hunters?

By 1.5 million years ago, *Homo erectus* had evolved. *Homo erectus* was so successful that he migrated from Africa throughout Asia even to the pre-

Peking man

sent-day island of Java. By 400,000 years ago, in caves at Zhoukoudian, China, just outside Beijing, Peking man (*Homo erectus*) was cooking food and staying warm and safe at night by using a camp fire. I would think that to control fire, language would already have to be quite developed. Certainly enough for the hunter-scavenging parties to communicate and daily camp life to be organized.

CHAPTER FIVE

From Caves to Cowsheds

125,000 Years Ago to 3500 B.C.

Neanderthal

B Y 125,000 YEARS AGO, Neanderthal man (*Homo sapiens neanderthalensis*) was in Europe and the Middle East. Neanderthal immediately preceded modern man (Cro-Magnon or *Homo sapiens sapiens*) in Europe. Therefore, the differences between the Neanderthals and ourselves is what makes our civilization possible. In other words, the differences between ourselves and the Neanderthals is what permits us to send men to the moon, build cities, sail the oceans, and the Neanderthals to live in cave mouths by campfire light.

Therefore, if we study Neanderthal's characteristics, his lifestyle, how he lived, and contrast it to how we and our ancestors lived, then the difference between the two will give us the causes that permit our modern civilization to exist. In effect, the difference between Neanderthal and modern man is the key to what makes modern man the dominant animal of this planet. It will be the cause that enables us to go to the supermarket and virtually treat ourselves to whatever we have a taste for, as opposed to living life in a cave mouth, with wild man-killing beasts outside. These differences are the causes not only for all of modern man's (Cro-Magnon) achievements, but also the key to our humanness.

Neanderthal man

Neanderthal, who is named after a site in the Neander Valley in Germany, has been found in a number of sites in the Middle East and Europe, beginning approximately 125,000 years ago. The majority of the finds of their habitations show them to have lived in rock shelters and cliffs. It is not possible to live in caves as we might picture because bad things happen to one in caves. For instance, one comes down with arthritis when one spends a great deal of time in caves. They lived in rock overhangs mostly and seemed to inhabit the site periodically throughout the year. Meaning they probably wandered; they were probably nomadic. Many of their sites are found with bones that appear to be, by scientific analysis, previously chewed upon by an animal, which means that Neanderthal was most probably, at least partially, still a scavenger. The change to hunting had not been completed with Neanderthal. The average age of the bones of Neanderthal is 30 years old, not a very long life expectancy. If Neanderthal reached puberty at the same age as we do today, at twelve or thirteen years old, it certainly did not leave much time to raise a family. Neanderthal had control of fire. To control a fire and to keep a fire going, one has to be concerned about the future. However modestly, one must have some concern for the future. Neanderthal must certainly have had a good command of language and communication. Brain sizes were as large as or larger than ours today, 1620 cc. So the difference in intellect, therefore, must be one of quality and not quantity. They had a sufficient amount of brains, but ours must have a unique quality to it. The forehead of Neanderthal was more sloped than ours. Behind our foreheads lie our pre-frontal lobes, that portion of the brain that permits us to think about the future.

Neanderthals also display a modest amount of thinking in the future by preparing their dead for burial. They coated the corpse with red ocher, which is iron oxide, more commonly known as rust, which serves one of two possible purposes: 1) to inhibit the action of insects or 2) to restore the bloom of life to a corpse (according to a hypothesis by anthropologists). Whichever purpose it was, it demonstrates, however dimly, thinking in the future. Nevertheless, throughout the 90,000 years that Neanderthal was on the planet, he showed no evidence of cultural advancement. In the most telling evidence we have, the stone tools Neanderthal used, there is only one type of tool construction technique. The same Mousterian tool culture was in use throughout the entire 90,000 years of his existence. Neanderthals, generation after generation, sat down and chipped their stone tools the exact same way, no change. Upon the arrival of modern man, every few thousand years a new and improved way of chipping tools was created (see the chart below for the continuing improvement in tool construction techniques used by modern man).

TOOL CULTURES IN ICE AGE EUROPE		
HOMO SAPIENS	**TOOL CULTURE**	**YEARS BEFORE PRESENT**
Neanderthal	Mousterian	125,000 - 35,000
Neanderthal & Modern Man	Chatelperronian	35,000 - 30,000
Neanderthal & Modern Man	Aurignacian	34,000 - 30,000
Modern Man	Gravettian	30,000 - 22,000
Modern Man	Solutrean	22,000 - 18,000
Modern Man	Magdalenian	18,000 - 11,000

In comparison to Neanderthal, and in the time frames in which we have been thinking, modern man created a bewilderingly rapid pace of technological improvement. Therefore, we can draw some conclusions about Neanderthal: He was content with his way of life. There is no evidence to show that Neanderthals ever thought up one improvement except the burying of the dead. They certainly did not think about the future and apply those thoughts to improve their technology. That is the key. Once again, we see it is thinking in the future—making a plan and having the social organization to carry out the plan—that makes the critical difference.

Modern Man (Cro-Magnon Man)

As early as 40,000 years ago modern man had entered Spain, perhaps crossing from North Africa, and by 35,000 years ago modern man had entered western Europe, probably migrating from the Middle East. For a short time, some 2,000 years, modern man coexisted with Neanderthal. There is some evidence that they occupied the same sites and that Neanderthal, before disappearing from the record, adopted modern man's tool-using culture.[19] Modern man's record of tool use is one of continuous improvement. Five times in 25,000 years there was a substantial improvement in the manufacture of tools.

But what was modern man's life truly like in this period from 35,000 years ago to 10,000—12,000 years ago when the Ice Age ended? What was the lifestyle of modern man in Europe?

Early Homo sapiens

This question interested me greatly because I knew that the answer to that question would confirm or deny my conclusion about the keys to our humanness. I knew that the individuals who had painted in the caves in the Dordogne region of south-central France near the end of the last Ice Age had left thousands of artifacts relating to their culture. With the large quantity of facts available, it should be fertile ground for the Black Box Technique to discover what their lifestyle was like.

They were clearly a very successful group of people in that they had the free time to paint the beautiful, beautiful paintings on the walls of the famous caves of Lascaux, Font de Gaume, and many others. After reading several books in the United States about these caves, I traveled to France in the early 1980s and was taken through Font de Gaume by a Dutch doctor of anthropology who is a specialist in cave paintings. He is a very courageous man because he knew that by the age of 45 or so, as a result of his working extensively in the caves, he would come down with arthritis and the latter years of his life would be accompanied by crippling pain. While showing me through the caves, the Dutch doctor of anthropology told me, "We anthropol-

---

19. The significance of the overlap of the Chatelperronian and Aurignacian tool cultures is not currently understood by anthropology.

ogists have a problem. And the problem is: Why no reindeer?" Of the various representations of animals on the cave walls—wild horses, woolly mammoths, wild cattle, bison—fewer than 5 percent are of reindeer. Yet, when the anthropologists dug up the cave floors and analyzed the remains of the meals, they found that in some caves, over 99 percent of the protein portion of their diet came from reindeer. Yet fewer than 5 percent of the paintings were of reindeer. Rather curious.[20]

Also, the remains of their meals show that the reindeer were two- and three-year-olds killed only in the winter. In addition, many of the cave paintings are rather high up on the cave walls. Cro-Magnon had constructed scaffolding in order to reach the high places. A notch containing petrified wood has been found, along with imprints of a rope in the clay floor of the cave and even preserved rope itself.

I began to work the cause-and-effect relationships. First, I reasoned, we must be dealing with gourmet cave painters who have the ability to cull from the herd, whenever they wished, the tenderest and youngest animals. Second, from the skeletal remains of Cro-Magnon, we know that they were anatomically identical to us even in cranial capacity and shape. Therefore, their capacity for reasoning probably was identical to ours. Therefore, I could conduct an Einsteinian Thought Experiment and substitute my brain for the brain of a Cro-Magnon. By determining what I would do in a given situation, it should give me great insight into what Cro-Magnon would do in the same situation. If I had sufficient control over the reindeer herd to cull the two- and three-year-olds, and I had rope and timber, I would build a corral and herd the two- and three-year-olds into it. It would be very odd if Cro-Magnon had developed a rope and timber technology solely for scaffolding purposes in order to paint pictures and not applied it to the all important problem of staying alive.

---

20. This is an excellent example of an anomaly in the data, as discussed in #8 of the logic section on page 19.

If Cro-Magnons actually built corrals, then this would make them reindeer-herders instead of hunters, as is generally believed. I asked the Dutch doctor of anthropology if any excavations had been conducted on the ground outside the caves. He replied that there had been. What did they find? He responded that they had found one post hole. Aha! One post hole does not a corral make, but at least it was supporting evidence, as opposed to there being no post hole at all.

I continued my cause-and-effect reasoning. What is the significance of all the two- and three-year-old reindeer being killed only in the winter? Since all reindeer calves are born at the same time—the spring—then by knowing the age of the reindeer when it is killed (by comparing the bones to modern reindeer bones) it can be easily determined in what season of the year it was killed. All were killed in the winter. I could think up no plausible reason why a proud painter would not visit the caves in the summer if he were around. That means the caves were not used in the summer. Therefore, I reasoned, the cave painters were not there in the summer. Where would I be in the summer were I Cro-Magnon? If over 90 percent of my protein came from reindeer that I had control over, I know where I would be in the summer. I would be with the reindeer herd. This conclusion stands to reason because reindeer are known to migrate long distances between summer feeding grounds and winter ranges. Therefore, at least some Cro-Magnons of the late Magdalenian period were probably reindeer-herders rather than hunters.

Cro-Magnons must have followed the reindeer on their yearly migratory cycle. If this were true, then it becomes quite easy to derive what the lifestyle of Cro-Magnons must have been in virtually any particular in which we are interested. For instance, Cro-Magnons no doubt wore clothing of the readily available reindeer skin. Since nomadic people must travel light, and since we know Cro-Magnons did not live in the caves, they may well have lived in tents also of reindeer hides. Among the many Cro-Magnon artifacts are large numbers of highly decorated portions of reindeer antlers with holes drilled through the top end. Almost all are broken. The French anthropologists call these objects "Batons du Commandment," meaning that they believe them to be symbols of authority. Insofar as the individuals in the small bands of migratory reindeer- herders would have seen one another every-

Baton du Commandment

day, and everyone would have known everyone else's relative social position, this explanation seems implausible to me. Instead, they appear to be broken tent stakes. We are beginning to build a sizable preponderance of evidence.

Now, we can answer the Dutch doctor of anthropology's question, "Why no reindeer?" There would have been little excitement or adventure in reindeer-herding, but almost all outdoor people engage in hunting for sport, for fun, and for relief from boredom. Reindeer-herders, being nomadic, had no way to carry a trophy of the hunt with them on their migration. Therefore, Cro-Magnon hunter-artists memorialized the thrill of the hunt on the walls of the caves. There would have been no desire to paint pictures of reindeer because there was no thrill, no glory, no excitement in butchering semi-domesticated animals. Just as, if we were to visit the farm house of a Wisconsin dairy farmer, we would expect to see the head of a deer over his fireplace mantel, but not the head of a cow.

What happened to this very successful society? As the Ice Age ended, the lichens, which fed the reindeer that fed Cro-Magnon, would have retreated farther and farther north. By 7,000 B.C. the ice cap had withdrawn from the Scandinavian Peninsula and the Baltic Sea had filled—first with fresh water from the melted ice cap and later with sea water. The reindeer would have entered the Scandinavian Peninsula from the Karelian Peninsula. If they were to eat, the reindeer-herders would naturally follow.

In 1985, I traveled to Scandinavia and, after consulting with Dr. Pekka Aikio, I was shown rock carvings in the northernmost part of Norway. These rock carvings were very similar to the paintings done in the caves of the Dordogne some 10,000 years earlier. It strikes me that a culture that was so successful as to create the cave paintings of France would not vanish from the Earth without an echo or a remnant. It is possible that the Lapps of northern Norway, Finland, Sweden, and the Soviet Union are the direct descendants of the Cro-Magnon cave painters of France.[21] The majority of the other residents of Finland are Finno-Ugric people who came from the Volga River area of Russia as the Finns, Estonians, and the Magyars of Hungary 1,300 years ago. My hypothesis is that the Lapps were already there and adopted the Finno-Ugric tongue merely as an expedient means of surviving with the warlike Finns. If that is true, the Finns, not being reindeer-herders, would not have a vocabulary as extensive as reindeer-herders would to describe reindeer-herding. Therefore, the Lapps should not have Finno-Ugric words for reindeer-herding. In fact, that is the case. The woman who did the studies on the Lapp language, Marjut Aikio, has determined that the words that the Lapps use for reindeer-herding are not of Finno-Ugric origin. Therefore, I hypothesized that the Finno-Ugric language was an overlay language adopted by the Lapps as a survival mechanism. There is no current scientific test that would permit us to solve the question whether the Lapps are the direct descendants of the French cave painters or not. Many peoples must have been on the move across Siberia seeking a new way to make a living as the last of the woolly mammoth herds became extinct at the end of the last ice age. It is alternately possible that the Lapps are one of those peoples. We must await a defin-

---

21. The author believes that the hypothesis that the Lapps of Scandinavia are the direct descendants of the Cro-Magnon cave painters of France is new knowledge in the field of anthropology and is first revealed in this book. If someone else has previously advanced this hypothesis, the author apologizes and indeed welcomes it as further evidence of its correctness.

itive test to be developed by science that could tell us whether Cro-Magnons, the cave painters, are the ancestors of the Lapps of Scandinavia.

STOP PRESS

A few weeks before this manuscript was completed, the author came across a book published under the auspices of the American Museum of Natural History, The First Humans, *volume 1. On page 92 was the statement, "British Archaeologist Paul Bahn has suggested that the way of life of Upper Paleolithic people in Southern France and the Pyrenees was probably very similar to that of present reindeer hunters and herders in Siberia. . . . Bahn is therefore open to the suggestion that Magdalenian hunters may have tamed part of the Reindeer herds." Needless to say, I was elated. I immediately contacted him and he confirmed that indeed we shared "a view that I (Paul Bahn) believe to be absolutely correct." Paul offered helpful suggestions, such as an updating of the dates for the tool cultures in Ice Age Europe, that the Batons du Commandment resemble parts of harnesses used by modern Siberian reindeer-herders, and several articles from the recent scientific literature. He also informed me that the hypothesis for reindeer-herding first surfaced in the 19th century but was rejected by mainstream archaeologists, not to be resurrected until 1979 by his investigations. The article he sent me showed the current debate on this issue amongst archaeologists to be particularly acrimonious, bordering on the vitriolic, which through my personal experience I thought was reserved for "amateurs" armed primarily with logic sticking their noses into professionals' turf. I wish Paul and his colleagues luck in changing science's currently accepted reality. I guess the saying is true, that much of what science accepts as reality changes only when older generations of scientists die. Whatever the outcome of the current debate, the fact that the debate exists is additional validation of the power of the Black Box Technique.*

The cave painters of France clearly exercised great foresight and thinking in the future. They used the Four Critical Abilities, which permitted them to build corrals, maintain control of their food supply, and gave them the free time and a level of comfort and security never before known by any previous group of hominids.

The record of modern man in Europe from 35,000 B.C. to 13,000 B.C. is one of a culture continually improving its technology. We have the invention of harpoons, of saws and the needle by 22,000 B.C. The needle allowed humans to wear clothing fitted to the individual, making the person a more efficient hunter or herder or whatever. By 13,000 B.C., the artistry combined on modern man's utensils and tools is of a very, very high order indeed. It shows an observational sense, a sense of manipulation, of tool and hand-eye coordination equal to or better than the best today.

It is apparent that the difference between Neanderthal Man and modern man is the ability to think in the future, which is the ability to invent, the ability to create. Every act of creativity involves thinking in the future. To create something, you must first conceive of it as an idea. The idea can only become a reality in the future. Every invention, and every act of creativity, whether inventive or artistic, involves thinking in the future. This is the key. This is what makes modern man the dominator of the Earth. Thinking in the future is what permits us to be human, permits us to live in this society, in this culture, in a life of relative ease. We are no longer bothered with seeing our children torn apart by wild beasts. The ability to think in the future is the key to our humanness. The story of human history is the story of our advances, our improvements, and our accomplishments, all of which involve thinking in the future.

With the arrival of modern man, it becomes possible to accurately analyze brain function. It is apparent that amphibians, reptiles, and birds rely heavily upon their inherited instincts to determine their actions. Only with the arrival of the mammals can thinking, complex learning, and retaining of relatively large quantities of memory be recognized. Lemurs make only one leap. Monkeys perform them in uninterrupted series. Perhaps, the lemur can think only one jump in the future, whereas the brain function of monkeys has evolved to the point of sufficiently rapid signal processing combined with being able to think far enough in the future to conceive of a series of jumps. The monkeys contributed very high-speed thinking, superb hand-eye coordination, and thinking farther into the future. Our ancestors who came between the monkeys and Neanderthals gave us an ever-increasing capacity for memory and a modestly increasing capacity for thinking in the future. Neanderthals, with a cranial capacity larger than ours, presumably could remember even more things than we can. Probably, Neanderthal was nomadic and could remember very well such things as the game trails, mental maps of where he or she had been, lessons learned as a youth, stories told around the fires at night, where the best rock overhangs to stay dry were, etc. However, the ability to remember more than we can was a dead end. It was far outweighed in the struggle for survival by our ability to think in the future. Our ability to think in the future permitted us to plan, to prepare sophisticated traps, to project into the future and therefore to be prepared.[22] In short, it permitted humankind to utilize the Four Critical Abilities and conquer the animal kingdom to the point of making virtually all large animals extinct if we do not use those same Four Critical Abilities to protect them. The ability to think in the future has made us so powerful that we have changed from risking our own lives to kill an animal, to making our fellow animals extinct. We are in the final stages of doing what the hard bodies did to the soft

---

22. The author believes that the superiority of Cro-Magnon's advantage (thinking in the future) to Neanderthal's advantage (larger amounts of memory) is new knowledge in the field of anthropology and is first revealed in this book. If someone else has previously discovered that fact the author apologizes and indeed welcomes it as further evidence of the correctness of the fact. Anthropology currently believes that the advantage enjoyed by Cro-Magnon was language.

bodies, what the fishes did to the hard bodies, what the reptiles did to the amphibians, what the mammals did to the reptiles—we are making extinct not only many other species, but our fellow mammals as well.[23]

Further analysis of the difference in brain function between Neanderthal and us leads us to a very interesting conclusion. We have little to no evidence of change in the 90,000 years of Neanderthal occupation of the Earth. With the arrival of modern humans, there is an explosive growth of change that continues to this day. It is well understood that the rate of change is currently increasing exponentially. We know that the cause that permits us to be able to create change is our ability to think in the future. Inherent in thinking in the future is concern about the future. In modern individual humans, concern about the future varies from a modest amount of concern to an increasingly larger amount of concern, until finally, in more extreme cases, it reaches in ascending order, unease, anxiety, worry, fear, and dread. With Neanderthal's very limited ability to think in the future, presumably Neanderthal could not be very concerned about the future. Neanderthals were probably not very worried about the future and probably did not question their lot in life, but merely accepted what was and went about their daily lives

As I have traveled around the world, I cannot recall ever meeting even one human being who was not trying to improve his life, which is to say, change his life. From ex-headhunters in Borneo concerned about rats eating their rice, to Middle Eastern multimillionaires trying to make another 100 million dollars, they were all concerned with changing their lives for the better. Whenever I have asked people what they want out of life, the overwhelming response was, "To be happy." Upon further questioning about what happiness means, it always included achieving some permanent, unchanging condition in

---

23. The above was the reasoning about brain function that led the author to conclude that a Komodo dragon could be approached.

which they would not have to worry or be concerned about the future. Therefore, the ability that is responsible for all of humankind's achievements and progress, thinking in the future, with its concomitant concern about the future, is the very same ability that prevents humans from ever achieving the permanent state of happiness we all seek. We are destined by the very characteristic that makes us human never to be able to achieve a state of permanent happiness. In other words, what motivates us to continually seek improvement is exactly what prevents us from ever achieving the desired improvement—permanent, unchanging happiness. Therefore, an inherent characteristic of the human being is never to be able to achieve unchanging permanent happiness.

Moreover, Neanderthals, living in difficult conditions that would make us miserable, were probably permanently happy, or at least, permanently content. They lacked the desire to change or improve. In addition, it becomes easy to understand the response of John D. Rockefeller, who was the wealthiest man in the world and could not possibly spend all the money he had, when asked by a reporter in the 1920s, "Mr. Rockefeller, how much money do you have to have to be happy?" Mr. Rockefeller's response? "Just a little more."

Furthermore, it also becomes easy to explain why people seeking happiness through the teachings of Indian gurus invariably fail to reach the permanent state of happiness called Nirvana (absolute truth). Remember how the music group, the Beatles, after achieving the pinnacle of fame, wealth, and adulation by millions of groupies, sought happiness by traveling to India to learn from an Indian guru how to achieve Nirvana? In a short period of time, they returned to the west, unable to find happiness. Many Indian gurus seek to achieve Nirvana by attempting to train the conscious reasoning portion of the brain to suppress the innate human brain's characteristic of thinking in the future, thus freeing the person from concern about the future, which includes want and desire. The attempt is almost universally doomed to failure. When the enormous amount of

concentration required is successful, the person has only succeeded in suppressing the very characteristic that makes him
human and reverting to Neanderthalic brain function. More
usually what does succeed is the guru's achieving a temporary
state of happiness because of the large sums of money extracted from the acolyte. Therefore, the only possible way for
humans with normally functioning prefrontal lobes to achieve a
state of permanent happiness is by redefining happiness from a
static state of "no change and no concern about the future" to
one of deriving happiness from a "changing state of continuous
improvement." We have already learned how to control events
so that we can create the future we want, in this case continuous improvement, by applying the Seven Steps of the Black Box
Technique.

Farming

B eginning around 13,000 to 12,000 B.C., the Earth's climate
   began to warm due to an eccentricity in the Earth's orbit
around the sun, which occurs on a 100,000-year repetitive
cycle. While the Ice Age was lifting from Europe, in North
Africa and the Middle East the climate was beginning to dry
up. Rock carvings of men with bows and arrows hunting ante-
lope, gazelles, and herds of wild animals, are inscribed on the
Ahoggar Mountains in the Sahara Desert, around which empty
desert stretches for miles. What is currently the Sahara Desert
was a verdant, luxurious, almost Edenlike realm 15,000 years
ago. As the Ice Age lifted and the Earth warmed, the Sahara
dried up, causing a massive dislocation of animals and humans.
Of course, the humans and animals gravitated, as would only
be natural, to permanent water sources such as the Nile, the
Tigris, and the Euphrates rivers. Then, approximately 13,000
B.C., two wild grasses crossed, which produced an ancient
wheat known as emmer.

We can imagine in an Einsteinian Thought Experiment
groups of nomadic hunters in the desert in a drying climate

being driven to, for instance, the Nile, along whose banks emmer was growing. The women probably gathered these wheat kernels. Perhaps they accidentally spilled some in a given area and when they came through the following year, noticed that emmer was growing abundantly in the area where they dropped it the year before. No doubt they carried some of the emmer with them, spilling it in other locations on their routes and noticing that the following year it would grow also. Eventually, they might even sow some of the grain in locations at which they knew they would be the following year when it would be ripe. It is very likely that the initial farming and cultivation of grains would have been invented by women. As the desert dried more and more, it became more important to stick close to the year-round water sources. Some of these people would have decided to settle down on a permanent basis at the water's edge and attempt to cultivate the wheat over which they, for perhaps generations, had control. Thus began a settled life and the beginnings of farming.

Farming in and of itself, by definition, involves thinking about the future. A farmer plants something now, in the present, the reward for which may or may not occur four, five, or six months in the future. The farmer sacrifices his labor in the present for no current reward with the hope that there will be a reward in the future—a relatively long time in the future. So farming is by definition a quintessential act of thinking about the future. The very act of working in the present to achieve a future goal involves the act of sacrifice. The individual forgoes present rewards for rewards to be gained in the future when the plan is completed. The farmer invests literally months of labor waiting for a future payoff.

We can hypothesize, using Occam's razor, that some of the nomads did not come out of the desert. Whenever there are groups of people and change occurring, some people will want to continue doing what they were doing regardless of consequences. They are not going to be able to change. Times must have become more and more difficult out in the desert as it became more desiccated. The nomads would have come out of the desert to a river, where people would be living in some sort of permanent houses, probably made of mud and sticks. It would not have taken long for the nomads to realize that it was far easier to attack a village and take away the things that the farmers had, than it was to make a living out on the desert. In very short order there would have been warfare between those who chose the sedentary life and those who continued to be nomadic. For protection, the farmers would probably have thought up the idea of building walls around their villages. Of course, there would be more people in some villages than in others. The nomads would naturally pick on the smaller, easier villages. It seems to me a very logical next step that the smaller villages that were being picked on would go to a larger, more powerful village that was not being bothered and say something like, "If you come and help us when we are attacked, we will give you 10 percent of all our grain." The beginnings of tribute—and a good deal for those who otherwise would have had all of their grain taken away and possibly faced extinction.

In very short order, there would have been petty alliances between small villages, with the leader of the village who could field the most followers being perhaps the most powerful in the region. The nomadic bands could only reach a certain size, whereas the settled people could achieve much denser concentrations of people, which meant more warriors to defend themselves than the nomads could concentrate to attack them. In a sense, warfare promoted civilization. It caused the towns to form alliances. This, in combination with larger irrigation projects than one village could construct, caused a rise in proto-petty states—agglomerations of small villages of an area. With the threat of the nomads reduced or eliminated, these petty states were free to begin fighting and arguing amongst themselves over such things as land, water, and irrigation systems.

By 8000 B.C., with the founding of the city of Jericho in modern-day Israel and other cities, centers of trade were developing where herders could bring their sheep, goats, and cattle for trading, and farmers could trade their grains and produce. Catal Huyuck, in Turkey, was by 7600 B.C. a large city devoted to the raising of cattle. Around 4000 B.C., in Mesopotamia, a method was developed for recording business transactions, involving hundreds of sheep and tons of grain, that were too important to consign to memory alone. A number of balls were put into a clay vessel and sealed. If anyone needed to know what a particular contract was about, they would break the bottle and count the balls to determine how many sheep were traded from whom to whom. Not the most convenient method but the first recorded non-verbal business deal in the world. The recording of contracts was followed much later by the invention of money. I mention money at its invention because it is such an important component of modern society. One of the most basic motivations of our society is the accumulation of money. It was used as a medium of exchange. At first, money had value in and of itself. It was made from silver or other precious metal. Money today is merely a representation of value. In and of itself it is absolutely worthless, except as a piece of paper and ink. Its only purpose is to be circulated among people in a symbolic representation of wealth, not the wealth itself. This fact will be important to us later. But let us continue with our story.

The Rise and Fall of Human Societies

3500 B.C. to A.D. 1492

History

HISTORY BEGAN APPROXIMATELY 5,500 years ago, 3500 B.C. The Sumerian invention of cuneiform writing marked its dawn. The first writing was done with a split reed on wet clay. Sumerian priests needed to keep track of the immense quantities of grain and sheep flowing into the temples. Writing was later chiseled into stone and painted on papyrus. Humans, for the first time, communicated from generation to generation in a non-oral form. There were empires before writing, but we have very few means of discovering much about them except through the excavation of old cities. The earliest cultures that we can investigate through the use of written language are the Middle Eastern and Egyptian cultures.

Narmer's Palette. The oval created by the two intertwined necks is for ladies' eye shadow.

Egypt

The first pictographic writing from Egypt dates from approximately 3000 B.C. and is called Narmer's Palette. It describes the victory of King Menes, who for the first time united Upper and Lower Egypt. Up until this time Egypt had been a collection of warring states. There must have been bitter fighting, because the Egyptian Pharaoh is shown clubbing captives to death.

Later statues show the Pharaoh holding a hook and a flail. The hook is the staff of the shepherd, the flail is the tool used to flail wheat and extract the kernel from the chaff. In other words, the Pharaoh is king of both the herders *and* the farmers. The Pharaoh probably ended the conflict between the herders and the farmers that had continued since the Nile Valley was first settled. The Pharaoh's costume shows they are both under his control.

The Pharaoh (King Tutankhamen) with hook and flail, symbolizing mastery of both shepherds and farmers

The same battle was still raging when the American West was settled. The Lincoln County wars in New Mexico, in which the infamous Billy the Kid took part, was a conflict between sheepherders and cattlemen. The Johnson County wars in Wyoming were even more extensive battles between the sheep men and the farmers.

The Pharaohs of ancient Egypt were not just kings. The Pharaoh was not like a sovereign in the Middle Ages who ruled by the divine right of kings, the right God supposedly gave to kings. The Pharaoh *was* the living god. He was god himself. It was believed that if a commoner touched the Pharaoh, the commoner would immediately die. The Pharaoh was all power-ful and lived forever. When one of the Pharaohs died, the next Pharaoh claimed that he was the same Pharaoh in a different human form. Then the new Pharaoh could claim on his monu-ments all the past achievements of all the other Pharaohs because he was the same Pharaoh and had never died.

The Pharaohs of Egypt clearly thought about the future. The Pharaohs were not content with the Neanderthals' method of burial—just sprinkle a little red ocher on a body and bury it with a few possessions. The megalomaniacal Pharaohs thought in the future about their eventual deaths and had the prerequisites of a social organization that gave the people a large quantity of free time. For five months out of the year the Nile flooded. The entire Nile valley was under water. A vast farming civilization of two to three million people could not farm for five months of the year. However, the Nile in flood made it extremely easy to transport heavy blocks of limestone. The Pharaoh had literally hundreds of thousands of able-bodied people looking to him for protection who did not have anything to do. Also present was the social organization which permitted the free time to be applied to a single purpose. A Pharaoh thinking about what happens after he dies, with the ability to induce hard labor in up to three million people for five months a year, created a tomb we call a pyramid. The labor for the pyramids probably was not forced, as there was a gigantic surplus of labor. It may even have been considered an honor to work on the pyramids. Nonetheless, thinking about the future was present. The social organization was present that allowed the time to be devoted to the pyramids, and the people could be induced one way or another to perform the labor.

Think about that for a minute in an Einsteinian Thought Experiment. Become the Pharaoh of ancient Egypt, the living god, and have the surplus of labor and be able to command them to do anything you want. With the surplus of labor, with the ability to induce sacrifice to his plan by his people, the succession of Pharaohs could have accomplished enormous things over the approximately 2,300 years of the Egyptian Empire. Instead, the Pharaohs produced vainglorious egotistical monuments to their own megalomania. What would the reader have commanded the people of ancient Egypt to do?

The history of the Egyptian Empire over 2,300 years is characterized by two conditions: 1) Egypt was almost impossible to reach by land. Its position was isolated. On the

west was the Sahara Desert, on the east was the much smaller Eastern Desert, and the only connection between Egypt and
the Middle East, the rest of Asia, and Europe was a narrow
strip of land called the Sinai Desert. The Sinai had at one
point a 92-mile stretch without water in it. No one could cross
the 92 miles of waterless desert without assistance from the
Pharaoh, who could order the burying of pots of water in the
sand. Egypt enjoyed an excellent defensive position. 2) Egypt
was one of the most fertile regions in the world. Every year
the monsoons that bring rain to India also cause rain in the
mountains far to the south of Egypt. Massive amounts of rain
would fall, and the charging, turbid water would carve the
rock into soil. Every year the silt-laden flood water renewed
the topsoil of the Egyptian farmer, or fellaheen. They never
had to worry about soil depletion or lack of water. After the
Nile receded, they harvested three crops in only seven months
of the year. Egypt was a forever fertile place to farm. The population of ancient Egypt has been estimated to be between two
to three million people, which is only about the size of a medium-size metropolitan area today. The 1994 population of
Egypt is 60 million and is growing at a rate in excess of one
million people per year (2.8 percent). Modern Egypt is an
extremely poor country. However, were there two or three million people in Egypt today, it would still be one of the richest
and greatest countries in the world. The wealth of Egypt is
divided up not three million ways, but 60 million ways and
growing. Now Egypt is poor. It is interesting to look around
the world at the very poorest of countries. One notices that in
past times, many were extremely prosperous and rich lands.
For instance, Bangladesh is one of the poorest countries in the
world. The population density of the land is over two thousand
per square mile. Think of how rich that land must be to support that population density compared to the population density in the United States, which is only 70 per square mile.
Over the years the population of Egypt increased and multi-

plied because of its wealth. Now, the Egyptians are at the limits of their abilities to cope with the problem. It is a recurring
story that the richest of countries oftentimes become the poorest of countries.

For instance, Haiti. During Napoleonic times Haiti was a
rich and lush country. Until Haiti achieved its independence
in 1804, it supplied two-thirds of the wealth needed to fuel
Napoleon's war that raged across Europe. The little country
of Haiti, so lush and so bountiful, paid two thirds of the bill
for Napoleon. Today it is a treeless, rocky, hilly, extremely
poor country. The people are absolutely impoverished. What
happened? They did not protect their topsoil; it washed into
the Caribbean Sea. Now with a population density of over 600
per square mile, all the topsoil washed away and all the
wealth washed away with it. It is an amazing coincidence
how many of the poorest of nations were once the wealthiest
of nations. China and India are further examples of countries
with rich farmland that have overpopulated themselves into
poverty. Evidently, the law of the universe that we tentatively
created in the section on animals applies even to humans,
"When a creature develops even a modest advantage over its
fellow creatures, not only it but its variants increase until the
available resources are fully exploited." It is ironic that in the
very richness of the land lie the seeds of destruction of the
society which those same rich lands brought to greatness.

Over the 2,300-year history of the Egyptian Empire there
were many vicissitudes in the fortunes of the culture. There
were three Pharaonic periods: The old kingdom (2676–2194
B.C.), the middle kingdom (1991–1670 B.C.), and the new kingdom (1568–1085 B.C.), separated by short periods of chaos
and/or foreign invasion, from which very few writings have
come down to us. It is assumed by the scholars that Egypt was
thrown into turmoil and chaos reigned in the land. We do have
one writing that has survived from one of the periods of chaos.
A man complained that society had become so decadent that

the wealthiest person in the culture was a female dancer. (Sort of makes you wonder: Anyone checked Madonna's income lately?)

The fortunes of the empire rose and fell due to simple cause-and-effect relationships. Egypt was isolationist, and oftentimes the technology of its neighbors overwhelmed it. The Hyksos came with the chariot, the Romans came with their new battle formations, and the Assyrians came just for the fun of killing. By and large the entire Pharaonic period was one of conservatism. The state art of Egypt is very stereotyped art that did not change much. Most of the public art was ritualized art in which the same body positions were used century after century after century. When there was a prolific amount of monument building and statue-making, we find it was caused by a Pharaoh who was building a great number of monuments to himself. The art appears to have been ordered out of a factory. It is a case of art not having served the same purpose in the Egyptian society as it serves in our society. It was merely another object for a factory to make. It was a very conservative, non-changing society. Clearly those in charge did not want change. Every day the fellaheen would fight the sun to till the soil or be at the Pharaoh's beck and call to do what was required. For the entire lifetime of the average fellaheen there would not be one technological improvement. No change for an entire lifetime. We are very lucky to be alive today.

The Egyptian Empire came to an end in 715 B.C. through the invasion of the Assyrians. Except for one brief period, Egyptians did not regain control of Egypt until 1952, when Egyptians took control from the British. In the intervening 2,700 years Egypt was ruled by foreign powers. Needless to say, when a foreign power rules a country, decisions are made on the basis of the benefit to the foreign power and not the benefit to the subject country. By the time the Egyptians regained control, Egypt was an impoverished, overpopulated, and disheartened society. Although great progress has been made by the Egyptian government since 1952, many more years of misery will have to be endured by the Egyptian people because of their loss of control over their own society 2,700 years ago. It is appropriate for Americans, who currently have the leading culture on the planet, as we review history, to investigate other cultures that occupied the same position prior to us. We have much to learn from them. We have looked at the Egyptian civilization. Let us look at the Greeks.

Greece

The Greeks migrated from northern Europe at the beginning of the second millennium B.C. The relatively inhospitable terrain of the Greek peninsula caused the early Greeks to raise easily grown olives, grapes, and goats in great surplus. It also caused them to turn to the sea to trade for their other needs. In effect, the Greeks, of necessity, created a division of labor between themselves and other nations. The Greek surpluses of wine and olive oil were traded for the surpluses of other eastern Mediterranean nations. Initially, barter was used. However, barter trade has drawbacks in that the various agricultural products are harvested at different times of the year. Therefore, one of the merchants in a barter transaction oftentimes must accept a promise of payment in the future. No matter how earnestly given, the promise of reciprocal payment in the future could not always be kept because of war, pestilence, drought, etc. The imaginative Greeks circumvented the limitations of barter trading through the widespread introduction of metal coinage around 700 B.C. The wealth that subsequently flowed into the Greek city-states caused the flowering of a civilization that, in many attributes, has not been surpassed since.

The Greeks founded a society that was to be one of the greatest civilizations of all time. They were to reach heights that may not have been equaled yet in architecture. They attempted to build the perfect structure. The Parthenon was deliberately constructed to allow for perspective. To this day, when a government wants to overwhelm

Supreme Court Building—
Washington, D.C.

its people with its grandeur and its power, it copies the architectural style of the Greeks. Our Supreme Court building in Washington, D.C., is an example.

The Greek pottery was exquisite. In Greek society, art was admired for its beauty and perfection and for the grace that it contained. The shipwrights even removed their tool marks, which would never be visible, from the inside timbers of ships. Greek civilization is marked by a quest for excellence in athletics, the development of the human body, and also in the development of the human mind. They valued poetry, literature, philosophy and intellectual thought. Thales of Miletus (late 6th century B.C.) and his students began asking the question, "What is really going on around here?" and hence are credited with the founding of science and philosophy. They were quick to abscond with Egyptian mathematics and build on it. Greece gave us the earliest books of sufficient length to investigate a culture through—the *Iliad* and the *Odyssey* by Homer. The *Iliad,* the account of the ten-year war between the Greeks and Troy that ended around 1200 B.C., is worthy of investigation. You will learn that the ancient Greek heroes whose names are synonymous with the word "legendary"—Agamemnon, Achilles, Hector—were illiterate. The Greeks held games, such as chariot races, outside the walls of Troy, and the winner was deemed to have been assisted by some god or other, and the prize would be a highly esteemed

iron tripod used for cooking. This was considered to be a won-
derfully rich prize. We can see an economic level somewhat
lower than might be expected. However, it places the Trojan
War in perspective for us: the desperate struggle of men who
were prepared every day to fight and die for what presumably
was Grecian honor, but was more probably Grecian desire to
sack a wealthy city.

Troy never fell to the Greeks by force but through the trick
of the Trojan horse. The Trojans took a wooden horse
containing Greek soldiers inside the wall. The Greek soldiers
came out later that night and opened the gates. The rest of
the army entered and killed almost everyone. What they
could not get through force of arms, they obtained through
trickery. It is amazing. We see this over and over again
throughout history. The Chinese built the great wall of
China—the only man-made feature on Earth visible from the
moon—to hold back barbarians. The barbarians breached the
wall several times through bribery, not through assault. The
Romans voluntarily permitted a Germanic tribe, which would
later sack Rome, through its wall. The French Maginot line of
fortresses was not taken through assault by the Germans in
World War II, but rather was circumvented by superior tac-
tics. It seems that often societies sow their own seeds of
destruction.

The Greeks had, as a cultural trait, the striving for excellence in all things. They had the luxury of striving for excellence in all things because they were a slave state. They
existed on the labor of slaves. It is far easier to be a perfectionist when the work is actually accomplished by slaves than
it is when the perfectionist does the work.

The Athenians in particular achieved excellence in an
incredible array of things, not the least of which was how to
govern a people. From two Greek words, *demos* (the people)
and *kratos* (strength or authority), comes "democracy," rule by

the people. To decide an issue, the 18,000 male citizens of ancient Athens would climb a small hill near downtown named the Pnyx (tightly crowded together) and discuss the issues and then vote on them. A direct decision by the people. The population of ancient Athens was sufficiently small to permit direct decision-making by the people. They had no need for representatives to make their decisions for them. The earliest and one of the purest forms of democracy experienced on the face of the Earth. However, only adult males native to Athens were permitted to vote. Women and slaves were excluded from voting.

The Greeks also gave us one of the great thinkers of all time—Aristotle. Aristotle was the last in an intellectual tradition that included Socrates and Plato. To validate his brilliance, the man who was tutored by Aristotle became a warrior and a conqueror who is still regarded as the greatest of all time—Alexander the Great.

One of the city-states, Sparta, was a prime example of the Greek striving for excellence and the ability to sacrifice. The Spartans created a brave and efficient army. In 480 B.C., several hundreds of thousands of Persians commanded by Xerxes I invaded Greece from the north. Leonidas, king of the warrior society of Sparta, commanded a small contingent of Greeks at a narrow pass called Thermopylae. The brave Greeks held the Persians back for two days. However, when a Greek traitor, Ephialtes, led the best Persian infantry, "the Immortals," over a goat path to a position behind the Greeks, King Leonidas and his Spartans were slain to the last man.

The Greeks were not a single nation but a related group of rival city-states. When they were threatened by an outside force, the city-states were often inefficient in rapidly uniting together. This inefficiency was to cost the Greeks their civilization in 338 B.C., when Philip of Macedon, Alexander the Great's father, attacked Greece. Alexander finished the conquest of Greece in 336 B.C., when he inherited the throne. The untimely and ineffectual defense by the Greeks caused their civilization to pass into the control of the Macedonians. The Macedonians in turn were defeated by the Romans in 191 B.C. at the old battleground of Thermopylae. Hence the Greeks lost the ability to control their own destiny. The once proud Greeks had to dance to the tune played by others. To the future grief of the Greek people, the Turks were to play the tune for hundreds of years. In terms of the Four Critical Abilities, the Greeks lacked the cohesion, due to an inefficient city-state social organization, to efficiently coordinate and implement plans despite the obvious ability of at least part of the citizenry to pay the ultimate sacrifice. The appropriate social organization is vital to the continued success of a country because social organization determines what a country is capable of accomplishing.

The Greeks were a great culture and a powerful culture because of their drive for excellence in all things. If they were going to fight, they were going to fight excellently; if they were going to draw, they were going to draw excellently; and if they were going to talk, they were going to talk excellently. Being superior or successful in all things was the driving goal of ancient Greece.

Rome

We now come to Rome. The precise beginnings of Rome are not known, but the Romans themselves thought they were the descendants of one of two sons of the war god, Mars. Romulus, after killing his twin brother Remus, was supposed to have founded Rome in 753 B.C. Romulus and Remus were raised by a she-wolf. A she-wolf is renowned for its tenacity, particularly in defending its young. The Romans considered themselves to be the sons of the war god, meaning that perhaps their first inclination would not be to solve a problem peacefully. Their being raised by a she-wolf would make sure that the problem was not going to be solved peacefully. The population of early Rome consisted primarily of male outcasts and criminals from neighboring societies. Their most infamous atrocity was the rape and abduction of the Sabine women in order to secure suitable companionship. The Romans considered themselves great warriors and clearly very tough. With that attitude, they created an excellent army that was so well disciplined and trained that they could conquer anybody they could catch. They could catch almost everybody except the Scots and the Germans and the Persians.

The Romans viciously conquered the competing societies on the Italian peninsula. They then turned to more distant competitors. The Romans fought the second longest war in European history (the longest was the Crusades, 1095–1291). It was actually a series of wars called the Punic Wars (264–241 B.C., 218–201 B.C., 149–146 B.C.) spanning 118 years. It was fought with ancient Carthage ("new town" in Phoenician), which was founded in 804 B.C. by the Phoenicians in what is now modern Tunisia. The two warrior states battled for some five generations. With victory the Romans killed 450,000 people and enslaved the remaining 50,000. They tilled salt into the land of the Carthaginians. In effect, the Romans did to the Carthaginians what the hard-bodies did to the soft-bodies, what the fishes did to the hard-bodies, what the mammals did to the dinosaurs. They made their competitors extinct by means of the greater efficiency of the Roman society. After the fall of Carthage, the Romans took over other states, including Egypt, and spread the Roman system of rule by defeating armies, by killing anyone who gave them trouble. As the Roman historian, Tacitus, quotes Calgacus, leader of the Scots, referring to the legions of Rome, "*Facient solitudinem, et pacem appellant*—They make an emptiness and call it peace." They were sons of the war god Mars, raised by a she-wolf, and acted like it.

For a period of time Rome was a republic. It held elections and had a Senate composed of the patrician class. The republic became corrupt, and the government became a monarchy with the Emperor Augustus in 27 B.C. The Senate of Rome continued in existence, but the emperors emasculated it by destroying the patrician families that had guided Rome since its inception. In one memorable scene from Edith Hamilton's *The Greek Way* (Norton), she reports that the seven-year-old daughter of a Roman family was being taken away to be killed. As the soldiers led the frightened, sobbing little girl through the streets, she pleaded with her fellow citizens, "What had she done wrong? If they would tell her, she would never do it again." Of course, she had done nothing wrong. Life can be unfair when one lives in a society nurtured by a she-wolf. The Senate's fortunes fell so low that the Emperor Caligula (37–41 A.D.), to embarrass the senators, appointed his horse to the Senate of Rome.

The greatest achievement of the Roman Empire was the Pax Romana, the Roman Peace, which lasted from 27 B.C. to A.D. 180. Although the borders of the empire continued to expand, and there were occasional disturbances in the provinces, it was a period of peace and prosperity unrivaled by any other empire in the history of the world. The internal tranquility and stability permitted the Roman civilization to make unparalleled progress in a wide variety of areas of social development: the arts, sciences, public works, etc. The Pax Romana was the high-water mark of western civilization, at least until present times. It is interesting to note that the crushing military cruelty of Rome resulted in the longest period of peace and human progress ever known; an interesting cause-and-effect relationship.

It is generally assumed that the reason the Roman Empire fell is that it became decadent; that the Romans began engaging in orgies, drunkenness, and all sorts of licentious and libertine behavior. However, an examination of the facts shows us that the moral conduct of the Romans was the same prior to reaching its peak as it was after. The decadent reigns of Caligula (A.D. 37–41) and Nero (A.D. 54–68) occurred while the empire was still expanding. The Roman Empire reached its peak under the emperors Trajan (A.D. 98–117) and Hadrian (A.D. 117–138). The only conclusion possible is that moral conduct is not necessarily a relevant ingredient in the success or failure of a society.

The Roman Empire fell because it agreed to a request by a German tribe, the Visigoths (western Goths), for protection behind the Roman wall. The Visigoths needed protection because the Huns (Hsiung-nu) were invading Europe. The Huns were fleeing the grasslands of Mongolia, where they faced extinction at the hands of the Chinese and their wall. They had already butchered the Ostrogoths (eastern Goths) in the Ukraine. The Huns, even more than the Mongols and Vikings, may well have been the most feared warriors ever known. Although they were superb horsemen, their inhuman appearance coupled with unspeakable cruelty oftentimes caused superior forces to flee before them. Their heads were reported to be misshapen, bulletlike lumps. Swarthy complexions and horrific scarring further heightened their terrifying appearance. At birth, male infants were cut in the face by swords so that a male child would know pain before experiencing the comfort of his mother; so that he would taste blood before tasting the sweet milk of his mother. The Visigoths were trapped between the Roman wall on the Danube River and the invading Huns. If the Romans had not allowed the Visigoths to seek safety behind the Roman wall, the Visigoths would have been massacred also.

Why did the sons of the war god Mars, raised by a she-wolf, care whether the Visigoths were butchered by the Huns or not? I do not know the answer to that question except to note that perhaps the Romans no longer regarded themselves as the sons of Mars. In A.D. 313, the Roman Emperor Constantine I (A.D. 312–337) legalized Christianity in the Edict of Milan. In A.D. 381 the Emperor Theodosius, banned pagan ritual, making Christianity the only legal religion of the Roman Empire. Perhaps the Christian virtue of turning the other cheek caused the Romans to admit the Visigoths. In any event, as the historian Will Durant notes, "A great civilization is not conquered from without until it has destroyed itself from within."

For whatever reason, in A.D. 376 the Emperor Valens permitted the almost one million Visigoths to cross the Danube and enter the Roman Empire. The Romans planned to disarm the Germanic tribe, but the plan was never implemented. The Roman officers supervising the arrival of the Visigoths charged them exorbitant prices for food, stripping the Visigoths of their highly prized jewelry. After the jewels, gold, and silver ran out, the Roman officers forced the Visigoths to sell their children into slavery in exchange for food. When the Roman officers demanded that the Visigoths turn over their weapons, the Visigoths bribed the officers with their last remaining children in order to retain their arms. The Visigoths then turned on their Roman protectors and slew them. Emperor Valens led the legions against the Visigoths, but was defeated, and the wounded emperor himself was burned alive in a cottage where he had sought refuge. The Visigoths were appeased temporarily, but finally rampaged through the Roman Empire. Alaric the Brave, king of the Visigoths, not only spoke Latin, but had converted to Christianity and had made two visits to Rome. In A.D. 410, the Visigoths sacked Rome. In terms of the Four Critical Abilities, the Romans, at a pivotal point, clearly lacked effective plan implementation. The decadent Roman officers would not sacrifice their own greed to implement the plan of disarming the Visigoths for the long-term benefit to the

Roman Empire. As has been stated before, it seems that many societies sow the seeds of their own destruction.

The Middle Ages—A.D. 410 to A.D. 1492

With the sack of Rome by the Visigoths in A.D. 410, the ancient world comes to an end. We pass into the area of western history known as the Middle Ages. The Middle Ages is noted for the large number of petty kingdoms that swelled and shrank over time. By the way, what happened to the Visigoths, the conquerors of the greatest empire western civilization has ever known? When the Romans stripped the soldiers from their wall to defend Rome from the Visigoths, hordes of barbarians entered the empire. The German Franks seized what is now France, hence its name. The Alans (originally from Iran), the Germanic Suevi (Swabian), and the Germanic Vandals (Wanderers) took Spain. The Visigoths entered Spain, where they conquered the Suevi and in A.D. 429 forced 80,000 Vandal and Alan warriors and their families under King Gaiseric to flee from Andalusia (land of the Vandals) across the Straits of Gibraltar to North Africa. The Vandals ravaged North Africa and re-crossed the Mediterranean to rampage through Italy and sack Rome in A.D. 455. This rampage is memorialized in the word "vandalism" (wanton, senseless destruction without benefit to the destroyer). The Visigoths ruled Spain from their capital Toledo, and they put together a mini-kingdom consisting of southern France, Spain, Portugal, and part of North Africa. Despite frequent skirmishes with the Franks, a period of relative peace ensued. The Visigoths converted to Christianity and adopted a sedentary life in which art and architecture flourished. However, in A.D. 711 the Muslim Moors attacked Spain and quickly defeated the Visigoths at the Battle of Guadalete, driving them into small pockets in northern Spain and the Pyrenees. For 700 years the Visigoths, with the assistance of other Christians, slowly reconquered Spain, culminating in their victory at Granada in A.D. 1492 under Ferdinand and Isabella of Christopher Columbus fame. If you would like to see what remains of the Germanic Visigoths, descendants of the conquerors of the Roman Empire, one need only look as far as the closest Spaniard.

It is remarkable to survey the completeness of the Germanic conquest of the western part of the Roman Empire, modern-day Western Europe. The Germanic Suevi managed to maintain their existence in the western Iberian Peninsula and became the roots of the modern Portuguese. As we have learned, the Germanic Visigoths became the modern Spaniards. The Germanic Franks and the Germanic Burgundians became the modern French. The Germanic Flemish settled in part of what is modern Belgium. The remnants of the Germanic Ostrogoths and the Germanic Lombards (long beards) settled in Italy along with the non-Germanic Huns. The Germanic Angles (from whom the word "England" is derived) and the Germanic Saxons (from whom come the names of the English counties of Essex [East Saxony], Sussex [South Saxony], and Wessex [West Saxony]) settled in southern and central Britain. The Germanic Dutch (*Deutsche*; in old German, "of the people") settled in Holland. The Germanic Vandals and the non-Germanic Alans populated much of North Africa. The closely related Scandinavians, the Danish, Norwegians, and Swedish remained in the ancestral home of the Germans for a while. It would be several centuries before they ravaged much of Europe as the greatly feared Vikings and Norsemen (men of the North or Normans) and settled on the coast of France (Normandy). In A.D.1066, under William the Conqueror, they even conquered their Anglo-Saxon cousins in Britain. A large island off the east coast of Sweden is to this day still called Gotland (land of the Goths) and is the original homeland of the Goths. Of course, some Germanic tribes remained behind to become the modern Germans and Austrians. The massive movement of the Germans out of Central Europe created a vacuum that permitted the Slavs, who were to become the Poles, Czechs, Serbs (who adopted Eastern Orthodox Catholicism), Croats (who adopted Roman Catholicism), Ukrainians, Russians, and others, to move into Central Europe. In exceptional cases, ancient Celtic peoples, such as the Scots, Irish, Welsh, Helvetii (Swiss) and the non-Celtic Basques, retained their homelands. Although there has been a subsequent intermingling of many peoples, it would not be too much of an oversimplification to state that the foundation of modern Western Europe is Germanic peoples who adopted Roman civilization to varying degrees. Therefore, it is apparent that the Germanic peoples clearly won the struggle for the survival of the efficient in Western Europe.

The most illuminating method of investigating the Middle Ages is to examine the lifestyle of the average person. This would, of course, be the peasant. This poor guy had nothing but troubles. First of all he was illiterate. Second he was for all intents and purposes bonded to a feudal lord of one rank or another. The peasant worked in primarily agrarian pursuits all day long, the rewards of which he shared with his boss. Working in a field in the Middle Ages produced the same dirt and grime that it does today but, without the same effective means of removing dirt and grime at the end of the day.

The life of the peasant of the Middle Ages was short and nasty. The average life expectancy was 40 years. Diseases were oftentimes rampant in the society with very mixed results insofar as cures were concerned. Plague, known as the Black Death, scourged Europe from 1347 to the 1660s. Since the cause of the disease was unknown, the only defense against the Black Death was for a city, town, or village to isolate itself. No one was allowed in or out. It is estimated that one out of every three Europeans perished from the Black Death. The survivors must have been terrified. A terror that lasted spasmodically for over 300 years. Is it not nice to be alive today?

Relief from a life of never-ending toil in dirt and squalor in some sort of rude hut would occur when a peasant's lord called him to serve in a military capacity. If one has had the opportunity to peruse a suit of armor worn by the upper classes during these military adventures, it becomes apparent that when an opponent lord fielded a peasant army to fight, he was doing the other lord a favor by presenting him with suitable targets whom his horse could trample and his lance could spear and his sword could chop into as many pieces as he had time for.

Life was unimproving. One could not expect life to get better. Generation after generation there would be no change in lifestyle, no improvement for one's children. We are very lucky to be living in today's society. Even with all the problems that confront us in our daily newspapers, we are far, far better off than at any other time in history and beyond comparison to any time since the beginnings of life on Earth. We should cherish and protect our comfortable and prosperous society.

Some of the Fundamental Laws of the Universe that Apply to Human Societies

In the three cultures upon which we have briefly touched, we can see some of the advantages that caused their greatness. Rome, being warlike, created through conquest a massive empire and ruled it well for some 400 years. The Greeks, with their advantage of striving for excellence, were a great culture for 900 years. They contributed immensely to the culture of humankind. They gave us a standard for the highest form of government, gave us a standard in beauty for which to shoot—perfection—and invented the rational investigation of nature. The Egyptians, in their protected position, and receiving the gift of the Nile of new farms for everyone every year, remained a very strong and wealthy empire for 2,700 years. The Egyptian culture was more efficient most of the time at defending itself than the culture that could attack it. The Greek culture was more efficient than, for instance, the Persian culture that it battled and finally defeated. The Persian culture fielded an army of one million, whereas the Greeks could only put 120,000 men into the field. The Greek army won and won easily because they were more efficient. It is apparent that the story of societies (we would call them countries today) in conflict, with some winning and most losing, is the story of history. If we compare the number of cultures that have vanished over the course of history to the number of cultures that still exist in this world, we will find that over 99 percent of them have vanished. Of the thousands and thousands of human societies that have existed on this planet, only a few hundred are extant today. The cause-and-effect relationship, the Law of the Survival of the Efficient, has operated as brutally on the extinct societies as it has on over 99 percent of the animal species that no longer exist. Like the animals who still exist, the societies that still exist are greatly evolved from their ancestors.

Darwin's principle applies just as assuredly today, only in modern industrialized societies it applies to societies. If we look within our own society, it appears that the law of the Survival of the Efficient cannot possibly apply because there are handicapped people, some people are smarter than other people, and all people seem to be surviving. Survival within a society may not depend on how efficient an individual is, but the success of individuals within a given society may well depend on individual efficiency. The Law of the Survival of the Efficient does not operate within a society; it only works extra-societally, among societies. History demonstrates that societies with certain traits and characteristics are favored. Just because we cannot see the law operating from within an individual society does not mean it is not at work. The Law of the Survival of the Efficient applies to our society on a scale and over a time frame that is not apparent from the viewpoint of one individual lifetime within this society.

Remember the bees? How the bees divided labor into drones, worker bees, and the queen bee? How investigating an individual bee is not a very enlightening thing to do? The real organism is the entire beehive. The same is true of human beings. Humankind is not an individual organism. Humankind is like the bee. A culture may be made up of many individuals but we are all interdependent. We have divided labor. To look at the life or death or success of one individual is really not important because the society has divided labor. Take the average American citizen and remove all man-made objects from him or her and drop him or her out in the forest. He or she will die very shortly, almost assuredly. Most of us would. Very few of us would be able to survive because we depend upon the rest of our society for our survival. In all three civilizations, the Egyptian, the Greek, and the Roman, labor had been widely divided into hundreds of different occupations from soldier to shopkeeper to artisan to shoemaker, etc. As long as each of the divisions of labor was relatively efficient compared to its competitors in performing its function, then the society could continue to survive. As long as the army, the government, the businesses, and the farming all remained competitively efficient, then a given society had an opportunity to survive. In modern industrialized societies our divisions of labor are most often performed by institutions. We will discuss more about institutions later.

The ancient societies were large enough that their efforts could be directed into enormous and important undertakings. The social organization was present to achieve what the society deemed as its goals, whether by democratic Greece or autocratic Rome and Egypt. The citizens of these societies, due to the social organization present, were induced to sacrifice to achieve these goals. Hence, these were the great and leading cultures of their times.

All societies are in competition with other societies. The most extreme form of competition is war. If we follow the history of nations we see that it is a history of warfare, of expanding and shrinking countries based upon the advantages that they have at the moment in time, just exactly like the animals. When they no longer have the ability to maintain those advantages that keep them a large powerful nation, then they succumb. They are taken over by another society and they fall or they shrink.

It is apparent that the story of history is one of societies in competition. The competition is resolved, just as it has been throughout the course of life on Earth, along the Darwinian principles of the Survival of the Efficient. Each one of these societies could be assessed in the same manner as we assessed the animal world. What occurred to the Romans is exactly what occurred to the hard-bodied trilobites; when they had the advantage they increased and multiplied. However, in the case of humans, it is not a physical improvement that brings an advantage, but rather cultural traits. The important cultural traits are 1) How has the society, consciously or unconsciously, arranged itself (social organization)? How efficiently has the society divided labor? How efficient is its army? How efficient is the society's government? How efficiently does the government think in the future? How efficiently does the government plan? In short, the answer to "How efficient are the institutions of a given society?" is critical to the survival of that society. 2) And just as important, what are the values, beliefs, attitudes, and perspectives held by the people of the society? How efficient are the people at adapting to change? How efficient are the people at carrying out goals? How efficient are the people at being cohesive? In short, how efficient are the people of a society at sacrificing to carry out the plan to achieve the goals of the society?

The same Four Critical Abilities that caused humankind to become the unquestioned masters of the animal kingdom are the same Four Critical Abilities that cause a society, or in historical times a country, to survive and succeed.

Four Critical Abilities

1) The ability of the government to *think in the future efficiently*.

2) The ability of the government to invent a *plan efficiently*.

3) An *efficient social organization* to implement the plan.

4) The ability of the people to *sacrifice* to carry out the plan *efficiently*.

How efficiently does a society need to utilize the above Four Critical Abilities in order to survive? At least as efficiently as its competitors. How efficiently does the society have to utilize the above Four Critical Abilities in order to prosper? *More* efficiently than its competitors.

It is obvious that the unrelenting Law of the Survival of the Efficient applies equally mercilessly to human societies as it does to microbes and wildebeests. It is interesting to note that, insofar as the Four Critical Abilities required for human societies to prosper have been disclosed in this book for the first time, then it follows that no human society could ever have been consciously designed with them specifically in mind.

Now that we have discovered how societies prosper because of the Four Critical Abilities, let us analyze why societies fall.

All extinct societies, by definition, have gone out of existence and therefore failed in the struggle for survival. Only the countries existing today have a possibility to continue to survive. However, societies are extremely unstable, even though, from the perspective of one lifetime of one individual in the United States, countries may appear to be relatively stable. Think of the large number of countries that have experienced a fundamental change in government, or devastation by war, or social upheaval, or disappeared entirely in just one lifetime, say from World War I until now. It is a very large number when one realizes that a normal lifetime for a society is usually counted over hundreds and even thousands of years. Since a far greater number of societies has become extinct than continue to survive, it must be very easy to become extinct and very difficult to survive.

There are two causes of the collapse of a society—external and internal. External causes are those cause-and-effect relationships that originate outside of the society, such as earthquakes, floods, volcanic eruptions, changes in climate, changes in commerce, natural disasters, and, most important, conflicts with neighboring societies. The extreme form of this conflict is, of course, warfare. If we apply the Four Critical Abilities needed by a society to the conduct of warfare, we can easily see that the society that 1) thinks about the future; that 2) plans for the future; 3) has the appropriate social structure necessary to implement the plan most effectively; and 4) has the necessary degree of sacrifice to carry out this plan will invariably defeat the less effective societies despite even very large differences in numbers or technology. Classic examples come to mind: the Greek defeat of the Persians, the Israeli defeats of the Arabs, the Vietnamese defeat of the U.S.

The internal causes and effects of the collapse of a society are usually lumped into the catchall word, "decadence." *From* what, *to* what, does a society decay? To answer what decadence means, let us look at a classic example of decadence and see what we can learn. Let us take the hypothetical case of a 35-year-old wealthy bachelor who eats too much, drinks too much, takes drugs, and womanizes. What is wrong with that? The bachelor may feel great. He may be enjoying himself immensely today. No problem. The problem comes in the future when a heart attack kills him, his liver stops functioning, his personality becomes warped, and medical science can no longer cure his venereal diseases. Clearly, the bachelor could not forgo present pleasures for future ones. He could not sacrifice today for a better future tomorrow. He did not think about the future. He did not plan for the future. He did not have the necessary degree of sacrifice for a better future. Therefore, the bachelor will come to a premature end.

Now let us apply what we have learned about decadence to a society. A society becomes decadent when it can no longer think in the future, when it can no longer plan, when it no longer has the appropriate social structure for its time and place, and additionally, when its members can no longer make the appropriate sacrifice. Therefore, decadence is precisely the reverse side of the coin of the Four Critical Abilities a society requires to prosper. All things being equal, a society will prosper if it efficiently employs the Four Critical Abilities, and it will decay and come to a premature end if it employs the Four Critical Abilities inefficiently. Therefore, it is inconsequential to the survival of a given society what sorts of babble the pre-adolescents choose to call music. It is also inconsequential what painters paint, or what sculptors sculpt. As we learned from ancient Rome, it is also inconsequential to the survival of a society what internal patterns of morality are adopted, as long as the Four Critical Abilities are followed.

If ancient Egypt, Greece, and Rome had efficiently utilized the Four Critical Abilities, all would exist today. If they had been able to accurately perceive the future, they would have been aware of the threats to their societies. Then they could have made plans to avoid the impending disaster. With the appropriate social organization and willingness on the part of the people to sacrifice to implement the plan, all three societies could have continued to exist to the present day. Equally, if the government of the United States of America were to begin to utilize the Four Critical Abilities, then we could continue to exist and prosper indefinitely.

Although history may seem very long and very complex, in the overall view it is the story of societies in competition with one another, and the winners have the advantages, and the losers do not have sufficient advantages to overcome the winners. History is merely an extension of the competition amongst animals played out by human animals organized into societies. It is about as simple as that.[24]

Therefore, that country that is more efficient will continue to exist, whereas those countries that are less efficient and/or decadent will cease their existence. A perfect example is the break-up of the Soviet Union. The question becomes, how efficient are we, the United States of America?

---

24. The author believes that the concept that history in its largest sense is the study of the Law of the Survival of the Efficient applied to societies over long periods of time is new knowledge and is first revealed in this book. When the author attended school, it was taught that the Law of the Survival of the Fittest does not apply to humans and our societies. If someone else has previously discovered this fact, the author apologizes and indeed welcomes it as further evidence of the correctness of the fact.

CHAPTER SEVEN

Democracy Triumphant

1492 to 1952

A
S WE CONTINUE OUR QUEST in chronological order, we must narrow our focus to the United States of America. For if we attempted to maintain a global analysis in our investigation of the past, this book would become so long and convoluted that it would be virtually impossible not to become lost. If the reader has an interest in analyzing other societies, then the following can be used as a model.

Therefore, in this chapter we will investigate the recent past (1492–1952) as it relates to the United States of America. We know what has happened in the distant past and will shortly know the recent past. We will next learn about the present. Then it should be relatively easy to predict the real future of the United States. We can then compare that real future to an idealized future and see what the differences are. If the two futures are relatively similar there is no problem. If, however, there is a significant discrepancy between the two futures, then we must determine what causes must be changed to bring about the idealized future. The changes to be made will naturally give us the plan. In other words, we will apply the incredibly powerful Seven Steps of the Black Box Technique to the United States of America.

An Extremely Short History
of the United States of America

Since it is required that every high school graduate in the
United States complete one year of U.S. history, I will presume that the reader is generally aware of our history.
However, every country has skeletons in its closet that are not
usually brought out for the high school students, such as
Japan's failure to teach that Japan is responsible for starting
the war with the United States in 1941. This places the
author in the unenviable position of recounting historical
events that cast the United States of America in a less favorable light than the one in which we are normally used to viewing ourselves. For we must know the past accurately for our
extremely powerful problem-solving techniques to work. What
follows in this section is not motivated by any unpatriotic
motive, but rather the reverse.

Humans entered the Western Hemisphere from Asia
across the Bering Sea land bridge some 14,000 to 25,000 years
ago. After the Viking "re-discovery" of America in A.D. 1000,
Christopher Columbus "re-re-discovered" America in 1492.
The first permanent European settlement in the thirteen original colonies was the Pilgrim settlement of Plymouth, Massachusetts, in 1620.[25] Why did it take 128 years to permanently
settle here? The European nations were concerned farther
north, initially over Newfoundland, a large island off the coast
of Canada.

It was the easiest place to set up fish-salting and packing
operations for the cod being harvested by the boatload from
the waters of the Grand Banks. When John Cabot discovered
the Grand Banks in 1497, he reported that baskets full of fish
quite literally could be simply pulled up over the sides of the
vessel. The Grand Banks is an area partly controlled by the

---

25. Jamestown, Virginia, was settled in 1607, but no longer exists.

United States and was up until recently the most productive
fishing grounds in the world. I understand that it is now
utterly exhausted. North American cod was a cheap and reliable source of food for the Europeans, and control of Newfoundland so vital that a pact was signed barring permanent
settlement in the New World. Things got off to a slow start.

The Pilgrims were seeking freedom to practice a religion
that dictated a very rigid lifestyle. In light of the later
witchcraft trials, I presume it to be considered odd by modern
standards as I am not aware of the religion's continued existence. Therefore, I suppose, if today's media were reporting
the Pilgrims' landing in the *Mayflower,* it would refer to them
as a "religious cult," as they did when Jim Jones moved his
religious cult to Jonestown, Guyana.

The Pilgrims were beset by problems, not the least of
which was landing in Massachusetts in the winter when their
destination was Virginia. Of the 102 arriving Pilgrims, only 50
survived the first winter. Extinction was fended off only by the
timely intervention of the local Indian tribe, the Wampanoags.
We celebrate this charitable act in our national holiday,
Thanksgiving. The repayment for this act of kindness was to
come when New Englanders massacred hundreds of Indians
in the Pequot War in 1637. The Pilgrims were not particularly
successful, but their numbers increased through continued
immigration. It is interesting to note that neither of the two
societies present at our society's founding survived until the
present. They are both extinct.

Colonies under royal charter from England became the
thirteen original colonies. To work the tobacco crop in the new
land of few people, a labor force was needed. Black Africans
were forcibly abducted from their homelands and brought to
the American colonies as slaves. In the North, the climate
was neither sufficiently benign, nor were the forests and
stones sufficiently yielding, to permit a surplus of cash crops.

Additional labor was not required. Slaves were not valuable to a family on its own farm in not particularly good farming country. It is easy to understand the stereotype of the hard-working and stoic character of rural New England.

Boston, New York, Philadelphia, Baltimore, and Charleston were the trading centers for the commerce with England. Land transportation between colonies was abysmal to non-existent. In fact, when the king of England wanted to punish someone, he would have the person summoned to an official meeting in a distant city. Travel could take several weeks one way and several weeks back.

From 1620 to 1775 the colonists clung to the relatively narrow strip of coast between the Appalachian Mountains and the Atlantic seaboard. The time between the Pilgrims' settlement and the settlement west of the Cumberland Gap was 155 years (283 years after the re-re-discovery of the New World by Columbus). The colonies of the New World got off to a slow start. It was not until 1775 that Daniel Boone cut the Wilderness Road out of the dense forest and led settlers through the Cumberland Gap. The Indian territory that was to become Kentucky and Tennessee was first settled one year before the Revolutionary War. The expanding population forced new territories to be opened. The population had increased to 2.5 million, mostly through immigration. Not only did the colonists forcibly take the land from the Indians, they stole from one another as well. Daniel Boone's home and property were unjustly taken from him when unscrupulous lawyers and magistrates caught up with the advancing frontier. It was a common story. After the often illiterate settlers cleared and worked the land and subdued the Indians, unscrupulous lawyers in league with newly appointed magistrates would produce phony deeds and evict the struggling settlers' families.

England looked upon its colonies as a way to profit rather than as an extension of England itself. As we learned from ancient Egypt, when a foreign power rules a country, decisions are made on the basis of benefit to the foreign power and not benefit to the subject country. Therefore, the proceeds of a required stamp on all business transactions might have seemed beneficial if you lived in London. Less so if you lived in Boston and actually paid for the stamp. Since all trade by law had to be with England, England controlled the prices. As the colonists chafed under unfair treatment, more troops were needed to maintain order. It was cheapest to house these troops in civilians' homes, which only added to the discontent.

By 1776, a sufficient number of the colonists had decided that the injustices being done to them by an absolute monarch, who made judgments based solely upon their benefit to another society, warranted war in order to set up a new society. However, some 20 to 33 percent of the citizens of each colony were Tories and sided with England. It seems likely that those who were prospering under the English rule would be reluctant to revolt, but enough of the prosperous George Washingtons and Thomas Jeffersons favored independence.

The Revolutionary War was fought. It was a very close war. The Americans were hampered by innumerable problems but were aided by the French. At Valley Forge the flames of rebellion almost flickered out but were rekindled by new recruits and European officers to lead them. The war ended at the Battle of Yorktown, where we defeated not only the British but also, interestingly enough, the remnants of the ancient Hittite Empire, who had been hired as mercenaries. (Around 1900 B.C. a very warlike but illiterate tribe entered Turkey. They conquered the indigenous society, adapting the writing of the conquered people to the phonetics of their own spoken language, which was German. They conquered most of the Middle East and even attacked the Egyptians. When the Hittite Empire was defeated by Assyrian King Sargon II in 717 B.C., the Hittites returned to Germany. In A.D. 98, the Roman historian, Tacitus, included them as the Chatti in a report entitled *de Germania* about the German tribes on the borders of the Roman Empire. Some 1700 years later, the prince of Hesse[26] found he could enrich himself greatly by hiring out his virile and obedient young men as mercenaries to England. Hence, when we defeated the British and a regiment of Hessians at Yorktown in 1781, we in actuality defeated some of the descendants of the Hittite Empire.)

With the war won, the real trouble began. The newly independent Americans were unified in their dislike of a foreign monarchy that dictated their laws, but uncertain exactly what form of government they should create. The opinions ranged from a monarchy, with George Washington as king, to no central government at all but thirteen separate countries. The thirteen future states all had functioning governments which, as would be expected, did not want to give up power. The first attempt at forming a central government resulted in the Articles of Confederation (1777). The Articles of Confederation merely created a league of independent states as opposed to a central government. Its inadequacy impressed everybody. I will bet that the reader has never read the Articles of Confederation, not even in the required U.S. history class. Why? Because the Articles of Confederation are so blatantly ill-conceived, they are an embarrassment to our Founding Fathers and to all who read them. The lack of a properly functioning central government resulted in Shays's Rebellion. The rebellion of debt-ridden Massachusetts farmers was crushed by the end of February 1787. To avoid further chaos, George Washington supported a convention because, as Washington put it, "Good God...there are combustibles in every state, which a spark might set fire to."

---

26. Hesse is the region of Germany that includes the modern city of Frankfurt.

A constitutional convention was rapidly convened from only twelve of the thirteen states in Philadelphia in May of 1787. The original intent of the convention was merely to amend the Articles of Confederation. Rhode Island never sent a delegate to the convention, and both it and North Carolina finally ratified the Constitution only after it went into effect. Rhode Island was concerned about the small role it would no doubt play in a new government. George Washington presided over the convention, and the only other patriots in attendance whose names most of us would recognize were Benjamin Franklin of Pennsylvania, James Madison, Jr., of Virginia, and Alexander Hamilton of New York. Conspicuous by his absence was a major component of the brainpower of the Founding Fathers, Thomas Jefferson. Thomas Jefferson was a brilliant thinker and may be the only American who can be placed in the same category as Aristotle, da Vinci, Newton, Mill, and Einstein.

His writings on difficult social issues are so convincing and lucid that they tend not only to resolve the issue but also to become the definitive statement on the issue. For instance, on how much public dissent should be tolerated, Thomas Jefferson stated: "... Let them stand undisturbed as monuments of the safety with which error of opinion may be tolerated where reason is left free to combat it." In 1789, the first year the Constitution took effect, Thomas Jefferson promulgated the idea that each generation should re-write the Constitution for itself. As Jefferson remarked, "no society can make a perpetual constitution or even a perpetual law...the Earth belongs to the living, and not to the dead...." In 1816 Jefferson further stated "Each generation has a right to choose for itself the form of government it believes most promotive of its own happiness ... a solemn opportunity of doing this every nineteen or twenty years, should be provided by the Constitution...." In other words, Thomas Jefferson, our wisest Founding Father, thought that each generation of future Americans should be able to create for itself the form of democracy under which it wanted to live.

He was also an expert horticulturist, botanist, scientist, inventor, and architect, in addition to being the gentleman who founded the University of Virginia and served as one of the very best presidents of the United States. The presidency of Thomas Jefferson (1801–1809) was noted for 1) the expansion of the United States through the Louisiana Purchase and the farsighted Lewis and Clark expedition, and 2) extreme frugality—his budgets actually reduced the national debt when a new expanding nation needed almost everything. From the inception of the Constitution, presidents had the right of impoundment (in modern terms: line-item veto). This meant that they could either refuse to spend, or spend in another way, money budgeted by Congress. In 1801, Thomas Jefferson refused to spend money that Congress had voted for the purchase of warships. Instead, he reduced the national debt.

Thomas Jefferson was on assignment as the Minister (Ambassador) to France at the time of the constitutional convention and therefore never attended. Many of the other patriots with whom we are familiar were already serving in the government under the Articles of Confederation and therefore were not chosen as delegates by the sovereign states. For instance, John Adams was the Minister to England. The sovereign states that sent delegates naturally desired a government to which they would give up as little power as possible. Had these more famous men been in attendance, the Constitution probably would not be very different, for the discussions of the delegates focused not on lofty ideals, but on compromises. In our required high school U.S. History classes, we are given the impression that the Constitution is such a perfect document that it should be regarded with only slightly less reverence than the Ten Commandments. The truth is far different. The great issue at the constitutional convention involved the discrepancy in size and therefore population between the large states and the small states. If America was to become a democracy in the truest sense of the word—one man (ladies were excluded), one vote—then the small states with their small populations would have a very small say in the new government. The small states wanted a one-state-one-vote type of democracy. As indeed the voting at the constitutional convention itself was one-state-one-vote. Therefore, nothing could be passed without the approval of the small states. The large states, on the other hand, wanted a one-man-one-vote type of democracy.

James Madison, Jr., of Virginia brought to the constitutional convention a proposal he had authored called the Virginia plan. It provided for a one-man-one-vote system excluding women. The bulk of the constitutional convention was not spent discussing lofty ideals of government, nor was it spent attempting to put in place a government to stand for all time and serve as a model for future governments. It was spent compromising the Virginia plan to make it acceptable to the small states. Hence, the inefficiency created by having two houses of Congress: the House of Representatives elected by the one-man-one-vote system, and the Senate, with two senators from each state, originally elected by the state legislatures. In effect, the states controlled the legislative branch of government by their election of the Senate. Both houses of Congress have to agree to pass any legislation. If the Senate did not approve, then the legislation could not become law. The Senate also was given the task of confirming nominations to the Supreme Court. By controlling the Senate, the states also controlled who could be appointed to the Supreme Court. Therefore, in our government as originally designed by the Constitution, the state legislatures controlled two of the three branches of government by their election of the Senate. In other words, the Constitution was not the highest and purest form of democracy by any standard, but rather a patched-together compromise that resulted in an inefficient and relatively undemocratic government. It was a far cry from the participatory democracy of ancient Greece. Early in the constitutional convention, Alexander Hamilton walked out in disgust.

The incredible compromises contained in the Constitution become readily evident when one reads in Article 1, Section 2, Paragraph 3 that for purposes of electing representatives, each slave will be counted as three-fifths of a person. I can see the logic behind counting one person as one person. I can even follow the logic of not counting certain people. But there is no logic that can make a person three-fifths of a person. Only compromise can do that. However, that particular compromise may well have been the best solution to a given problem at that time and at that place. But then we must give up all pretense of the Constitution's being a hallowed and sacrosanct document that can at all times and under all circumstances be the blueprint for the highest and best form of government. The framers of the Constitution themselves recognized this fact when they permitted the state legislatures and the two houses of Congress to amend the Constitution.

A lengthy discussion of the Constitution is possible here, but rather than do that it would be more enlightening for the reader to read the Constitution. The reader should view the Constitution as an effect caused by the following factors: 1) a dislike for a strong central government due to maltreatment by King George III of England; 2) the necessity of a central government due to experience under the Articles of Confederation; 3) the desire of some states to retain slavery and others to end slavery; and 4) the desire of the states to cede to the central government as little power as possible. The result was a very compromised piece of work resulting from the competing factors at that time and at that place. As we see what the Constitution in turn caused, we must realize that it was a result of compromises between competing forces as opposed to an enduring statement of how governments should eternally be organized. For instance, the Constitution's inability to resolve the slave issue resulted in the Civil War. However, it was probably the best that could be done under the circumstances.

As for the actual type of government that the Constitution created, it must be remembered that the Constitution was the first attempt in 850 years to create a democratic form of government.[27] It is revealing that the countries that have followed us in creating democracies almost never duplicate our form of government.

Most of those democracies that have come after us are of the second-generation model of democracy, the parliamentary form. The parliamentary form of government is an inherently more efficient form of government than our quarrelsome, divided power system of checks and balances. We have two houses of Congress because of a compromise between the big colonies and the little colonies. As we recall, the senators were actually elected by the state legislatures until 1913. The typical modern parliaments have one-house legislatures elected by the people, and are therefore more efficient than our two-house legislature. Additionally, the prime minister (equivalent to our president) has been elected to the post by a majority of the members of parliament and therefore always has a majority of votes in parliament to pass whatever laws the prime minister and his cabinet want. When the prime minister can no longer obtain a majority vote in parliament for an important piece of legislation, then new elections for prime minister must be held. Very democratic and very efficient. A prime minister in a parliamentary government can direct the government much more efficiently than our president can in our system. A prime minister has the majority of

---

27. The Icelandic Vikings set up a democratic institution known as the Althing in A.D. 930.

votes in parliament to pass his legislation, whereas our president needs his party to have a majority in the two houses of Congress to enjoy the same power as the prime minister. Indeed, it has been very rare in modern times that the party of the president had a majority in both houses of Congress. Therefore our system of government from its inception gives us a weak executive branch compared to a parliamentary system. Moreover, our system gives us a weak executive branch compared to the legislative branch.

By design of our Constitution, the legislative branch of government is stronger than the executive branch. If the president wants a law passed but Congress does not, no law is passed. If Congress wants a law passed and the president does not, the law is passed. The president may veto the law, but Congress can override the president's veto.

More efficient democracies usually have a legislature composed of only a single house instead of two houses, such as our Senate and House of Representatives. Until 1913 under the Constitution, the Senate was elected by state legislatures and not the people. This is a manifestation of the states' desire to have a weak central government. In other democracies, the single legislative house elected by the people is more democratic, involves less compromise (the House and Senate do not have to compromise further to reconcile their differences), is simpler and capable of more rapid decision-making, and is therefore more efficient than the system given to us by our Constitution. Additionally and most important, in a parliamentary system the prime minister (president) and the legislature (Congress) cooperate. They are in harmony working toward the same goal. Whenever the prime minister and the majority of the legislature disagree on legislation, an election must be held. By the way the people vote in the election, the people, in effect, decide the issue upon which the prime minister and legislature could not agree. Very democratic and just as important, very efficient. In fact, more democratic and more efficient than our system. By now, we should all be aware of how important it is to be efficient. The form of government given us by the Constitution is a slow[28] and cumbersome compromise that attempts to reconcile the conflicting goals of: 1) the states that appointed the delegates; 2) a central government of limited power; and 3) the people. Of the three, the people's rights were least attended to. The Bill of Rights, which gives us all of our great freedoms—freedom of speech, the press, religion, from false imprisonment, etc.—was not part of the original Constitution. It comprises the first ten amendments to the Constitution. Therefore, the Constitution, instead of giving us an enduring government for all time merely gave us a government that was the best compromise that could be worked out at the time. The best parts of the Constitution, the enduring part of the Constitution, the part of the Constitution to which we pay homage in our backyards on the Fourth of July, was not even part of the original Constitution and was added onto it two years after the first meeting of Congress.

When we think of the Bill of Rights, most of us think of the rights of freedom of speech, freedom of the press, freedom of religion, the right to bear arms, and the right of due process. However, Thomas Jefferson thought that, "The 10th Amendment is the bedrock of the Constitution." The 10th Amendment states:

> *The powers not delegated to the United States by the Constitution, nor prohibited by it to the States, are reserved to the States, respectively, or to the people.*

---

28. Given the condition of the roads in early America, it would take weeks for people in the more remote parts of the country to receive news of what the government was doing. Therefore, slowing down governmental decision-making was considered beneficial as more people would have the ability to follow what was being considered as opposed to being presented with a fait accompli.

The 10th Amendment strictly limited the power of the central government to those few powers listed in the Constitution. Therefore, our Constitution created a weak central government. Within the weak central government, the Constitution created a weak presidency and a strong Congress. Further, with the election of the Senate by the state legislatures, the strong Congress was controlled by the states rather than the people. All in all, our central government as set up by the Constitution was neither very efficient nor very democratic. As has been stated, it was a far cry from the democracy of ancient Athens.

As we have seen, the government created by the Constitution was deliberately designed to be relatively weak and slow-moving. The powers of government were split into three branches: the executive, the legislative, and the judicial. In an effort to ensure that no one branch of the government accumulated too much power, a system of checks and balances was installed. However, sadly for us, much of the system of checks and balances was not actually written into the Constitution itself. For example, 1) the president's traditional right of budgetary impoundment wherein Congress voted the total amount of money to spend, but the president spent the money as he so chose, and 2) the Supreme Court's power to review the actions of the two other branches for constitutionality. Our Founding Fathers made a tragic error by not including the system of checks and balances in the Constitution as we shall see later.

Apparently even as powerful a thinker as wily 81-year-old Benjamin Franklin evidently became befuddled over the compromises that created our government, when, during the proceedings he declared: "It is therefore that, the older I grow, the more apt I am to doubt my own judgment and to pay attention to the judgment of others." But Dr. Franklin was absolutely correct when, upon emerging from the final day of the secret proceedings, he was asked by Mrs. Samuel Powell in the crowd outside the hall, "Well Doctor, what have we got, a republic or a monarchy?" Ben replied, "A republic, if you can keep it." We will see what Ben meant more clearly later.

Six years after the end of the Revolutionary War, on the second attempt, after much compromise in secret sessions, the Constitution was signed by only 39 delegates out of 65 certified to the constitutional convention. The next step was for the states to ratify the Constitution. It is interesting to note that the Constitution was never put to a vote of the people but only of the state legislatures, demonstrating once again that the Constitution was created by sovereign states to form a weak government and not an idealized government with a clean sheet of paper.

It was evidently fairly well understood that the Constitution was a seriously compromised document, because in 1788 Tench Cox, a member of the Continental Congress, stated: "The people, who are made and held supreme by the Constitution, will change and amend the Constitution when errors are found."

The Federalist Papers

Three of the patriots wrote extensive articles in the newspapers of the day to explain the Constitution to the people. They were Alexander Hamilton, John Jay, and James Madison. Collectively, these newspaper articles are known as the Federalist Papers. In one of them, the relatively powerful role given to the legislative branch was justified by citing the fact that in the state legislatures of the day approximately 50 percent of the legislators were replaced every election. This fact was used to demonstrate the successful and healthy operation of democracy.

The Constitution was approved by eleven of the thirteen states, with Rhode Island and North Carolina ratifying only after the Constitution went into effect. In 1789, George Washington won the first presidential election and our nation was born. In 1794 President Washington had to take the Army to Pennsylvania to suppress the Whiskey Rebellion. A group of Scottish farmers in western Pennsylvania evidently enjoyed strong drink, but did not enjoy paying the liquor tax on same. The farmers altered their opinion on the subject upon George Washington's arrival at the head of the United States Army. The Whiskey Rebellion collapsed and the United States government passed its first test.

The Early Years

With our independence from England came our independence to trade anywhere in the world with anyone for anything. The traders centered in Boston, with a population of 18,000 in 1789, and sailed anywhere a quick profit could be turned. Whalers from New Bedford, Massachusetts, roamed the oceans in decrepit vessels manned by the scum of the seaports. They despoiled not only the great marine mammals but also local native populations. Many coastal Eskimo settlements in Alaska are today still hostile to "white men" because of the brutality of whalers, which included the rape and kidnapping of their women and the introduction of disease.

The Boston merchants also introduced guns and liquor to native populations in many parts of the world. The Russians, who were our close friends at the time that they owned Alaska, incessantly complained that the "Bostonians'" illegally supplied the native population with guns and liquor.

But far and away the most egregious trade into which we entered was with China. England wanted access to the silver and silk of China, which had been coveted by the West since Roman times. China with its large civilization was self-supporting and neither desired nor needed trade with the outside world. The enterprising English found the solution to this problem by surreptitiously introducing opium from their colony in India to the Chinese. It grew to a staggeringly large trade. By the 1830s, opium was the single largest trade commodity in the world. This trade, which the Chinese government was too weak to prevent, was far too juicy with profit for the Bostonian "Captains of Commerce" to pass up. As early as 1817, the American firm of Russell, Sturgis & Co. was supplying some 10 percent of the opium to China from farms in Turkey. The Chinese government, powerless to stop the destruction being wrought upon millions of its citizens, appealed to the humanity of the British government. Its letter, although written to the British, it could equally well have been sent to us.

Lin Tse-Hsu's Letter to Queen Victoria

. . . There appear among the crowd of barbarians both good persons and bad, unevenly. Consequently there are those who smuggle opium to seduce the Chinese people and so cause the spread of the poison to all provinces. Such persons who only care to profit themselves, and disregard their harm to others, are not tolerated by the laws of heaven and are unanimously hated by human beings. . . . If we trace the crime of those barbarians who through the years have been selling opium, then the deep harm they have wrought and the great profit they have usurped should fundamentally justify their execution according to the law. . . . There are barbarian ships that strive to come here for trade for the purpose of making a great profit. The wealth of China is used to profit the barbarians. That is to say, the great profit made by barbarians is all taken from the rightful share of China. By what right do they then in return use the poisonous drug to injure the Chinese people? Even though the barbarians may not necessarily intend to do us harm, yet in coveting profit to an extreme, they have no regard for injuring

others. Let us ask, where is your conscience? I have heard that the smoking of opium is very strictly forbidden by your country; that is because the harm caused by opium is clearly understood. Since it is not permitted to do harm to your own country, then even less should you let it be passed on to the harm of other countries—how much less to China! . . . Suppose there were people from another country who carried opium for sale to England and seduced your people into buying and smoking it; certainly your honorable ruler would deeply hate it and be bitterly aroused. We have heard heretofore that your honorable ruler is kind and benevolent. Naturally you would not wish to give unto others what you yourself do not want. . . . In several places of India under your control such as Bengal, Madras, Bombay, Patna, Benares, and Malwa has opium been planted from hill to hill, and factories have been opened for its manufacture. For months and years work is continued in order to accumulate the poison. The obnoxious odor ascends, irritating heaven and frightening the spirits. Indeed you, O Queen, can eradicate the opium plant in these places, hoe over the fields entirely, and sow in its stead the five grains [i.e., rice, millet, barley, wheat, etc.]. Anyone who dares again attempt to plant and manufacture opium should be severely punished. This will really be a great, benevolent government policy that will increase the common weal and get rid of evil. . . . He who sells opium shall receive the death penalty and he who smokes it also the death penalty. Now consider this: if the barbarians do not bring opium, then how can the Chinese people resell it, and how can they smoke it? The fact is that the wicked barbarians beguile the Chinese people into a death trap. How then can we permit these barbarians to live? He who takes the life of even one person

still has to atone for it with his own life; yet is the
harm done by opium limited to the taking of one life
only? Therefore in the new regulations, in regard to
those barbarians who bring opium to China, the penal-
ty is fixed at decapitation or strangulation. This is
what is called getting rid of a harmful thing on behalf
of mankind. . . . The barbarian merchants of your
country, if they wish to do business for a prolonged
period, are required to obey our statutes respectfully
and to cut off permanently the source of opium. They
must by no means try to test the effectiveness of the law
with their lives. May you, O Queen, check your wicked
and sift your vicious people before they come to China,
in order to guarantee the peace of your nation, to show
further the sincerity of your politeness and submissive-
ness, and to let the two countries enjoy together the
blessings of peace. How fortunate, how fortunate
indeed!

With the reader's newly acquired ability to predict the
future, I will let you predict what effect this appeal to honor
and justice had. It should be redundant to inform you that
when the Chinese government attempted to stop the continued opium smuggling by burning the opium warehouses, the
ensuing Opium Wars (1839–1842 and 1856–1860) forced the
Chinese to permit the British and Americans to continue
their "free trade."

The Boston merchants were in fact drug dealers, gun
smugglers, rum runners, and slave traders. It would not
be too much of an overstatement to assert that the Boston
merchants played roughly the same role in their day that
North Korea plays in international affairs today. It is the
height of irony to note that 150 years later it is America and
Great Britain who have the drug problems, whereas China is

virtually drug free. I cannot but perform an Einsteinian Thought Experiment and conjecture that if the Chinese government had been stronger, it might have sent an army to arrest the "blue bloods" of Boston or possibly even the president of the United States, as we did General Manuel Noriega of Panama. I also wonder if the extremely high moral standards, such as the banning of books, for which the City Fathers of Boston have been historically noted are not a consequence of the immoralities faced by the "Captains of Commerce" daily behind the closed doors of their board rooms. The whorehouse owner's daughters always have the strictest upbringing.

It is so personally distasteful to the author to continue with the narrative in this vein that the author proposes to strike a deal with the reader. If the reader will cede to the author the following points, then the author need not continue in the foregoing manner:

1) America has *no* historical basis upon which to claim a morality superior to that of other nations;

2) The cause of our historical wealth lies in a relatively small population's plundering the rich resources of an immense virgin continent. In the initial stages of this country's history, we did not need governmental planning. We needed Daniel Boones to carve out the wilderness. Later, we needed Andrew Carnegies, Henry Fords, and John D. Rockefellers to take the economic risks to build large industrial concerns;

3) Our continued existence was until recently due primarily to the difficulties involved in sending an invading army 3,000 miles across the Atlantic, or 7,000 miles across the Pacific, and that no more powerful nation shares our land mass. Other countries were weeks or months away from the United States even by the fastest means of transportation available, the sailing ship. Competition, both political and

economic, was many, many orders of magnitude less than it is today;

4) Much of our success was due to the advantage of a democratic form of government over an autocratic form. As recently as the end of World War I in 1918, many of the other industrialized countries of the world had monarchies for governments. Our democracy was clearly superior to the monarchies, but when England, Germany, and Japan converted to democracies, they adopted the more efficient parliamentary system; and

5) Whether we continue to prosper and be a leader among nations depends upon our present and future conduct as opposed to any inherent right we have merely because we are "good," or somehow morally superior to other nations. Then the author will only briefly list some of the major transgressions of our past. I will take the reader's silence as acceptance of the deal.

(1) 1759–1813. Four invasions of Canada, our benign neighbor to the north. Some of these were actually understandable as we were at war with England, of which Canada was a colony. We also threatened invasion in 1844 during the drawing of the western end of the boundary between the United States and Canada during the infamous 54′40″or fight incident.

(2) 1776–1865. Slavery

(3) 1776–?. Treatment of the Native American population

(4) 1836. Texas War of Independence. Astoundingly enough the Texas War of Independence, in which Davy Crockett, Colonel William Travis, and Jim Bowie died defending the Alamo, was in fact a war over the issue of slavery. The Mexican government had a welcoming, open-

door policy toward the Americans who arrived in Texas. However, the Americans were predominantly from the southern states and therefore practiced slavery. Colonel Travis even had his manservant Joe with him at the Alamo. A greater profit can be made using slave labor than paid labor. Slavery was prohibited by the enlightened Mexican government. Hence, the conflict.

(5) 1846–1848. Shooting by firing squad of non-combatant women and children during the Mexican War by U.S. troops.

(6) 1846–1916. Three invasions of Mexico, our benign neighbor to the south:

1846–1848. Mexican War

1914. Occupation of Veracruz

1916. General Pershing's pursuit of Pancho Villa

The point is that although we, of course, view ourselves as good neighbors, it is easy to understand how others might view the evidence differently, particularly if you had been invaded an average of 3.5 times.

(7) 1847–1849. Abraham Lincoln, who campaigned as "Honest Abe," cheated the government when he padded his expense records as a member of Congress before being elected president. In our contemporary political environment, Abraham Lincoln could not be elected president today, but he could serve a long and distinguished career in Congress.

(8) 1870–1920. Labor conditions during the robber baron days. Child labor abuse; female labor abuse; male labor abuse.

(9) 1898–1899. The Spanish-American War specifically,

and Latin American policy in general. It is interesting to note that both countries that came under our care, the Philippines and Cuba, are faring poorly and both display varying degrees of resentment toward us. By the way, the stated cause of the Spanish-American War was to assist the citizens of the two poor, suffering countries. This was precisely the identical reason the Soviet Union gave for assisting the citizens of Afghanistan. Gee, we better not help out any other countries like we helped out those two. If the United States had extended a friendly, helping hand to our neighbors to the south, instead of permitting the United Fruit Company (formerly the Boston Fruit Company) to dictate "banana republic" foreign policy, our Latin American neighbors would not be impoverished and wracked by revolution as they are today. There would not be a multitude of poverty-stricken people literally hurling themselves at our southern border every year.

(10) Racial discrimination.

(11) Being the largest polluter and generator of garbage per capita on the planet, poisoning and trashing the place where we live. How smart we are.

I think the foregoing list is a sufficient preponderance of evidence to make the points. To summarize, the United States of America has probably acted neither better nor worse than any other rapidly expanding power.

The Civil War (1861–1865) was about slavery and economics, but it was also about something else. It was about whether the supposedly sovereign states were still the equals of the federal government that they had created. The answer carried by force of arms was a resounding, "No! The states are subservient to the will of the federal government."

Interesting. The weak central government created by sovereign states achieved unquestioned superiority over the states that had created it. The weak central government made itself a strong central government while retaining the governmental structure of a weak central government. Needless to say, that condition (cause) would lead to trouble (effect) later. Only the 10th Amendment, which we will recall limits the federal government's range of permissible activities, checked the federal government's power. Jefferson called it "the bedrock of the Constitution." How right he was.

Let us proceed with the history of the United States from the point where we lost our democracy for the first time. As we have already discussed, our Founding Fathers designed us a governmental system with a strong legislative branch with two houses. One was elected by the people, the House of Representatives, while the other, the Senate, was elected originally by the state legislatures. The Industrial Revolution had come to America and the robber barons rapidly realized that profits can be maximized by the formation of monopolies or, as they were called in the late 1800s, "trusts." There was the steel trust, the beef trust, the railroad trust, the coal trust, and the oil trust—over 200 trusts in all.

The federal government had been given by the Constitution the power to regulate interstate commerce. Because of the ease afforded interstate transportation by the introduction of railroads, the trusts all operated in interstate commerce. Therefore, the power to regulate the trusts belonged to the federal government. The federal government needed both houses of Congress to agree to pass legislation. As we also recall, the senators were elected by the state legislatures at that time. The original purpose of the Senate was to give the small states power over the weak central government, but the central government was no longer weak. The states had become subservient to the central government as a result of the Civil War. The Senate was not elected by the people and felt no need to

"The Bosses of the Senate" by Joseph Keppler, 1889, a cartoon printed in the media of the day, clearly demonstrates that it was widely known and understood that the Senate of the United States of America was being bribed by special interests. Please note in the upper left-hand corner that the door marked "Peoples' Entrance" is securely barred and padlocked. The sign on the gallery reads, "This is a Senate of the Monopolists, By the Monopolists, and For the Monopolists!" Democracy was not returned to the United States of America until twenty-four years later with the ratification of the 17th Amendment to the Constitution in 1913, which took the right to elect the Senate away from the state legislatures and gave it to the people.

represent their interests. However, the Senate had the power to prevent the federal government from taking action.

Our government had an inappropriate structure for its new power. It had a powerful branch of government that had no purpose. The trusts were quick to open their wallets and ply the senators with bribes. The Senate blocked any and all attempts at ameliorating the situation.

Needless to say, the trusts were immensely profitable. Meanwhile, the working conditions for the people who worked for the trusts were abominable to the point of being deliberately oppressive. As one of the robber barons, William

THE BOSSES OF THE SENATE.

Vanderbilt, put it so charmingly, "The public be damned!" In a brilliant book, *The Jungle*, written by Upton Sinclair and published in 1906, working conditions in the Union Stockyards in Chicago are poignantly and accurately described. In the book, an immigrant family comes to Chicago seeking a better life and instead encounters the horrors of working for the Beef Trust. I highly recommend the book to everyone. However, Mr. Sinclair, after writing a truly great book, suggests that the answer to the inhuman working conditions was a socialist form of government. He was wrong. The correct answer, according to the form of government set

up in the Constitution, is for the legislative branch of government to pass laws protecting working people. Why did the
legislative branch not do its job? Because the Senate had
allowed itself to be bribed by the trusts. The trusts had effectively stolen our democracy.

Furthermore, insofar as the Senate was elected by state
legislatures and not the people, the people had no direct
means of altering the situation. Benjamin Franklin's response
to Mrs. Powell waiting outside the constitutional convention
comes to mind: "A republic, if you can keep it." We had not
kept it. We lost it.

The return of our democracy was accomplished by accident—assassination actually. President McKinley (1897–
1901) was shot in 1901 by someone our history books call an
"anarchist." If I had witnessed the conditions in 1901 as related by Upton Sinclair in *The Jungle*, I probably would have
been an "anarchist" too. Theodore Roosevelt (1901–1909)
ascended to the presidency. A headstrong and fearless man,
Teddy Roosevelt was not favored by the political bosses of his
party, but through rambunctious energy and charisma forced
himself up in the ranks of his party to become New York
State's governor. He finally was offered the seemingly dead-
end job of vice-president. Upon the assassination of President
McKinley, the bear was let out of his cage. As Theodore
Roosevelt stated in his autobiography, the United States had
become "A riot of individualistic materialism, under which
complete freedom for the individual . . . turned out in practice
to mean perfect freedom for the strong to wrong the weak . . . .
The power of the mighty industrial overlords . . . had
increased with giant strides, while the methods of controlling
them, . . . through the Government, remained archaic and
therefore practically impotent."

Teddy used the "bully pulpit" of the presidency to inform
the people of the error in our government. The public enthusi-

astically responded, giving Teddy overwhelming support. Teddy put into place anti-trust legislation (read anti-monopoly legislation), busted the trusts, and was instrumental in having the Senate elected by the people. Thank you, Teddy. We owe you. You are the second father of our democracy.

In 1913, the 17th Amendment to the Constitution was ratified, giving the people the right to elect the Senate. The Senate lost its constituency, the state legislatures. The Senate lost its reason for being. Therefore, the Senate was part of a government in which its reason for being no longer existed. The people already elect the House of Representatives. Why have two houses of Congress? With the ratification of the 17th Amendment, the Senate became an outdated anachronism. The Senate became a needless elaboration on the process of governing, which was already complicated and difficult enough.

Its democracy restored, the country bounced along with its powerful but limited central government, still constrained by Article 10 of the Bill of Rights. Then came the First World War, Prohibition, the Roaring Twenties, the Stock Market Crash of 1929, the Great Depression.

Strong Central Government

To counter the devastation wrought by the Great Depression, a newly elected president, Franklin Delano Roosevelt (1933–1945), rushed through Congress a flurry of legislation that attempted to stimulate the economy by job creation but also, by the sheer size of the intervention, to vastly increase the power and influence of the central government. To look upon it from a cause-and-effect, constitutional viewpoint, our Founding Fathers never envisioned the Industrial Revolution, let alone the America of the 1930s. They never provided the weak central government for action in an economic crisis, particularly one of the magnitude of the Great Depression. The forces that caused the Great Depression were very large, very powerful economic forces that, once set in motion, required a strong and pervasive power to counteract. The constitutional thing was to do nothing and let the Great Depression run its course. That, in turn, would mean the government would be abandoning its fundamental job, which is, as we now know, to look into the future and plan in order to head off disaster.

Therefore, President Franklin Roosevelt was correct in transforming the limited central government into a strong central government, but he had one problem: The legislation he proposed, and which was passed by the Congress, far exceeded the boundaries set in the Constitution for the weak central government under Article 10 of the Bill of Rights. We will recall that Thomas Jefferson said "the 10th Amendment is the bedrock of the Constitution." All of Roosevelt's legislation was declared to be unconstitutional by the Supreme Court, and rightly so. However, the president threatened the Supreme Court. He threatened to increase the number of members of the Court who, of course, would be nominated by President Roosevelt and confirmed by the Senate. In other words, President Roosevelt and Congress were threatening the nine members of the Supreme Court with the loss of their personal, individual power and relegation to a minority position on the bench. Can the reader predict the outcome of the quandary facing the Supreme Court Justices when, on the one hand, they had sworn to uphold and protect the Constitution and were faced with clearly unconstitutional legislation, but, on the other hand, if they declared it unconstitutional a second time they would lose their personal power to be the individuals who decide the supreme law of the land?

Yes, that is right. The Supreme Court Justices declared unconstitutional legislation constitutional in order to preserve their own power. As we witnessed during the framing of the Constitution when the states gave up as little of their power as possible to form a weak central government; as we have just witnessed in the Supreme Court Justices, and as we have witnessed with Ferdinand Marcos in the Philippines, neither dictators nor democratic institutions give up their power voluntarily. They must be forced to do so if a change is to be made.

It would be easy to chastise the Supreme Court Justices for lack of personal courage in the face of threats to the Constitution, but in reality what they did was best for America. Nowhere in the Constitution did it mention that the government had the power to respond to a broad-scale economic crisis. Therefore, two branches of our government, the legislative and the executive, teamed up and threatened the individual members of the third branch, the judicial, in order to circumvent the Constitution for the good of America. The Constitution then, by the consent of all three branches of government, was ignored at least insofar as limiting the power of the central government was concerned. Therefore, amazingly enough, what occurred in the 1930s was, by definition, a coup through conspiracy by the three branches of government that seized powers previously reserved for the people. However, this should be only modest cause for alarm, and rather a belated recognition that the world for which the Constitution was created no longer exists. It reflects the change from a frontier society in which rugged, rural individuals struggled to create their own independent destinies. They wanted and needed no interference from a government, especially if it meant paying taxes, as in the Whiskey Rebellion. We have evolved into a large, complex, interdependent, urban society that expects the federal government to solve its problems. Indeed, there is no institution in our society with the power to solve our problems except the United States government. Therefore, the upshot is that we have a strong central government even though the Constitution is deliberately being ignored to achieve it. The Constitution should be amended to be brought up to date to at least conform to the current reality. It is rather ridiculous for us "Champions of Democracy" not to be following our own Constitution. Until that is done, however, whenever you are stuck in rush hour traffic and are in need of some cynical humor, just remember that we are being governed by an unconstitutional and therefore outlaw government.

However, it also means that we have a strong central government operating with a structure that was designed for a weak central government. To have a strong central government clothed in the structure of a weak central government is to invite inevitable trouble. With the effective repeal of the 10th Amendment, the government could make laws about anything it wanted. Since Congress is that branch of government empowered to pass laws, in reality the power of Congress was enormously increased. As we discovered when we discussed the Constitution, the states created a weak central government structure but with the most powerful role in that weak structure going to Congress, which, having the most members, was least likely to reach a rapid and clear consensus. However, as long as the executive branch maintained control of budgeting through the right of impoundment (line-item veto), the president could virtually control public policy and thereby maintain the system of checks and balances. In any modern society, whoever controls the allocation of resources controls the public policy of that society.

From the massive unemployment of the Great Depression we entered the Second World War and encountered a labor shortage as our factories hummed along at full capacity. By war's end we were efficiently turning out war material at a prodigious rate from the only unbombed major economy in the world, thanks to the Atlantic and Pacific Oceans and the Navy. During World War II, the strong central government created by Franklin Delano Roosevelt and Congress became even stronger as the government virtually operated the entire economy, down to the rationing of every individual's food and fuel. The strong central government for the duration of the war became all-powerful. It clearly did a good job, as we won the war. (To be more precise, we were on the winning side. For the accuracy of the historical record, it should be noted that the Soviet Union paid the price to stop Adolf Hitler's armies: 26 million Soviet soldiers and civilians died, whereas 292,131 Americans perished in combat in the same conflict. The Soviets often could not evacuate their homes as the Germans advanced, because to do so meant certain death in the Russian winter. Almost 100 Soviets died for every American battle death. It is often thought that we supplied them with the bulk of their war materials, but in actuality we sent them only some three percent of their war materials, mostly jeeps and trucks. The Soviets used different caliber weapons from ours. Sending them our caliber weapons and ammunition would have caused a logistical nightmare. Therefore, the heroic sacrifice of the Soviet people should be recognized, and it should be acknowledged that they bear the major responsibility for bringing World War II to a successful conclusion. This fact in no way diminishes the valor and sacrifice exhibited by our own troops during the conflict. The purpose of war is not to see how many of one's own citizens one can get killed.)

With the war over, our unbombed industrial juggernaut was converted back to the production of civilian goods. Whereas the other industrialized nations' infrastructures all had to be rebuilt, our untrammeled economy soared, making us the wealthiest country on Earth. Our exclusive possession of atomic weapons made us the most powerful nation on Earth. Not only were we the wealthiest and most powerful nation on Earth, but we were the wealthiest and most powerful nation that had ever existed in the whole history of the

planet. And not by a little, but by far. We owe quite a debt to
the deep, wide, rolling Atlantic and Pacific Oceans.

President Eisenhower (1953–1961) presided over an increasingly wealthy America, and an America that was the
dominant world leader. His quiescent stewardship gave a
rapidly expanding economy the room to grow. Meanwhile,
Germany and Japan were getting back on their feet economi-
cally. The Marshall Plan distributed over $12 billion of foreign
aid to a large number of countries in Europe and Asia, but the
same two countries that were pre-war economic successes
returned to prominence. The two post-war governments of
Germany and Japan were able to re-evoke in their peoples the
cohesion and sacrifice that had brought them pre-war success.
The governments were able to accomplish this because the
people were cohesive and able to sacrifice, as demonstrated by
the Japanese kamikaze attacks. If more than a generation
had passed, these traits would have been lost to those societies. Imagine saying to the Italians, "If you want to have a
society like ancient Rome's, then you should behave as ancient
Romans did." They cannot behave like ancient Romans. They
do not know how. They only know how to behave like modern
Italians. The Germans and the Japanese knew how to behave—how to be cohesive and how to sacrifice. Their governments thought in the future and created good plans, and the
cohesion and sacrifice of the people fostered plan implementation. The sacrifice of the people was their hard work.
Therefore, the ascent of Japan and Germany as powers in the
1960s, 1970s, and 1980s can be easily understood.

However, there is a dramatic difference in the type of powers they represent. The new Japan and Germany are not military powers but rather economic powers. The Law of the
Survival of the Efficient has not in any way become inopera-
tive among societies. The weapons have changed, however,
from military ones to economic ones, at least among the indus-

trialized nations. Even though the Law of the Survival of the Efficient has not been abrogated by the change in weaponry, the effects could not be more highly applauded—a freedom from the carnage and destruction of warfare. Instead of the young men and women of different countries fighting one another with rifles, contemporary industrialized nations are fighting one another from their engineering design tables, from their offices, and from their factory floors, and the weapons are better designed products, automated factories, more efficient means of decision-making, and more efficient means of organizing work forces. Even though the weapons among the industrialized nations have changed, the effects of losing the struggle for the Survival of the Efficient have not changed. The countries that operate more efficiently will enjoy prosperity while those that do not, will not. Those that do not operate efficiently will eventually face social disorganization from the people's unwillingness to sacrifice for a society that is impoverishing them. Therefore, the effect of losing the struggle is still the destruction of the culture.

However, with the change in weaponry employed by the industrialized nations, the burden of our protection has shifted from the soldier to the businessman. We as citizens have the right to ask "How efficient are our businessmen?" Did our businessmen become decadent during the post-war years when they had no rivals, so that when efficient rivals appeared our businesses were no longer competitive? In fact, it is a matter of great importance how efficient our business people, and therefore our businesses, are. The future of our society and the future wealth of its citizens depend on the efficiency of our business people. Our businesses are institutions.

CHAPTER EIGHT

How Not to Run a Business

1952 to 1973

Institutions

OES THE READER RECALL our conclusion about bees? That because bees have divided labor among the drones, worker bees, and the queen bee, they have therefore created a society. In order to evaluate how well a bee society will do in the struggle for the Survival of the Efficient, it is necessary to consider the various divisions of labor because the various divisions are dependent on one another for survival. In modern human societies we call these divisions of labor "institutions."

Modern American society is primarily made up of institutions. The individual citizen spends the majority of life interacting with institutions. School is an institution. The business for which the citizen works, if it has more than approximately fifty employees, is an institution. The chain stores in which we shop are institutions. The television stations we watch are institutions. Our governments—local, state, and federal—are institutions. The police department is an institution. The library is an institution. McDonald's restaurants and the chain restaurants at which we eat are institutions. Gas stations are institutions. Banks are institutions. Professional sports teams are institutions. In short, unless you are interacting with your family or friends you are more than likely interacting with an institution. It is extremely important that we be able to judge our all-pervasive institutions, for they are our economy. They are our government. They are our defense. Like all nations, we will rise or fall based on the efficiency or decadence of our institutions. The most important of our institutions is our government. As we have recently discovered, if we are to continue prospering and surviving, our government is supposed to efficiently implement the Four Critical Abilities.

How can we determine if an institution is efficient? Or, to put it another way, how can we determine if an institution is inefficient and therefore decadent? The results of determining which of our institutions are efficient and which are decadent will lead us to by far the most astounding and amazing revelations in this whole book.

There are three tests to which an institution can be subjected to determine whether it is efficient or decadent:

1) A simple method of determining the efficiency or decadence of an institution can be derived by using the Black Box Technique just as we did in the factory when we attempted to determine what was behind the curtain. Only in this case we are not interested in *what goes on* behind the curtain, but rather in *how efficient* is whatever lies behind the curtain. Therefore, we will place the curtain in front of the institution (the present) and not know or care how the institution does whatever it does. Next we need to know what raw materials or resources the institution consumes (the past). In institutions the resources are always only people and money.

Then we need to know the actual results the institution produces (the future). Then we can compare the actual results of the institution with the stated goals or popularly expected results of the institution. If the expected results of the institution are roughly the same as the actual results of the institution, and the resources consumed compared to the size of the task are *moderate to small*, then everything is fine. However, if the expected results are widely divergent from the actual results and the resources consumed are *moderate*, then the institution is decadent. If the expected results are widely divergent from the actual results and the resources consumed are *great*, then the institution is extremely decadent. The more resources a decadent institution consumes the more decadent it is, and hence the less efficient it is. Although decadence and efficiency are not exactly opposites, all conditions of decadence contain a lack of efficiency. However, not all lack of efficiency is necessarily caused by decadence. Therefore, the more efficient an institution is the less and less decadent it can possibly be. The Black Box Technique is so powerful that it permits us to create a Decadence Meter.

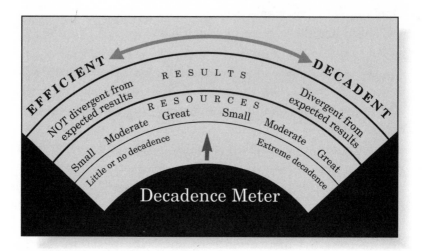

This simple little test will give us a foolproof method of evaluating our institutions and determining which of our institutions are efficient and which are decadent.

2) If the institution is not capable of forgoing present benefits (sacrificing) for future greater benefits, it is decadent.

3) The third test is a test for extreme decadence and is an extension of test #2. When we perform test #1 on an institution and we find the actual results widely divergent from the expected results, we should look inside the institution to determine if the institution has been taken over by its members. When the institution no longer has the ability to induce its members to sacrifice their own goals for the achievement of the institution's goals, then one has found the most decadent of institutions. Imagine a football team that cannot induce its members to pay the sacrifice of blocking and tackling to achieve the institution's goal of winning football games. Imagine an army, whose duty it is to defend the citizens of a country, operated for the benefit of the enlisted men who place their own concerns first and who will not sacrifice for the country. All who are dependent upon an institution that has fallen into the self-serving hands of its members are going to suffer greatly. Imagine a police department that can no longer instill sacrifice in its officers to fulfill the department's duties. The result is widespread corruption, with enormous suffering on the part of the citizens. Imagine a McDonald's fast-food restaurant wherein the employees, instead of rapidly serving the public, eat the food themselves. Imagine a Congress in which the members care more about re-election and personal power than about the people they serve. Remember the inability of the Roman officers who could not sacrifice their own enrichment in order to disarm the Visigoths and thereby caused the collapse of the Roman Empire? Therefore, the test for extreme decadence is if the institution's goals are subordinated to the personal benefit of the members of the institution.

Now we have two tests for decadence and one test for runaway, galloping decadence. Let us analyze individual behavior.

Individual Behavior

All human beings always act in their own best self-interest as they perceive it to be. For instance, Mother Teresa, who has devoted her life to the care of the poor in Calcutta, India, is acting in her own best self-interest as she perceives it. Mother Teresa would not be happy with herself if she were anywhere other than Calcutta helping the poor. From her point of view, there is no better way to spend her life than dedicating it to the poor. To those who value material possessions, her life appears to be one of sacrifice. However, one who perceives material possessions as not having any value and human beings as much more important than material possessions, can appreciate why Mother Teresa chooses to help the poor rather than do anything else with her life. Mother Teresa could have chosen to do a large number of other things with her life. She chose to help the poor in India because she wanted to, not because she was forced to. Therefore, she was acting in her own best self-interest as she perceived it when she chose to help the poor in India because, as she perceived it, the best thing she could do with her life was devote it to humankind. If at any time Mother Teresa had found some other way to spend her life that she would have preferred, she would have left India and pursued it. But she did not. She did what she preferred to do. Amazingly, we all always do what we want to do, or else we would not do it.

The condemned man voluntarily walks down the hall to the electric chair and sits in the chair and lets himself be strapped in. Why does the condemned man cooperate in his own death? We would expect that the condemned man's survival instinct would cause him to resist his own death at all costs. However, he does not. He prefers to cooperate with the people who will kill him because it is in his best self-interest. If he resists, he may become injured. He will be restrained and killed anyway. Therefore, as the condemned man perceives the situation, it is in his best self-interest to cooperate in his own death. Another way of putting it is he does not want to suffer the consequences of prolonging his life a few seconds or minutes. He prefers not to pay the price to act in another way because it is not in his self-interest.

Let us take, for example, a man who works in an office standing around the water cooler complaining that over the weekend he had to visit his in-laws. He complains that he hates visiting his in-laws and that it is the last thing on earth that he would like to do. However, the man is wrong because he did exactly what he perceived to be in his own best interests. The man had the option of not visiting his in-laws, but he did not want to suffer the consequences of not visiting them. Whatever the consequences of not visiting them would have been—heaps of abuse from his wife, perhaps—he was not willing to pay the price. Therefore, the man acted in his own best interests as he perceived them. Then why does the man complain? He should not complain. The man is a fool. Therefore, even when we do something we think we do not want to do, we are really acting in our own best interest as we perceive it to be.

For another example, let us look at the young woman in her office daydreaming of living in Hollywood and becoming a movie star. She perceives it to be in her own best self-interest to remain working in the office rather than to move to Hollywood. If and when her perception changes to believing that moving to Hollywood would be in her own best self-interest, she will, in fact, move to Hollywood. If we knew more facts about the woman's specific personality, then we could make an educated guess as to whether or not she would ever perceive moving to Hollywood to be in her own best self-interest. In approaching human behavior armed with this knowledge, much of the mystery and seeming randomness of human behavior disappears. In fact, individual human behavior and, in particular, group (institutional) behavior become subject to highly accurate prediction and therefore can be easily processed by the Black Box Technique.

To summarize the above: All human beings all around the planet twenty-four hours a day always act in their own best self-interest as they perceive it. Additionally, if we know how a given human perceives a given situation, accurate predictions concerning human behavior can be made. The behavior of institutions and the behavior of individuals in an institutional setting are even easier to predict, as the goals, rewards, and punishments of an institution are usually very clear. This fact makes it far easier to understand the perceptions of individuals in these institutions, which therefore makes the prediction of individual behavior in an institution very easy; which then makes the prediction of the behavior of the institution itself very easy.

We have already learned of the paramount role played by institutions in our society. Institutions shape our lives, make decisions for the society, and therefore most critically shape our future.

Business

To Black Box American business, we must first analyze what resources (money and personnel) are consumed. The money is the Gross National Product, $6.3 trillion, and the number of people is all of those employed by the private sector, 100 million people. The resources consumed are great.

The consumption of resources of this magnitude makes American business the largest economic institution in the world. What do we expect from American business? We would expect the highest quality goods and services at the lowest prices. We would expect service and efficiency to set the standard for the world. We would expect American products and services to be desired all around the world. We would expect American business to be expanding and to be extremely prosperous. What is the reality? American business is virtually out of the high-tech consumer electronics industry and is in full retreat in automobiles, steel, clothing, footwear, and scores of other industries that only continue to exist in this country because of government-imposed quotas on the importation of these products. Foreign products are generally viewed as being of higher quality and better value than American products. Americans buy some $100–150 billion a year more of foreign goods than foreigners buy of American goods. The actual results are widely divergent from the expected results. Therefore, American business is extremely decadent.

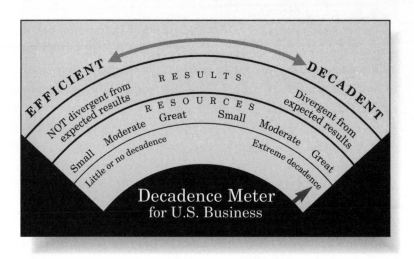

Why is American business in such a sad state of affairs? Insofar as this is a book for the general reader, a thorough analysis of American business is not necessary or even desirable, as the length of that analysis would exceed the length of this entire book. Let us pick up the story after the Second

World War when American businessmen were virtually unrivaled on the planet because we had the only major economy that was not ravaged by the war.

In the early 1950s, many American businessmen were still proud of the fact that they did business on the basis of a handshake only. No written contract was needed because the businessman's spoken word was his bond. In today's international business world, if you still cling to that method of doing business, you had better leave your hands at home. The returning servicemen and the factory workers who worked overtime to churn out the war materials were laden with unspent cash and pent-up demand from the sacrifices of rationing and military life. The factories were unbombed and rapidly reconverted to civilian production. The economy steadily grew. It was not very difficult, if one were in business, to be in a growing business.

Internationally, except for a handful of industries like soft drinks and oil, American business in general failed to forge alliances and enter overseas markets. They preferred instead to reap the profits available from the world's largest economy. I recall an interesting story from business class about two American Army generals who shortly after World War II were offered control of a German car manufacturer. After investigating the proposition, the two generals reported, "What they are offering us does not amount to a hill of beans." They turned it down. The German car company was Volkswagen.

American business remained a national institution and failed to capitalize on its position to become an integral and indispensable part of the world economy. American banks lent money to foreign concerns to invest in their economies. If the deal had been good enough for an American bank, it should have been good enough for an American business partner to make the investment.

Then a new factor entered the business environment—the visual impact of television replaced radio. By the purchase of

TV advertisement, even a relatively small regional manufacturer could, at the speed of light, become known in tens of
millions of households nationwide. Those businesses that
could appropriately utilize TV advertising grew, and those
that could not or did not went the way of the proverbial
buggy whip. In the rapidly growing economy, the advertising
companies on Madison Avenue in New York became the gurus
of greater profitability and expanded market share. By the
1960s, the word "gimmick" became popular. The saying in
advertising circles was "you have to have a gimmick." At one
of the two universities I attended in order to study the science of business, I was taught a famous example of marketing. A pharmacy was not having much success selling toothbrushes at 60 cents apiece, but when it changed the sign over
the toothbrush display to "2 for $1.29," the pharmacy sold out
of toothbrushes in short order. Two or three books touted this
example. Presumably, the lesson to be learned was that marketing trickery was an excellent method of obtaining profits.

In 1950s Japan, meanwhile, the Japanese were producing
and exporting to the United States cheap and inferior quality goods. To read "Made in Japan" on an article immediately
triggered the thought that the article was cheap and poorly
made. The Japanese government recognized the reality of the
situation and drew up a plan that involved calling the heads
of business together and advising them that for Japan to
prosper, the businesspeople must change their attitude and
manufacture goods to the highest quality standard. After
obtaining the agreement of the businesses, the government
advised the Japanese people that the highest standards of
quality should be employed in their jobs. Because of the cohesive nature of Japanese society, the people were willing to
make the sacrifice to implement the plan. In short, the
Japanese government utilized beautifully the technique recommended in this book for individuals and societies to solve

their problems. It was as if the Japanese people were dinosaurs who could think like humans and realized that if they
did not change, that they would become extinct. Therefore
they consciously and deliberately decided to change into birds
and not only survived, but prospered. Thus was wrought the
Japanese economic "miracle."

The concepts used by the Japanese to improve their quality and productivity were borrowed from an American mathematician from Chicago, W. Edwards Deming. In fact, the
Japanese government awards a prize every year to that company which sets the standard for the highest excellence in
quality. It is called "The Deming Prize." Mr. Deming first
attempted to induce American business to accept his ideas
but was rebuffed. When he presented his ideas to the
Japanese, they were eagerly accepted.

In America, by the early 1970s, Wall Street analysts and
stockholders had become accustomed to companies with
large rates of growth. The unchallenged 1940s and 1950s and
the TV-driven 1950s and 1960s gave companies very impressive rates of growth. To achieve or maintain impressive rates
of growth, some companies chose to grow by purchasing other
companies in other industries. These groupings of companies
from diverse industries are known as "conglomerates." This
means that the Chief Executive Officer (CEO) of company A
who purchased company B did not know much about company
B's market, manufacturing operations, etc., because company
B is from a different industry, in which the new CEO by definition has no experience. Conglomerates break the first commandment of business, which is "Know thy business." As
would be expected, most conglomerates have not fared very
well in the long term. Expansion by purchasing companies
from unrelated industries means the CEO must split his time
and energy. That is not as efficient as a CEO thinking solely
about one industry. Therefore, expansion by purchase of a

company in an unrelated industry is the quick and cheap way to grow, but in the long term it will usually mean trouble. The CEO of a conglomerate only superficially knows the various industries for which he is required to make decisions. He will probably never even enter some of the manufacturing facilities for which he will have to make decisions. The CEO then typically tends to become a "numbers man."

A "numbers man" is a CEO who attempts to operate a conglomerate or large company primarily by analyzing the financial statements of the individual companies under his control and attempting to mold the unrelated companies to fit an idealized consolidated financial condition. This idealized financial condition always and most importantly includes a continuing and ever increasing amount of profit. Insofar as publicly held companies must make their profit figures available to the public quarterly, the next quarter's profit figure becomes the most important number to the "numbers man." The stockholders, through the board of directors, ensure that the CEO remains transfixed on the profits of the next quarter because they most often pay the CEO the bulk of his income by a stock option plan. A stock option plan permits the CEO to purchase large quantities of company stock at a fixed low price. The difference between the fixed low purchase price of the stock and however high the CEO can drive up the price of the stock multiplied by perhaps the millions of shares that the CEO is allowed to purchase determines the majority of the typical CEO's income. The stock price is most directly affected by the most recent quarterly profit of the corporation. As earnings increase, the price of the stock must also increase. For if the stock price does not increase, then the stock is undervalued (or cheap) relative to the earnings that a purchase of stock in another company would control. Therefore, all things being equal, the stock is a bargain, and in short order a sharp "numbers man" such as T. Boone Pickens will be along in an attempt to purchase the company. Needless to say, present management of the company likes the present owners of the company because the present owners of the company have chosen the present management to manage the company. But, if the stock price does not rise with earnings, the CEO's job is in jeopardy from two sources: the stockholders and a hostile takeover. Moreover, the bulk of the CEO's personal income is derived from an increase in stock price through the previously described stock option plan. Therefore, the CEO's income and job itself depend on the CEO's ability to drive the next quarter's earnings higher than the last quarter's, which in turn will cause the stock price to increase. Failure to increase next quarter's earnings jeopardizes the CEO's personal income and his very job itself.

Now let us perform an Einsteinian Thought Experiment— which, we remember, permits us to go anywhere at any time and use our imagination to observe or participate in cause-and-effect relationships. Let us place ourselves as the CEO of a large group of companies in unrelated industries of which we do not know all the details. In fact, we probably have not even visited every facility and manufacturing plant and probably do not know in much detail the manufacturing sequence of those products manufactured. The cause-and-effect relationships in essence dictate that we (the CEO) will achieve the greatest personal benefit if we drive up next quarter's earnings. And we face the relentless necessity of having to increase next quarter's earnings not just once but every quarter for years and years—perhaps seven or eight or ten years or until we turn sixty-five and retire. The easy solutions as to how to increase profits have already been exploited by our predecessors. Nonetheless, we must increase profits next quarter! As we review our options of possible actions, one of the few that can give us a sufficiently rapid response is advertising. Let us increase the advertising budget. Let us

put a toy in the bottom of every cereal box. Let us run a
sweepstakes. Let us offer rebates. Let us raise our prices and
offer 0% financing. Aahh, we sigh with relief. The next quarter's earnings are up. The stock price increased $1\frac{1}{2}$ points on
news of sharply higher earnings. We have just become one
and a half million dollars richer due to our stock option.

But there is no time to rest on our laurels. For now, we
must increase profits next quarter! Hurry, let us save money,
and therefore increase next quarter's profits, by decreasing
our spending on engineering. Let us not re-engineer our products, let us just change the packaging. Let us cut 10 percent
of the scientists from the staff. Aahh, we sigh with relief. We
did it. The next quarter's profits are sharply higher. Wall
Street is buzzing. The stock price increases again. The board
of directors votes us a bonus. Our spouse and children are
proud of us. But nonetheless, we must increase profits next
quarter!

Hurry, our increases in advertising expenditures are no
longer increasing our sales. We have cut the budgets of
research and development, engineering and design as much
as possible. Oh, what to do? For we must increase profits next
quarter! Hurry, because we do not know the detailed work-
ings of the companies in our conglomerate, not having served
a 40-year apprenticeship in each industry in which we have a
company, let us call a meeting with the vice-president of each
division and offer them a bonus of say $10,000 for each per-
centage point of savings that they can make in their divisions. Each percentage point of savings would save the company $1 million more than the $10,000 bonus paid to the vice-
presidents. Therefore, profits will continue to increase next
quarter.

After two or three meetings, the vice-presidents begin to
focus on the fact that their most important job is to cut costs
and thereby increase profits. The vice-presidents, whose personal income is now directly affected by how much they can

reduce costs, begin to contribute ideas. Part of the meeting might go like this:

CEO: Vice-presidents, as you will recall in last week's meeting wherein I explained the need for severe cost cutting, trimming the fat, and running a tight ship in these increasingly competitive times, I asked you to formulate plans to reduce your divisional costs and receive $10,000 for each percentage point of reduction. Frobisher, what is your plan to reduce costs in your division?

Frobisher: Sir, by reducing the size of the patty in our hamburgers we can make a nine percent savings in costs next quarter.

CEO: Excellent, Frobisher. That is the kind of bold, innovative thinking we need around here. If those savings are actually made, that is a $90,000 bonus for you. A hearty job well done! Limburger, what are your plans to reduce costs?

Limburger: Sir, my division can reduce the thickness of the metal used on all of the widgets and save three percent while at the same time we can increase prices four percent. Giving us an overall increase in profits of seven percent.

CEO: Excellent, Limburger! You are a genius. If your plan materializes you will receive a $70,000 bonus. Farquahar, what is your plan to reduce costs?

Farquahar: Sir, in our division we plan to cancel all capital improvements, stop the purchase of new, automated equipment for our factories, and cut back on our maintenance of existing equipment. I expect a ten percent savings for the next quarter.

CEO: Farquahar, I am proud of you. I like the way you can run a tight ship. Next Wednesday afternoon, clear your schedule and we will shoot a round of golf at my club. We will discuss your $100,000 bonus and your future with the company. Great job! Caulfield, what is your plan to reduce costs and save the company money?

Caulfield: Sir, I have a plan that does not save the company any money, but if you will let me explain, sir—As you know, my consumer electronics division is consistently one of the largest producers of income for the company. We have 14 manufacturing facilities across the United States, employing 75,000 people. Across our entire product line our customers are informing us that Japanese companies are calling on them, offering to sell our customers a higher quality product than we can manufacture and at a lower price than we can sell at. Therefore, my division needs new, state-of-the-art, precision, automated equipment immediately. The new equipment will permit us to reduce our work force by 20,000 and reduce our price while increasing our quality to above the Japanese standard. Then our products will be better than the Japanese products. Our factories are closer to our customers than the Japanese factories, therefore transportation costs, service, and response to delivery requests will be much better than those of the Japanese. Therefore, our customers will buy from us and the Japanese will have no market in this country in our product line. However, to make the necessary investment in new equipment and to increase the engineering, design, and research and development departments, my division's contribution to the profit of the company will only be fifty percent of what it has been. The other fifty percent my division will have to reinvest in equipment for the next two years. After these two years, however, my division will be able to contribute at least $1\frac{1}{2}$ times what it currently contributes to corporate profits for an indefinitely long period of time. If we do not make the investment, then my division will be closed in five years.

CEO: Caulfield, your plan calls for the company profits not to grow in the next quarter. That is out of the question! Did you not hear Farquahar's plan? His division is in a similar situation to yours, but he found ten percent in savings for the company. I suggest you revise your plan and find the same ten percent savings that Farquahar found and join us for a game of golf.

CEO (thinking to himself): This Caulfield is an idiot. He does not understand the first thing about business. Does he not realize that we must increase profits next quarter? I must remember to tell the staff to begin looking for a replacement for Caulfield immediately. I will tell them to look for a real *team player*.

Caulfield was fired. Next quarter the profits went up again. The stock price rose dramatically after the announcement of sharply higher earnings. We, the CEO, made another two million dollars.

Now let us change our Einsteinian Thought Experiment and become the CEO of a Japanese company during the same time period. In order to accomplish this, we must understand the cause-and-effect relationships that operate on a Japanese CEO. The most important is, What drives a Japanese CEO? What is the goal? We know that American CEOs are driven by "nonetheless, profits must be increased next quarter." In Japan, the primary purpose of a business is not to make the most money possible; usually it is translated as "the reputation" or "good name" of the company. However, it also means much more than that. It is the "honor" of the company. It is "how the company is regarded by others," it is the Oriental concept of no "loss of face," it is an employee's personal pride. The Japanese CEO's top priority is not next quarter's earnings but rather that his company be held in the highest respect by his customers, by his employees, by his bankers, by his suppliers, and even by his competitors. This fact causes an effect, particularly in decision-making, that causes decisions to be made far differently from the way they would be made in the United States.

With company honor being the primary motivation of the Japanese CEO, he without question must make decisions with company honor as the goal. The average Japanese CEO of the early 1970s was male and had lived through the Second World War as an adult, which means that almost certainly he would have killed himself had his superior asked him to in a ritual suicide called *seppuku,* often mistakenly referred to as *hara kiri.* A few years ago, a Japanese ship captain rammed a dock, damaging both the dock and his vessel. The Japanese ship captain committed *seppuku.* A Japanese architect who designed a building in Shanghai, China, that was some inches out of tolerance committed *seppuku.* Even school children in Japan commit suicide when they cannot meet the enormous expectations that they conform.

The Japanese CEO is extremely self-disciplined and therefore capable of extreme forms of dedication—a cultural trait that was demonstrated by the Japanese troops during World War II by making kamikaze or suicide attacks. This dedication continues in the CEOs of today. Insofar as the "honor" of the company is his primary goal, if the CEO causes the company to be dishonored or "lose face," many Japanese CEOs would feel duty bound to commit *seppuku.* A very different and far more severe form of punishment for failure than that which is experienced by the American CEO.

With the ability to be extremely dedicated, the Japanese CEO also has the ability to demand extreme dedication from his subordinates, and so in turn down the line to the lowest levels of the company. It is easy to understand the Japanese business phrase, "We will control and perfect everything in the company down to the last grain of rice in the employees' lunch boxes." Contrast this with the American CEO, who has not even been in all of his factories.

We have learned the factors upon which the Japanese CEO bases decisions. Additionally we know that otherwise he is a human being more or less like us, driven by the same causes as we are. Let us mentally transport ourselves to the garden of a Japanese estate outside of Tokyo. It is night and there is a full moon. The reflection of the moon quivers hypnotically on the surface of the pond. A rhythm of ripples caused by a waterfall makes the reflection pulsate. The garden, although appearing totally natural, has in fact been meticulously planned down to the placement of each individual stone. We, the Japanese CEO with stern, self-disciplined countenance, sit cross-legged on a slightly raised platform staring across the pond at a white rock, which in the bright moonlight seems almost incandescent. There is moss growing on the rock that reminds us of age, of the immortal timelessness of a moss colony, of the frailty and shortness of our own lives, and of the fact that all a person ever really has is his or her own honor and the honor of the group to which the person belongs.

We, the Japanese CEO, have been thinking about a comment we heard at a conference sponsored by the Japanese government. The comment was that it would be very much to Japan's benefit if Japanese companies were pre-eminent in the world in automobiles, electronics, and computer chips, among other things. It just so happens that the company of which we are the CEO is one of Japan's largest electronics firms. Therefore, we will think about the future and formulate a plan to invade the American electronics market that will be of the highest honor and credit to our company, and will eventually lead to higher profits. The plan, which would be to our greatest honor, would be to annihilate the American electronics industry totally and completely. Therefore, the absolute destruction of the American electronics companies and the taking over of the American electronics market must be our goal. Additionally, because making money is not our primary goal, we need not concern ourselves very much with how much money we lose, if any, while we are carrying out our plan. For when the plan is successful, we will supply the Americans with all of their electronic goods for decades to come, which will make any amount of short-term losses insignificant in comparison. We will order our highly dedicated and motivated staff to draw up plans (causes) that will result in the destruction (effect) of the American electronics manufacturers and the conquest of their market by us. We will instruct them that the plan must be controlled and perfected down to the last grain of rice in the workers' lunch boxes. The length of time we will give them is seven years to conquer 50 percent of the American market and fifteen years to capture the entire market.

Now let us step back from our two competing CEOs and watch them collide in the no-holds-barred arena of international business. The reader has had a substantial amount of experience by now in observing how cause-and-effect relationships operate. The situation calls for predicting the future. All we have to do is operate the important cause-and-effect relationships and the future will be easily revealed. In the case of the Japanese electronics company in competition with the American electronics company, the Japanese have caused the struggle, by their decision to take over 100 percent of the American electronics market, to be a struggle for survival. Therefore, the most important cause-and-effect relationship controlling the struggle for survival is the Law of the Survival of the Efficient.

All we must know is which of these two institutions is more efficient at surviving, the Japanese electronics company or the American electronics company. We also already know that the highest and most efficient technique of ensuring survival for human beings is the Four Critical Abilities. More specifically: 1) Realistically view the future; 2) Make the best plan for the future that changes what would normally occur in the future into what we want to occur in the future by changing the causes to ones that will render the desired effect. The plan becomes those actions that we must take to change the normally occurring causes to the causes that we desire; 3) The structure of the organization must be capable of implementing the plan; 4) The society, or in this case the institution, must be willing to make the necessary sacrifice to institute the plan. Which of the two institutions locked in the struggle for survival is more efficient in doing the four things listed above? Let us analyze them one by one. The first one is to be capable of realistically predicting the future. The American CEO, driven by "nonetheless, next quarter's profits must be increased," is thinking primarily of short-range goals, no more than three months in advance. In terms of thinking in the future this is almost as bad as merely thinking in the present. The Japanese CEO, however, is planning seven and even fifteen years into the future.[29] The American CEO fired Caulfield, the one vice-president he had who realistically predicted the future and made a plan for years into the future. The Japanese CEO has a group of Japanese Caulfields as vice-presidents.

Therefore, the Japanese institution is far more efficient in being capable of realistically predicting the future and thinking in the future. Therefore, it follows that the Japanese

---

29. The author understands that Matsushita Electric Company (brand names: Panasonic, National, Quasar, Universal Pictures and Studios, MCA, et al.) has a corporate plan that covers the next 250 years.

institution is also far more efficient at planning the future. The first two requirements for surviving clearly are easily won by the Japanese institution, but how about numbers 3 and 4?

Number 3 is: An efficient organizational structure necessary to implement the plan. Once again, with an organizational structure that permits the Japanese CEO "to control and perfect everything down to the last grain of rice in the workers' lunch boxes," the Japanese company is far superior to ours, wherein the American CEO would most probably get himself lost were he by himself in his own factories.

Number 4 is: "The society, or in this case the institution, must be able to make the sacrifice necessary to implement the plan." We have already noted the Japanese tendency to dedication—what seems to us an almost fanatical dedication. A dedication so deep that in this country it is usually only observed in the meaningless devotion fans display for their favorite sports teams. An American company motivated by "nonetheless, next quarter's profits must increase" cannot even sacrifice next quarter's profits to invest in machinery that will increase profits next year. Therefore, the American institution loses number 4 also.

As a result, in a comparison of the traits needed for survival the Japanese business/institution is far superior to the American business/institution. Therefore, in 1973 we could have easily predicted with an extremely high degree of confidence that the Japanese manufacturers would, without much difficulty, drive the American manufacturers out of business. History bears out the accuracy of the prediction.

Thus it is easy to predict that our hypothetical electronics division went out of business. The profits of the American business declined. The stock price fell. The CEO was forced to retire. The stockholders sold to someone like T. Boone Pickens, who sold off parts of the company to finance the purchase, and the once proud conglomerate limps along heavily in debt. Being heavily in debt, it cannot raise the cash to re-engineer and re-design or re-invest in its remaining factories or in its products, which it has neglected for so long. Therefore it survives by seeking quotas from the U.S. government against the importation of foreign goods. The company claims that the Japanese are competing unfairly, which is true, but the important reality is that the company has been killing itself for the last twenty years. It failed to sacrifice short-term profits for long-term investments in engineering and productivity. In short, the American company reeks of decadence to the point of defining the word.

There are only a few major exceptions to the extinction of the American consumer electronics manufacturers. Motorola is one. Motorola not only survived but prospered because it, in effect, had a Caulfield as CEO and primary stockholder, in the person of Robert Galvin. Mr. Galvin realized that to sur-vive, Motorola would have to sacrifice its short-term prof-itability for increased investments in research and develop-ment, engineering, design, and automation of its factories. Because Mr. Galvin owned much of Motorola, he was able to make the sacrifice in short-term profitability without being fired or bought out. He traded short-term profits for long-term megaprofits.

American business was decadent by 1973. In business class, we students were told that America's factories were becoming older and more antiquated every year while America's competitors were building modern plants employing the latest technology. American business viewed factory and equipment expenditures as short-term decreases in profits, which decrease stock prices, which therefore decrease the bonus for the American CEO. Some of us students knew even then that trouble was on the way. Let us return to 1973 and continue with the story of American business.

That was the year of the first Arab oil embargo. The price of gasoline increased from 35 cents a gallon to 66 cents a gallon. Fifty percent of America's oil was imported.[30] With the explosive increase in the price of oil, American business found itself with skyrocketing energy bills, which decreased profits. The environmental movement was at its strongest, which also threatened profitability. We can imagine what the reaction of our hypothetical CEO would be to being forced by the government to reinvest profits in pollution control equipment that would never make a contribution to profits when the CEO even turned down Caulfield's plan to improve profits in the future. The combination of the Japanese invasion of superior goods plus the skyrocketing cost of energy plus the environmentalists, petitioning the government for mandatory pollution controls, meant that it was impossible for American business to increase next quarter's profit. The American CEOs became frantic. They were trapped like rats in a corner. They could not decrease costs any more because costs were actually increasing due to the Arab oil embargo. They could not increase sales any more because the Japanese, with superior products and lower prices, were causing the American companies to *lose* sales. Fighting back at the Japanese, as we have seen, took a large investment and took years to show profits. And to add insult to injury, the environmentalists were getting all the legislation they wanted through Congress and, from the CEO's point of view, the environmentalists were so ignorant they were not even aware of the most important reality in the world, which is "nonetheless, next quarter's profits must increase." The American CEOs were literally at wits' end. What is worse, they were powerless. They could not do anything about the Arab oil embargo. They could not do anything about the invasion of

---

30. Fifty percent of America's oil is still imported. However, because our economy is larger than in 1973 we are actually importing more oil now than in 1973. Was not a long-term goal of the United States government in 1973 to be energy independent by the year 2000? So much for the long-term plans of the United States of America.

Japanese imports. They could do nothing about these "annoy-ing" environmentalists. They were caught in a whirlwind of forces in which they were helpless. The CEO could do nothing to stop profits from declining. The American CEO's world was collapsing around him. He felt trapped with no way out. The game was over. Unless the CEOs could get the rules of the game changed, American business was finished. The CEOs packed their bags and went to Washington. The corridors of Congress were bustling with CEOs and their hired consul-tants begging, cajoling, and pleading for protection from the forces of the Japanese invasion of superior goods at lower prices, the Arab oil embargo, and these "nutty" environmen-talists. The CEOs were prepared to do anything to obtain pro-tection. Anything!

CHAPTER NINE

The Theft

The Pivotal Years—1973 to 1974

BEFORE WE BEGIN THE NEXT CHAPTER, the author would like the reader to consider the following question: "Can democracy exist in a given society if the elections in that society are unequal and unfair?" To put it another way: "If fair and equal elections do *not* exist, can there be a democracy?" My answer is no. A democracy cannot exist without fair and equal elections. Please remember your answer.

Let us briefly review the major events that have caused our government to be as it is.

1) 1789: The Constitution was the result of compromises. Rather than presenting us with an idealized, enduring governmental structure, it was the best that could be done given the exigencies of the time. Serious errors were made, such as not including the Bill of Rights, the First Ten Amendments to the Constitution, and not incorporating the entire set of checks and balances into the Constitution. A weak central government was created, but the strongest of the three branches of government was Congress. In addition, the states, by election, controlled the most powerful house of Congress, the Senate.

2) 1861–1865: The Civil War ended any claims to sovereignty by the states. The weak central government became the powerful central government constrained only by Article X of the Bill of Rights.

3) 1889–1913: Our democracy was stolen for the first time by the trusts, which had bribed the Senate. Our democracy was not returned until 1913, when the 17th Amendment was ratified. The 17th Amendment took the election of the Senate out of the hands of the state legislatures and gave it to the people. The Senate's function in government became redundant and therefore counterproductive and therefore the Senate makes government less efficient. It took over twenty-four years to wrest back our government from the hands of the thieves even after it was generally known that the Senate was being bribed.

4) 1932–1945: President Franklin D. Roosevelt and Congress pressured the Supreme Court into approving legislation that (1) was unconstitutional and therefore illegal, and (2) released the power of the federal government from any restraint by the 10th Amendment to the Constitution. The government could make laws about anything it wanted. In addition, because Congress is the branch of government empowered to pass laws, in actuality *the power of Congress was greatly increased.*

Let us continue our history by following the relationship of the president and Congress. Because of the strong leadership exerted by President Roosevelt and the emergency situation caused by the Second World War, our democracy continued to function well. President Harry "the buck stops here" Truman (1945–1953) also was a forceful leader in his relationship with Congress, as was the former allied commander in Europe, President Eisenhower. President Kennedy (1961–1963) was, surprisingly enough, a weak leader in his relationship with Congress. However, his inspirational leadership coupled with his short term of office did not affect the relative powers of Congress versus president. He was succeeded by the consummate arm-twisting, former congressional leader and master politician, President Johnson (1963–1969). Rare was the member of Congress who could stand up to President Johnson's combination of arm-twisting and trading of favors. Therefore President Johnson was a very strong president and able to get his way with Congress.

President Nixon (1969–1974), also a shrewd politician and former member of Congress, was able to be effective with Congress. However, in 1973 he was linked to the infamous 1972 Watergate break-in. He resigned in 1974 shortly before he would have had to face impeachment by Congress. The Democratic-controlled Congress smelled Republican blood in the water and wanted President Nixon brought to trial on criminal charges. Within a month of assuming office, Republican President Ford (1974–1977), who followed Nixon, used his power of pardon to spare the nation and the Republican party the debacle of an ex-President on trial. The Democrat-controlled Congress was enraged. They had raw meat on the table only to have it snatched away by President Ford. Congress firmly grabbed the bit of power in its teeth.

The illegal actions of President Nixon caused the Congress of the United States to embark on an orgy of power-grabbing and rape of the executive branch's responsibilities, which legislatively was equivalent to the Vandals' sack of Rome or the Mongol horde's destruction of a city to the last man, woman, and child. The point of critical importance to America's future about Watergate that is universally overlooked is that Congress systematically stripped the presidency one by one of its independent powers. Congress upset the delicate balance created by the Constitution and made itself supreme amongst the three branches of government. Congress effectively trampled the system of checks and balances that, we recall, our Founding Fathers had neglected to place in the Constitution.

In 1973, Congress passed the War Powers Act, severely curtailing the president's constitutionally provided role as commander-in-chief and thereby greatly hindering the president's ability to conduct foreign policy. Every president since the passage of the War Powers Act has declared it unconstitutional, even such presidents with widely differing political viewpoints as President Carter (1977–1981) and President Reagan (1981–1989). To further inhibit the president, Congress passed laws limiting and emasculating the CIA.

In 1974, Congress passed the Congressional Budget and Impoundment Control Act. This piece of legislation drastically altered the balance of power between the president and Congress in setting the budget and controlling spending, which in turn determines domestic policy. Prior to the passage of this law, Congress could basically pass whatever budget it wanted, but the president did not have to spend the money. The president could "impound" the money (in modern terms: line-item veto) and not spend it or, if he chose, redirect it. The president has done this many times throughout the history of the nation. In 1801, Thomas Jefferson refused to purchase warships with money provided by Congress, and instead reduced the national debt. President Franklin D. Roosevelt impounded funds for flood control in 1941. President Johnson impounded seven percent of the United States federal budget and redirected it to the Vietnam War. President Nixon impounded $19 billion from domestic spending for the Vietnam War. Therefore, the president in fact controlled the budget and spending process. However, when Congress passed the 1974 Congressional Budget and Impoundment Control Act, it removed the president's unilateral right to impound funds (line-item veto) and forced the president to spend the money budgeted by Congress for the purposes legislated by Congress, or go to prison. In short, the power over the budget and spending process had been taken from the president and Congress gave it to itself. In effect by controlling the budget, Congress controls domestic policy. Not one penny of the federal budget may be spent for anything other than the purpose designated by Congress. Imagine a president who would like to institute a far-reaching domestic policy. It is not possible without the approval of Congress. I challenge the reader to think of domestic policy changes that can be implemented without spending a single penny. The list is very short. Other than symbolic gestures and minor changes in emphasis by the bureaucracy, the president has virtually been stripped of control over domestic policy. Once again, as had been done with the Supreme Court, Congress unilaterally broke the traditional system of checks and balances, only this time from the only remaining equal branch of government: the executive branch.

STOP PRESS

Just before going to press, President Gerald R. Ford (1974–1977) has graciously responded to a list of questions submitted by the author. President Ford fully concurs with the central thesis of Future Perfect, *that during the post–Watergate period, an avenging, Democratic–controlled Congress was intent upon upsetting the system of checks and balances by stripping traditional powers from the Presidency. For example, the passage of the War Powers Act of 1973, which he and every President since has declared unconstitutional. A further example, the Congressional Budget and Impoundment Control Act of 1974 removed what we now call the line-item veto from the President, which in turn removed the President's ability to control and thereby balance the federal budget. These two laws (1) greatly hindered the President's role in foreign policy and (2) removed the budget from the President's control, which in a larger sense removed control over domestic policy.*

President Ford further stated "As a consequence of Watergate and Vietnam, there was a deliberate effort to weaken the power of the President. I do not believe there was a deliberate effort on the part of Speaker Albert or Senate Leader Mansfield to weaken the power of the Presidency. However, there were strong elements in the Democratic party in the House and Senate who were upset with the Nixon White House on Vietnam and Watergate. It was to a degree—a vendetta."

However, the Congresses of 1973 and 1974 had just started, and much, much worse was about to come.

Having sucked from the presidency its two main powers, restricting the president's ability to conduct foreign policy, and controlling the budgeting process and therefore domestic policy, the Congress had made itself supreme among the three branches of government. But even all of this paled in comparison to what was to come next. Congress was emboldened by the power it had amassed and was the unrivaled master of the government of the most powerful nation on Earth. Its power knew virtually no bounds, as its next step shows.

To understand the next step of the lawmakers, we will have to know what the operative cause-and-effect relationships are that cause members of Congress to behave the way they do. In order to understand the motivation and behavior of a member of Congress, the single most important thing to remember is that he or she is like any other human being. Therefore, we can be certain that members of Congress will act like other human beings, which is to say that a member of Congress can be relied upon to always do what is in his or her own best self-interest as he or she perceives it to be. Insofar as becoming a member of Congress is a voluntary act, it is clear that the individuals who run for Congress perceive it to be in their own best self-interest to be members of Congress. It is equally clear that members of Congress perceive it to be in their own best self-interest to continue being members of Congress, as recent history shows more than 97 percent of members of Congress run for re-election. Now, up to this point, nothing is unexpected or unusual. People who are successful want to remain successful. That is natural. We could go into a lengthy explanation at this point about how especially important it is to a member of Congress to remain being a member of Congress. They may be human beings just like us, but a member of Congress, unlike us average people, is treated with respect, courtesy, and deference by all who come in contact with him. People seeking favors, people seeking jobs, military personnel who need the member of Congress's vote for the military budget, bureaucrats, foreign ambassadors, congressional staff members, the press wanting a story. Taxi drivers are kind, even in New York. Maître d's in restaurants do not keep members of Congress waiting for tables. The member of Congress may not even be asked to pay for the meal. Lobbyists, the people, us, back in the home district, even the president who needs the vote, treat the member of Congress with respect. In short, the member of Congress is treated as all of us would like to be treated but are not. Everyone with whom the member of Congress comes in contact validates that the member of Congress is a special person to be treated with respect. It takes a very special and unusual type of person not to believe that he or she is in fact a special and unusual type of person when treated by one and all in this way.

We could also have a lengthy discussion of how, as Lord Acton put it, "Power tends to corrupt and absolute power corrupts absolutely." If the reader has never had the heady smell of power in his or her nostrils, it may be difficult to understand the literally intoxicating effect power has on people. Let me attempt to explain it in this way. Heroin and crack cocaine are supposed to be the most addictive drugs in existence. However, legions of people have kicked both habits. In all of the 5,500-year written history of humankind, I cannot think of one dictator who has voluntarily given up power—not Hitler, Stalin, Napoleon, Caesar, Castro, Ferdinand Marcos, Manuel Noriega, François Duvalier, or Saddam Hussein. Regardless of the amount of suffering humankind must pay to keep a dictator in power, the dictator clings to power at all costs.

Compared to power, drugs like heroin and crack cocaine are only mildly addictive.

To further validate the fervent desire of senators and representatives to be re-elected, we need only look at the lengths to which they go when there is a closely contested congressional election. These men and women, who between elections portray themselves as kindly, deliberative, self-effacing statesmen of integrity, resort to the basest levels of mudslinging, including racism, distortion of truth, dirty tricks, and slander. Anything to be re-elected.

At this point the reader may think, "Yes, all that is true. Members of Congress desperately want to be re-elected, but so what? America is a democracy and we, the people, decide who will be elected." We need to add two more facts before it becomes apparent what the problem is. The first is that Article 1, Section 4, paragraph 1 of the Constitution states:

"The Times, Places, and Manner of holding Elections for Senators and Representatives, shall be prescribed in each State by the Legislature thereof; but *the Congress may at any time by Law make or alter such Regulations*, except as to the Places of Choosing Senators." (Author's italics)

In short, Congress itself makes its own laws concerning how its own members will be elected. Therefore, the members of Congress, who, as we already know, desperately want to be re-elected, decide by themselves the regulations governing their own re-elections.

The second fact is, as you will no doubt recall, that we left our harried CEOs in 1973 in a desperate state. They were besieged and could no longer increase profits. They had been caught between the rising costs of energy because of the Arab oil embargo and environmentalists on the one hand, and the inability to raise prices because of the introduction of low-priced, superior-quality, imported goods produced by the efficient Japanese on the other. American business was trapped. What President Lyndon Johnson said about himself and the

Vietnam War applies to the CEOs of 1973: "I [they] felt like a hitchhiker in a Texas hailstorm—I cannot run, I cannot hide, and I cannot make it stop." The only possible solution for the CEOs was to have the cause-and-effect relationships that would damage them and their companies interdicted. The only institution powerful enough to intervene was the Congress of the United States. In long lines, the American businessmen came to the offices of their individual senators and representatives to tell their tales of woe and despair. All the tales ended the same way—the loss of American jobs, market, and businesses.

The businessmen were desperate and would do anything to halt or slow down the Japanese invasion. Being good businessmen, they were more than prepared to spend a few million dollars to protect billions of dollars of profits.

Looking at it from the viewpoint of a member of Congress, here were literally hundreds of businessmen lining up outside their offices not only willing, but eager, to give millions of dollars to members of Congress in exchange for protective legislation and special favors.

The members of Congress, being mostly lawyers, were sophisticated enough not to accept the money directly from the businessmen, as you will recall the Senate had when it stole our democracy the first time, at the turn of the century. Instead, utilizing their power under the Constitution to write their own campaign laws, in the Campaign Reform Act of 1974 as amended in 1976 and subsequently, Congress created political action committees whose sole political action is to give money to members of Congress. In short, Congress legalized bribery. The coming together of Watergate and massive amounts of money caused the Congress to steal our democracy again. In so doing, they have created a situation wherein the incumbent member of Congress can accumulate massive quantities of money. At election time, the incumbent has accumulated a campaign fund of perhaps $10 million to run against a challenger who has not had an equal chance to raise such massive sums of money. If the reader, for instance, wanted to run for Congress, how could he possibly raise $10 million? It is virtually impossible. Do you remember at the beginning of this chapter when you were asked, If there are not fair elections, can there be a democracy? If you answered, "No," then clearly we do not have a democracy in this country. We have been fooled by the fact that our Bill of Rights, our personal liberties, have been left intact, protected by the Supreme Court. However, the people's right to influence our government has been stolen by Congress and sold to the special interest groups in return for cash used to unfairly re-elect the members of Congress. Therefore, incredibly, the United States of America is no longer a democracy, but rather a tyranny of the U.S. Congress.

I am aware that this shocking conclusion may well emotionally stun the reader. The implications of the loss of our democracy are too overwhelming to permit belief. Congress, as we have already seen, has unilaterally severed any real control over itself by the other two branches. By creating an election process based on bribery, Congress unilaterally severed the last link of control over itself. It severed the most important link of all—the system of checks and balances held by us, the people. They no longer have to do what we want. All they have to do is what the special interests want them to do. Therefore, our problems do not get solved, and legislation to favor special interests or to further their own re-election sets the government's agenda.

Additional proof that we no longer have a democracy in this country is that the definition of democracy is rule by the people. If the reader were to go into the streets and ask passersby, "Who is in favor of continuing massive budget deficits?" I am quite sure he would not find one person who agrees in a whole day. However, year after year, Congress gives us massive budget deficits that will surely destroy this society. Therefore, what the people want is not what the people get. Therefore, the people do not rule. Therefore, we do not have a democracy.

Furthermore, the Federalist Papers, co-authored by James Madison, noted that approximately 50 percent of the legislators in the state assemblies were replaced every election. It was stated that a 50-percent turnover was healthy. Therefore, presumably, none other than the author of the Constitution, James Madison, would decry as unhealthy a situation wherein, historically, more than 97 percent of members of Congress are returned to office in spite of the fact that the citizens believe Congress is doing an incredibly bad job.[31]

Additional evidence that we no longer have a democracy in this country is that in a recent poll in which people were asked to rank occupations in the order of the amount of respect and trust the people had for them, belonging to Congress came out next to the bottom, only one step above used car salesmen. Do you see how smart your fellow citizens are? They only missed Congress's truly deserved rank by one position. At least a citizen knows the used car salesman will try to give him or her a bad deal. With members of Congress, we get bad government, while they tell us during campaigns how much they are going to improve things. I personally would be honored to have a person of integrity like a used car salesman as my friend, if my only other choice were a member of Congress.

---

31. Since the passage of the Campaign Reform Act of 1974, the re-election rate of incumbent members of Congress has climbed to 97 percent. The two exceptions have been the congressional election of 1992 wherein roughly 25 percent of the House of Representatives was replaced (rather than being a hopeful sign of the beginning of a new trend, this signals the expiration of a campaign law that lets the retiring members of Congress place re-election campaign funds in their pockets) and the election of 1994 (we will discuss this election later).

However, despite this very low opinion that the citizenry has of members of Congress, it remains a fact that, except in the last two elections, more than 97 percent of members of Congress were re-elected. Clearly, something is wrong. Once again the people's will is not being carried out.

Let us take a closer look at the election process that the members of Congress have set up for themselves. The Campaign Reform Act of 1974 created political action committees to channel money from special interest groups into individual members of Congress's campaign funds. A special interest, by definition, is an interest that is *not* in the general interest. If the special interest wanted the government to do what is in the people's best interest, then there would be no need for the special interest. Therefore, special interests seek to cause the government to act in a way that is out of the natural course of government and to act in a way that provides special favors that the special interest would not otherwise receive. It is obvious that special interest groups have been so successful that the general interest has been spurned in Congress. This has left many groups who represent the general interest (such as environmental groups, veterans' organizations, health related groups, and so on) to resort to forming special interest groups in an attempt to have the general interest done. Therefore, special interest groups at the present time do not all universally represent "bad" causes (i.e. not in the general interest).

Nonetheless, Congress set up a campaign system whereby those wanting special favors could legally bribe the members of Congress by donating to their re-election campaigns. With the money so obtained, the incumbent has an unfair advantage over the challenger. Challengers have not had special interest groups lined up outside their offices with briefcases full of money pleading for special favors in return for campaign contributions. As long as the incumbent member of

Congress continues to provide special favors to special interests, the campaign contributions continue. Therefore, the
incumbent member of Congress typically has many millions
of dollars more than the challenger. The incumbent member
of Congress then spends some of his money on political advisers, pollsters, and media advisers. A television campaign is
put together that typically has two objectives. The first is to
give the voters a positive, warm, likable emotional feeling
about the candidate without discussing any issues. To every
issue there are at least two sides, else it would not be an
issue. Some voters will be in favor of one side of the issue,
and some will be on the other. Therefore any intellectual posi-
tion-taking is to be avoided because some voters will be alien-
ated no matter what position is taken. This is what the
cognoscenti in Washington have named "Miller time" politics,
after the beer commercials: Give the voter in 30 seconds a
warm, positive feeling about the product, which in this case
just happens to be a member of Congress. The typical campaign attempts to avoid to the greatest extent possible any
discussion of the issues. In fact, the incumbent member of
Congress will not even debate the issues with his opponent
unless the polls show it to be a close race. Likewise, in inter-
view situations on television and radio, the incumbent member of Congress attempts to avoid definitive positions on
issues. The emphasis in the 30-second commercials is on a) a
vague better future, and b) vague personal qualities of the
candidate such as leadership, experience (of course, the
incumbent always has more experience than the challenger—
he is already in Congress), and what a great family person he
or she is. One can only wonder why, with all the great family
men running for office, so many spouses of politicians have
substance-abuse problems, but I will leave the reader to puzzle that out. Needless to say, this type of campaign leaves the
voters with very little substantive knowledge upon which to
make an informed judgment of the candidate.

The second objective of the campaign is to link your opponent to as many negative, bad concepts and feelings as possible. The effect desired by the media expert is to associate a
negative reaction to the opponent's name. Then when the
voter reads the opponent's name in the voting booth, the voter,
like one of Pavlov's dogs, will react in the desired manner
without thinking. The member of Congress avoids logical and
rational discussions that would inform us, the voters, because
so much of what the member of Congress does is neither rational nor logical. The member of Congress would have great difficulty defending the favors and votes given for money spent
on behalf of the special interest groups that result in the massive budget deficits threatening the continued existence of this
society. Instead, the member of Congress prefers to run a campaign based on the amount of money one has to spend. With
all the bribes the member of Congress has collected during his
term in office, he can smother the voter with positive ads
about himself and negative ads about his opponent. For example, let us analyze the results of the 1990 Senate elections. Of
the 35 seats up for election, four incumbent senators, or 11
percent, ran unopposed. Of the remaining 31 races, only one
incumbent senator lost. The winning incumbent senators
spent an average of $4.41 per voter, whereas the losing chal-
lengers, on average, spent less than $1.80 per voter. In only
three races did the challenger outspend the incumbent. The
incumbent senators lost one, or 33 percent, of those races in
which they were outspent. The conclusions to be drawn are 1)
the incumbent has a far greater ability to raise money than
the challenger, and 2) the candidate who can spend more
money has a far greater chance of winning. Therefore, the
incumbent has a far greater chance to win the election.

It is a far cry from the system envisioned by Jefferson
and Madison, of informed voters acting in their own enlightened self-interest. Congress writes its own re-election laws,
and it has written them to permit bribery and unfair elec-

tions. Congress has stolen our democracy and sold it to the special interest groups in return for cash, which is used in unfair elections to remain in office. In my book, this makes members of Congress far worse than prostitutes. At least prostitutes sell what is theirs. Members of Congress sell what they have stolen from us: our most important possession—our democracy.

If any institution other than Congress made the campaign laws, then what the members of Congress do would be illegal. As we have discovered, not only does Congress pass its own campaign laws, but they passed a law making it illegal for any other branch of government even to investigate Congress. Because they write the laws, they can make anything they want to do legal, and make illegal anyone else's efforts to stop them.

The incredulous reader may wonder, "How can this be? They seem like such nice men and women when you see them on TV." For con men to steal, they first need to gain the victim's confidence. After acting in a way to gain the victim's trust and confidence, the con man can induce the little old lady to withdraw her life savings and give it to him. The members of Congress act in the same way. Let me demonstrate how corrupt they are. One would assume, since we live in a violent and crime-ridden society, that our highly exalted lawmakers and guardians of the public trust would most surely be of high moral conduct, far higher than we lowly, average people. The opposite, however, is true. Recently seven senators were under investigation for ethics violations. Since there are 100 senators, seven percent of the Senate was accused of violating the rules by which senators swear to live. However, in 1988, the FBI reported that in the entire United States there were only 13.9 million arrests, including arrests for vagrancy, curfew violations, runaways, and the heinous crime of loitering, which means that only 5.6 percent of the general population of the United States is accused of violating the rules by which we are supposed to live. Therefore, the Senate of the United States had more accused crooks in it, percentage-wise, than the United States as a whole. Interestingly enough, five of the senators, known as the Keating Five, were accused of accepting bribes (or campaign contributions as they are known in Congress) in exchange for interfering in and delaying the executive branch's investigation of a fraudulently operated savings and loan. The defense used by one of these stalwart statesmen was that all the members of Congress do it and that if he was guilty, then all the members of Congress were guilty. Now, that I believe. One of them has finally told us the truth. They are all guilty.

The government of the United States, as President Abraham Lincoln stated so eloquently in the Gettysburg Address, is supposed to be of the people, by the people, and for the people. The members of Congress, by rewriting the election laws, have given away our right to contribute time and money—or not—as we see fit to election campaigns, and thereby affect the outcome. Congress severed the link between themselves and the people. They then sold the link to special interests for cash, which gives the incumbent an unfair chance to be re-elected.

If it is true that Congress stole our democracy in 1974, why has the reader not heard about it before?

The Media

Why is the theft of the American democracy reported for the first time in this book? Where is the supposed fourth estate, the "watchdog of the public," the media? Why did the media, after doing such a determined job in uncovering President Nixon's involvement in Watergate, miss the story of the century, the theft of the American democracy by Congress? In terms of importance to the future of this country, the Watergate break-in was a misdemeanor compared to the theft of the entire democracy by Congress. Why has it not been reported? I do not have any special expertise or knowledge about the media. However, the power of the Black Box Technique suggests that there are two possible explanations. The first is that the tens of thousands of newspeople in this country failed to realize what was going on and continue to do so. Though surprising, this would serve as confirmation that our logic is indeed very powerful. The second possible explanation is that some members of the media have figured out what is going on, but for some reason the story is never told.

What reason would there be for not running the blockbuster story that Congress has stolen our democracy, and that we therefore do not have a democracy in this country any more? Up to 680 million dollars are spent on crooked congressional elections every two years.[32] It is almost all spent on television, radio, and newspaper advertising. In short, the millions of dollars that the members of Congress receive in bribes are then given to the media. Therefore, if the first explanation is true, the media are unwitting conspirators in depriving the American people of our democracy. If the second explanation is true, they are witting conspirators, and Congress has succeeded in severing the last remaining check and balance by bribing the news media of the United States of America with windfall profits. Either way, conspirators the media definitely are.

We know that the media, like every person and every institution, will act in their own best interest as they perceive it. We also know that every two years the TV, radio, and newspapers in this country are deluged with hundreds of millions of dollars for unfair campaign advertising. It is therefore in the media's own best self-interest if this unfair type of

---

32. Though at the time of completion of this manuscript the total amount spent on the congressional election of 1994 had not been reported, it is estimated that one billion dollars was spent.

campaigning continues. It is therefore in the media's own best self-interest if Congress continues to sell our democracy to the special interests.

Have the media either 1) honestly overlooked the most important story in America—the theft of our democracy—and as soon as they hear about it (through this book, if no place else), can we expect them to make it the most important news story in America until something is done about it? or 2) can we expect the news media to remain silent and quash the story in order to continue to receive the bribe? If they remain silent, of course, then the integrity and credibility of the United States news media are absolutely nonexistent. Let us conduct an Einsteinian Thought Experiment. Let us imagine that we are observers in the newsroom of ABC, NBC, CBS, or CNN. The newsroom is a beehive of activity as the people scurry to prepare the next telecast. We move into the office of the anchorman—Peter Jennings, Tom Brokaw, Dan Rather, Ted Koppel, or Bernard Shaw. It is apparent that whoever our choice is, he is deeply troubled. He is staring at the wall, wrestling with a very difficult problem. He is trying to decide whether to go to his superior, the president of the news division, and request to run a continuing exposé on the theft of the American democracy by Congress. In so doing, he will help to alert the people and thereby help to save the United States of America. That is his job: to inform the public, us, what is really happening. These men are neither stupid nor naive. They know what is at stake. Their bosses, their employers, may be opposed to running the continuing exposé even though it is the most important news story in the United States of America, because if the American people are made aware of the theft of their democracy by the Congress, the American people will demand reform, and the network will lose its biennial multi-million dollar windfall profit.

Let us say that the anchorman decides to discuss the issue with his boss. He calls him on the interoffice phone system and tells his boss that he needs to see him as soon as possible. The anchorman takes the elevator up to the president of the news division's office. They sit down and the anchorman explains to his boss how important it is to run the exposé. The anchorman tells the president of the news division that the story must be run for three reasons: 1) It is critical that the story be told for the survival of the American people; 2) It is critical for the long-term health of the network to maintain its credibility in the eyes of the American people; 3) If the story gets out to the American people another way first, then the anchorman himself will lose his integrity and credibility and therefore his personal effectiveness in the eyes of the American people.

How will the president of the news division respond? Will the president of the news division respond that the story cannot be run? Because if it is, the following will happen: The American people will be enraged and demand reform, which will cause elections to be federally funded with much more sensible levels of spending; or the networks may even be required to supply the air time free of charge as a public service, which will in turn cause the network to lose money and make the heads of the network unhappy. The heads of the network will have to cut the news department's budget. That will in turn cause the anchorman and the president of the news division to receive less money when their contracts come up for renewal. In addition, if the heads of the network are sufficiently unhappy, the anchorman and the president of the news division will be fired.

Or will the president of the news division respond, "Good idea. I like it. Let's run the story until democracy is restored to America"? By now the reader should be an expert in predicting the outcome of cause-and-effect relationships. I will let the reader predict whether the continuing exposé on the most important news story in the United States of America will be run.

From the perspective of the average citizen, the purpose of the news media is to inform us citizens of the truth, of reality that we cannot experience ourselves first-hand. We, the citizens, cannot possibly be present at all important news events as they happen around the world. We are dependent upon the news media to inform us accurately of reality. Then according to Jefferson and Madison, armed with a clear picture of reality, we can vote in our enlightened self-interest. The critical nature of the citizens being informed of the accurate reality in a democracy is so great that freedom of the press is guaranteed in the Constitution to prevent the government from influencing the press. However, it should also be recognized that the Constitution does not guarantee a fair and impartial press. There is nothing in the Constitution that prevents the media from allowing themselves to be influenced by sources other than the government. From the perspective of the news media editor, the news media have an additional purpose—to make money. If the only two purposes of the news media conflict with each other, informing us of reality, or making money, which does the reader think the editor will choose? If it is making money, then are not our media subject to failing to report to us the truth, if it would gain substantial profits in so doing?

I can remember innumerable stories in the news media of the late 1970s and early 1980s of the threat to America of "Japan, Inc.," as it was often called. Those stories told of purchases of our real estate, unfair trading practices, dumping of consumer goods, refusal to permit U.S. goods to be sold in Japan, etc., and warned of dire consequences if it continued. It has continued, but what has not continued is the news media's continued trumpeting of our peril. Independent observers marvel at our stupidity.

As the prime minister of France, Edith Cresson, has said, "There is a world economic war on." "Japan is an adversary that does not play by the rules and has an absolute desire to conquer the world. You have to be naive or blind not to recognize that." "The Japanese have a strategy of world conquest. They have finished their job in the United States. Now they are about to devour Europe."

I would amend Prime Minister Cresson's remarks to include "naive or blind or *seeking a profit* not to recognize that." The economists, like Lester C. Thurow of MIT in his book *Head to Head* (published by William Morrow), warn of the peril. A highly respected print reporter, James Fallows, a long-time Japan watcher, convincingly warns us of the peril of Japan's economic policies in a recent book, *Looking at the Sun* (published by Pantheon). The author can assure the reader that virtually all of our business leaders, including Lee Iacocca and others, are well aware of the peril. Therefore, those who are in the front lines and in a position to know believe that Japan presents an economic threat. However, the news media fail to continue to report the peril posed by the Japanese. Why? Have the news media collectively decided that they were incorrect in warning us of the peril earlier and that Japan is not an economic threat to America now? If so, why do they not explain their reasoning to us? Or do they fail to warn us of the Japanese peril because the news media are now replete with advertisements for Japanese cars, Japanese computers, Japanese copiers, and Japanese stereos? The author will let the readers conduct their own Einsteinian Thought Experiments on the phone conversation between the news media editor, whether it be television, radio, magazine, or newspaper, and the head of the advertising agency representing a Japanese car company the morning after a news story was run depicting the Japanese as a peril to our society. With the threat of loss of significant ad revenue, would not the editor be forced to promise not to run stories that trumpet the Japanese peril? Although Japanese advertising is not the majority, five of the top 32 advertisers in America are Japanese companies: Toyota, Sony, Nissan, Matsushita, and

Honda.[33] Is it not, therefore, in the best interest of the news media to continue to fail to report this documented threat to our society in order to continue enjoying profits? When it comes to the news media, as we learned from the lions, "It is not the media bias you see that will kill you, it is the one you don't see."

A new trend is even more disturbing. The national media have clumped themselves into large media conglomerates. Their holdings range from television stations, radio stations, newspapers, magazines, book publishers, to cable channels. These media conglomerates have the right to operate their businesses the same as any other business, which among other things means at a profit. It also means that the media conglomerates, under the Campaign Reform Act of 1974, can legally bribe our politicians. And that is precisely what they do. For instance, Time-Warner, the publisher of *Time* magazine and the owner of a number of cable TV channels amongst other things, has recently been named as the single largest contributor of money, known as "soft money," to the Democratic party. Insofar as the president is appointed the head of the Democratic party, "soft money" received by the Democratic party can be spent by President Clinton for his own re-election; or President Clinton can give the money to Democratic members of Congress for their re-election campaigns in exchange for favors that increase the power of the presidency. What did Time-Warner receive in return for its roughly one-half million dollar legal bribe? The author is not privy to conversations in which such things are discussed, but a few weeks after the legal bribe, he read an extremely interesting news story. It was reported that at the economic summit of the G-7 nations in Naples, Italy, in the summer of

33. Japanese corporations purchase advertising in America through American subsidiaries such as Sony Corporation of America. Therefore, the author has not been able to find any statistics of what percentage of U.S. advertising is purchased by Japanese-owned corporations.

1994, President Clinton was strongly criticized by the other nations for introducing a proposal on only two weeks' notice that would have allowed virtually unrestricted access to the European TV market by American media companies, such as Time-Warner. The other nations of the world have legitimate concerns about being inundated by American TV programs because of the violence, sex, and "family" sitcoms in which family members are rude and sarcastic to one another. They point to the increasing violence in our society as justification for their refusal. The other nations have repeatedly and adamantly declined to allow our media companies unlimited access to their cultures throughout the eight years of GATT (General Agreement on Tariffs and Trade) negotiations. It was reported that the other G-7 nations ridiculed President Clinton and decried his proposal as amateurish, and American foreign policy lost credibility in the eyes of our allies; all that for a measly half million dollars in legal bribes. Meanwhile, we citizens send the government more than one trillion dollars in taxes every year and cannot get the government to attend to our problems. However, for a paltry half million dollars, it is evidently possible to purchase the foreign policy of the U.S. government. I wonder if the president does windows?

Therefore, a powerful member of the media, Time-Warner, also happens to be the largest single special interest using the "soft money" bribery channel. An institution charged with the responsibility of clearly informing us of reality is the largest user of one of the legal bribery channels that result in the theft of our democracy. The money so given to the politicians is then given back to the media to buy campaign advertising. The media and the politicians are creating a closed-loop system wherein the media can legally bribe the politicians in order to influence them, and then receive their money back with interest when the politicians, in turn, legally bribe the media by purchasing campaign ads with the legal bribes from the media and the other special interests. In short, the media legally bribe the politicians and then the politicians use the money to legally bribe the media! This cozy circular bribery scam functions very well in bringing profits and influence to the media and re-election for the politicians. But guess who suffers? We, the people, suffer as the theft of our democracy goes unreported. When can we expect to see a cover story of *Time* magazine trumpeting the theft of our democracy by the special interests? The week after a cover story informs us of the Japanese economic threat. When will that be? Right after a cover of *Time* magazine gives a favorable review to this book.

CHAPTER TEN

The Results of the Theft

1974 to the Present

THE FACT THAT CONGRESS has stolen our democracy is nasty and disgusting in and of itself. More nasty and disgusting is the effect that it has had, is having, and will continue to have on the United States of America. The special interest groups' profound ability to affect the outcome of elections means that what the people want, need, and desire is disregarded by Congress. Instead, what the special interests want, need, and desire is enacted by Congress. In short, Congress now responds to the special interest groups, not the people. To state that the results of Congress' placing itself in the hands of the special interest groups will be catastrophe for the citizens of the United States can be confirmed merely by reviewing some of the actions of our government from 1974 until now. Let us note the effects of the damage done by the three laws that have obliterated our system of checks and balances and thereby have caused the theft of our democracy for the second time.

1. 1974 Congressional Budget and Impoundment Control Act

Congress' passage of the Congressional Budget and Impoundment Control Act of 1974 was to cause the *excessive* budget deficits that began in 1975. In 1981, President Reagan assumed office along with a Republican majority in the Senate. President Reagan was determined to increase defense spending in order to either 1) force the Soviet Union into an arms race in which the inefficient Communist economy would destroy itself, or 2) if the Soviets chose not to follow our arms build-up, relegate them to a second-class and therefore relatively ineffectual military threat. The strategy clearly worked as, in the late 1980s, the Soviet economy disintegrated, causing the break-up of the Soviet Union. However, in 1982, the Democrat-controlled House of Representatives wanted a budget that increased domestic spending. President Reagan and the Senate refused to reduce defense spending. Neither side would give in. A compromise budget was finally passed that increased defense spending *and* increased domestic spending. The president, having lost the right of impoundment (line-item veto), was unable to unilaterally reduce spending to balance the budget. Hence, the beginning of our *massive* budget deficits. We have over 180 years of experience that clearly proves that when presidents have the right of impoundment (line-item veto), the budget is roughly balanced. We also have 20 years of experience that proves that when the president does *not* have the right of impoundment (line-item veto), we have catastrophic budget deficits. The passage of this one law, the 1974 Congressional Budget and Impoundment Control Act, has created $4 trillion in budget deficits that we would not otherwise have, as the accompanying chart shows.

ANNUAL BUDGET DEFICITS FROM 1969 TO 1994 (000's deleted)

MAJOR EVENTS	YEAR	ANNUAL BUDGET DEFICIT	TOTAL NATIONAL DEBT
Vietnam War	69	+3,200,000	-367,144,000
"	70	-2,842,000	-380,921,000
"	71	-23,033,000	-408,176,000
"	72	-23,373,000	-435,936,000
U.S. Leaves Vietnam; Watergate Scandal	73	-14,908,000	-466,291,000
Nixon Resigns; Congress Controls Budget	74	-6,135,000	-483,893,000
Excessive Deficits	75	-53,242,000	-541,925,000
Pres. Carter Elected	76	-88,476,000	-643,561,000
Excessive Deficits	77	-53,659,000	-706,398,000
"	78	-59,186,000	-776,602,000
"	79	-40,183,000	-828,923,000
Pres. Reagan Elected	80	-73,835,000	-908,503,000
Excessive Deficits	81	-78,976,000	-994,298,000
Military & Domestic Spending	82	-127,989,000	-1,136,798,000
Massive Deficits	83	-207,818,000	-1,371,164,000
"	84	-185,388,000	-1,564,110,000
"	85	-212,334,000	-1,816,974,000
"	86	-221,245,000	-2,120,082,000
"	87	-149,769,000	-2,345,578,000
Pres. Bush Elected	88	-155,187,000	-2,600,760,000
Massive Deficits	89	-153,400,000	-2,867,538,000
"	90	-220,400,000	-3,206,207,000
"	91	-269,521,000	-3,598,303,000
Pres. Clinton Elected	92	-290,160,000	-4,001,941,000
Massive Deficits	93	-255,300,000	-4,351,223,000
"	94 est.	-234,400,000	-4,676,000,000[34]

Source: Statistical Abstract

34. As the reader has noticed, the Total National Debt increases each year by more than the Annual Budget Deficit. The reason is that Congress plays a deliberately deceptive trick on us. It has created a group of expenditures that Congress has legally defined as "Off-Budget Expenditures." These expenditures, although exactly similar to all others, are not by law included in the budget, but are included in the national debt. This distortion is used to deliberately trick us into thinking the budget deficit is not as high as it actually is. If it were not so tragic, it would be humorous. It is like trying to hide an elephant under a handkerchief.

Whether the reader favored the increase in defense spending or the increase in domestic spending, the critical point is that massive federal budget deficits destroy us all.[35] Before the president lost the right of impoundment (line-item veto), the budget deficit averaged only $11.2 billion annually, even during the Vietnam War. If the 1974 Congressional Budget and Impoundment Control Act had not been passed and our budget deficits had remained the same as the principle of Newtonian Trends says they would, our total national debt by 1994 would be only slightly over $700 billion instead of almost $4.7 *trillion* and growing. Therefore, Congress' passing this one law has cost us roughly $4,000,000,000,000 in debt. This one law causes our massive budget deficits. This one law will do far more damage to us than all the wars the U.S. has ever fought combined. By upsetting the system of checks and balances, the power-usurping Congress is sending us into the future on a collision course with suicide. The catastrophe in progress from this usurpation of presidential power, by 535 members of Congress' creating a budget for which none of them is responsible, is of a magnitude that will easily, in one action, destroy the society of the United States of America. Congress is currently adding to the federal deficit at a rate of $9,600 per second. If you are a typical family of four, your share of the national debt is $73,000. Are you bankrupt yet? Perhaps not, but you will be.

The passage of the 1974 Congressional Budget and Impoundment Control Act was to wreak equally great devastation on the power of the presidency. For a person to be an effective leader amongst opposing factions, the leader must have the ability to reward and/or the ability to punish those

---

35. Lest the reader err in judging the author's political party preference, let me hasten to assure you the author holds both political parties in equally low regard. After all, are not their members the very people who have stolen our democracy?

whom the leader leads. Prior to the 1974 Congressional
Budget and Impoundment Control Act, the president could
reward a member of Congress with say, a dam, by not
impounding the appropriation. The president could also punish by impounding the appropriation. After the passage of the
1974 act, what influence, what pressure, what arm twisting
can the president bring to bear on Congress? Virtually none.
Congress can vote its own rewards and the president has to
spend the money as voted. What is the incentive for Congress
to cooperate with the president? The Congress can pork bar-
rel itself into hog heaven without the assistance of the president and, more important, without the president's being able
to stop it. With the passage of the 1974 Congressional Budget
and Impoundment Control Act, the president was stripped of
his levers of power over Congress. The president was stripped
of his powers and therefore his ability to fulfill his role in the
delicate system of checks and balances.

Whenever there is a presidential election, it is actually
humorous to watch the presidential candidates of both
parties scurrying from state to state pontificating on how their
programs will solve the problems of America. They solemnly
state to their cheering supporters how they will cure what ails
us. Their campaign promises always turn out to have the
same effect as the honking of a gaggle of geese, for the truth
is, Congress will determine what will happen. We have heard
these great promises before, and they never come true.
Prediction: Our government will continue to be grossly inefficient no matter who is president, even if we could elect George
Washington, Thomas Jefferson, or H. Ross Perot, because *the
office of president no longer has the power to direct the
nation*. Congress will force whoever is president to compromise whatever plan he may have to the point of utter stupidity. The office of president has been stripped of control over the
budget, and therefore control over domestic policy. As we will

discover shortly, the power of the president to conduct foreign policy has been greatly impeded. If control of domestic policy has been removed and severe limitations placed on foreign policy, what policy remains in the control of the president? What else is there? Very little. The president is expected to do a job for which he no longer has the tools. Anyone running for president today is an overambitious fool begging to be made a buffoon on the stage of history. As long as Congress retains its stolen powers, our problems will continue to increase, and the national debt will continue to grow.

2. War Powers Act of 1973

We already have learned that neither dictators nor democratic institutions voluntarily relinquish power. They will only yield to force or, in some circumstances, to a credible threat of the prompt use of overwhelming force.

For a president to effectively deal with a dictator, the dictator must have the understanding that the president has the ability to efficiently and promptly apply overwhelming force.

If a dictator has the understanding that the president cannot apply overwhelming force promptly without first consulting Congress prior to acting, then the dictator can be assured that within a body of 535 people there will be a wide range of conflicting opinions over how best to proceed in any given situation. The dictator also knows that for a consensus to gel amongst 535 legislators there will be debate, vacillation, and most important, delay.

If the dictator knows the above (and he does by observing the process when we deal with a previous case) then it is always in the best interest of the dictator to ignore the advice of a U.S. president, laugh at the president's threats, and thumb his nose at the inevitable first course of action, which is invariably sanctions. The sanctions are recommended by a legislature that has absolutely nothing politically to gain from a presidential foreign policy victory, but would suffer from having voted for a prompt invasion that resulted in casualties.

Insofar as saying no to the president of the United States always results in the dictator's remaining the dictator for the near term, then it is always in the dictator's best interest to say no to the president of the United States of America.

That is why a mediocre foreign policy consistently applied by one person with the power of prompt and sustained action is far superior to 535 legislators' ostensibly seeking a perfect foreign policy slowly.

That is why we have repeated failures in foreign policy when attempting to negotiate with dictators, as in Somalia, Bosnia, Haiti, Iraq, North Korea, Libya, Panama, Grenada. In the future the list will continue to grow. We are forced to launch a military invasion if a change is to be made. The passage of the War Powers Act of 1973 has caused the United States of America to have to invade, and thereby risk the loss of American soldiers lives, in order to effect changes in dictatorships. With the relative military power of the United States as compared to the dictatorship, in many cases, the United States should be able to cause change without resorting to invasion.

3. The Campaign Reform Act of 1974

Let us analyze what the members of Congress' catering to the special interests in order to receive campaign contributions (bribes) has done to the general interest. The causes that would result in the Campaign Reform Act of 1974 were already beginning to surface in 1973. Congress slashed NASA's budget from its 1965 level of $5.1 billion to $3.1 billion in 1973, the year of the Watergate scandal. Of course NASA, being a governmental agency, cannot bribe Congress. Additionally the results of any given year's budget allocation to NASA take years to come to fruition. As we have learned, the members of Congress are primarily concerned with being re-elected and have very little inclination to spend money on long-term projects when the next election is never more than two years away. It is in the members of Congress' best interest as they perceive it to spend our money on favors to the special interests that result in immediate campaign donations (bribes) rather than long-term projects that may take a decade or more to come to fruition. This is an important point. We will see this over and over again in Congress' actions. The members of Congress underfund, or do not fund at all, long-term projects. The supercollider is a perfect example.

In the case of NASA in 1973, the unexpected budget cut sent NASA into a frenzy. Projects had to be scaled back and droves of scientists and technicians had to be let go. Morale was severely damaged, as it continues to be to this day. One of the most dramatic effects was on a program that was then in the design stage—the space shuttle. Because of the budget cutback, the shuttle had to be redesigned to cost much less. In the original plan, the giant rocket-booster casings were to be cast in one solid piece. Because of the budget cutback, a cheaper design had to be found for the rocket-booster casings. The cheaper way was to make the rocket-booster casings in three sections joined by a rubber "O" ring. When the *Challenger* shuttle was launched in cold temperatures, the rubber "O" ring failed, causing the shuttle to blow up. The result was the death of the entire crew and additional delays in America's space program. Without the spending cut, the space shuttle would have gone into orbit. Although it may not be possible to find Congress guilty in a court of law, Congress is morally guilty of murdering the crew of the space shuttle *Challenger.*

Congress is also guilty of underfunding America's space program, which results in NASA's inability to retain qualified personnel, cost overruns (actually they are not cost overruns, as NASA does not believe it can do what Congress asks it to do with the money provided), and delays. I have watched America's space program go from a symbol of pride and accomplishment in the 1960s to one of failure and bungling in the 1970s and 1980s because of Congress' lack of funding. When the members of Congress are asked why they do not fund space programs at appropriate levels, the members respond that there is no constituency for the space program. As we know now from our new understanding of how Congress works, this means that there is no one to bribe them to do what is right—to do what the people want. This is why, if Americans ever reach the moon again, we will be greeted by Japanese scientists living and working there. Whether you are for or against the space program, the worst possible thing is to fund it in a way that blows it up.

The stupidity continues with the latest fiasco of NASA, the Hubble Telescope. Congress formed a committee to investigate this latest failure. After the bluster and posturing was over, the report blamed the manufacturer for not adequately testing the telescope. The reality, however, is to be found in an article in the September 1990 issue of *Scientific American*. C. Robert O'Dell, an astronomer at Rice University and the Hubble working group's chairman, is quoted as saying: "...the presumption was we were making the mirrors right.... [I was] continuously aware of the fact that we were being forced to make decisions on the basis of budget, and that meant cutting cost corners. The system forced even honest people to identify optimistically low prices" and then stick to them, because congressional appropriations committees were constantly charging that the telescope was costing too much. The failure of the Hubble is not one of science but rather one of funding by Congress. Congress harassed the management of the project with financial concerns and underfunded the project. The disaster

of the Hubble Telescope is clearly to be laid at the feet of
Congress. It also once again demonstrates very clearly
Congress' inability to adequately fund, and thereby insure
proper management of long-term projects.

Congress neglects and underfunds long-term projects
because the benefits of spending our money on long-term
projects will not be realized, by definition, for many years.
Congress faces an election within two years. Long-term projects will show no tangible results within two years. Therefore, they can be of no help in assisting the member of
Congress to win the next election. It is in the member of
Congress' best interest as he or she perceives it to spend the
public's money in a way that helps the member win the next
election. Therefore, members of Congress' best interest is
served by cutting the funding to long-term projects. The
money cut from the long-term projects can then be spent on a
favor to a special interest. The special interest group will
make a contribution to the supportive members of Congress'
campaign fund (a bribe). The long-term project is more likely
to be in the general interest. The reader will remember that
we have already learned in an earlier chapter that modern
humankind's greatest advantage over other creatures is the
ability to think in the future and plan. Upon successful completion of the plan at 5, 10, 15 years in the future, reality at
that time will be what we planned it would be. We can easily
see that this successful carrying out of a long-term plan for a
better future results in progress. Progress, by definition, is an
improvement in conditions. Hence it is the resolution of problems. Long-term planning is therefore an advanced form of
problem solving. Long-term projects are government's best
way of effecting progress or solving problems in a society,
whether it be a space shuttle program or a long-term project
to address educational deficiencies. The toughest problems
that a complex, modern society faces are by definition of a

large size and such severity that only long-term projects can even hope to address them properly.

Therefore, the fact is that Congress has traded away the people's right to have the people's government solve the people's deepest and most severe problems by successful long-term projects. In turn that means that our deepest and most severe problems will continue to remain unsolved and will continue to trouble us, such as the declining quality of education, increasing crime, and budget deficits. It becomes rather easy to predict that as long as Congress operates in its current mode, our deepest problems will not be solved. If we look back at Congress' inability to adequately fund (and thereby its practically assuring disaster for) all long-term projects, we see repeated failures since 1973. Remember how the 1973 Arab oil embargo brought the nation to the conclusion that we needed to be energy independent? It is now 1995. It is 22 years later. Almost an entire generation later. Today the United States of America imports more oil from overseas than in 1973. Needless to say that is a severely failed long-term project that would solve a very important problem. Needless to say, in the future we will suffer horribly for Congress' lack of solving the problem while it was still solvable.

However, in pre-Watergate days a president (Kennedy) who was relatively weak vis-à-vis Congress could launch a successful long-term project, namely the American program to land people on the moon. The goal of the moon-landing program, as stated by President Kennedy, was to land an American on the moon by the end of the decade. The first American landed on the moon on July 20, 1969, approximately six months ahead of schedule. However, with the members in the post-Watergate Congress having a natural tendency to underfund long-term projects, that same project could not be successfully accomplished today. It would end up like the shuttle.

Therefore, the members of Congress have traded away the ability to solve our most difficult problems—energy, the environment, education, toxic waste, the revitalization of American industry—which would all take long-term projects, in exchange for individual members of Congress' ability to be re-elected to Congress. The fiasco of the supercollider is a perfect example.

The supercollider was to be the greatest scientific project of the end of the 20th century. Sub-atomic particles were to be smashed together, which scientists hoped would reveal what the fundamental structure underlying all of matter actually is. The heat generated by the collision of sub-atomic particles would have brought us closer to simulating the conditions of the Big Bang than any previous method. Perhaps it would have enabled us to understand what occurred at the moment of the creation of the universe and allowed us to gain insight into what occurred prior to that. Who knows? Since the supercollider was canceled perhaps we will never know.

The $11 billion project would have cost far less had it been built at the Fermilab in Illinois where a particle accelerator already in place could have accelerated the particles and then injected them into the 54-mile tunnel in the ground. Why was it decided to build the supercollider in Texas? The real answer is probably because Speaker of the House Jim Wright and President George Bush were both from Texas. However, after Jim Wright and George Bush lost their jobs, the supercollider was canceled and three billion dollars, including cancellation costs, had been wasted, with nothing to show for it. Absolutely nothing. It was alleged that the supercollider was canceled because it cost too much. The only way the corrupt and decadent Congress would approve the supercollider was to build it inefficiently, so that it did cost too much. Then three billion was spent on it. Then it was canceled because it cost too much. All that was accomplished was that three billion of our dollars were wasted. Pretty efficient government we have! All long-term projects of our government are destined for failure. For Congress to approve long-term projects, they must be built inefficiently, so they cost too much, and then be canceled because they cost too much. Keep your eye on the space station. It will no doubt be next.

When the members of Congress sell our democracy to a special interest, they in a real sense sell our right to a better future. Our better future does not wind their clocks. Therefore, Congress has subverted the original purpose of Congress, which is to act in the people's best interest. Congress now acts in the best interests of the individual members of Congress and the special interests. As we have previously learned, the surest sign of gross decadence in an institution is when the institution's goals are supplanted by the goals of the individual members of the institution. Therefore, it is apparent that Congress is an extremely decadent institution.

It follows that an institution as decadent as Congress has become is also extremely inefficient in achieving its expected goals, which are to solve the people's problems and create a better tomorrow. Congress has taken the power that the people have given it and perverted it for the purposes of re-election. This perversion of power results in a very efficient re-election rate for members of Congress. However, the gross inefficiency in doing the people's business violates the fundamental law of the Survival of the Efficient. Therefore, under our current system of government, with no changes, it becomes easy to predict that the United States will succumb to the more efficient societies, such as Japan, Germany, and South Korea. The more efficient societies are able to successfully implement long-term projects that will bring solutions to their current problems and better tomorrows to their societies. The United States of America will not solve its current problems, and its tomorrows will be full of pain and suffering for the people.

The Great Sugar Rip-Off

All of these negative effects come from the members of Congress' neglect to do what is in the best interest of the people. The abuses of the public trust by Congress become far, far worse when Congress shifts from simple neglect and dereliction to active intervention on behalf of the special interests. The examples from which I have to choose could easily fill this book. I will only present a few egregious examples for the sake of brevity. Let us examine first the Great Sugar Rip-off. The 1994 world market price for sugar was eleven cents per pound. This makes sugar one of the cheapest processed commodities in the world. Only air and water come to mind as cheaper substances. Sugar cane is easily grown in tropical countries even on poor soil. In third-world countries like Jamaica and the Philippines, the time of the sugar cane harvest brings the only paid employment that hundreds of thousands of impoverished people will have the whole year: a few pennies a day for a lot of back-breaking labor. Therefore, sugar is not only typically abundant on the world market, but much of it is even destroyed by the third-world governments for lack of a buyer. That is the world sugar situation, but that is not the sugar situation in the United States.

In the United States, sugar is grown as sugar cane primarily in Florida, Hawaii, Louisiana, and Texas, and as sugar beets on poor farming land in such states as California, Idaho, Minnesota, Montana, Nebraska, North Dakota, and Wyoming. To make sugar beets grow on marginal land, precious ground water must be tapped and expensive chemical fertilizers must be used—which, incidentally, leach through the soil and contaminate the ground water. To force high yields from the poor soils, the ecosystem is further stressed with pesticides. Large quantities of petroleum and electricity are consumed to pump the water to the fields and operate the machinery to cultivate and harvest the sugar. It is expensive to grow sugar in this manner. The 10,000 sugar growers in this country cannot compete with sugar at 11 cents per pound. They must charge around 22 cents per pound. However, at 22 cents per pound, no one in his right mind would buy sugar when all he wanted is available for 11 cents per pound. So who buys this expensive sugar? The American people are forced to by Congress. Congress has placed quotas on the amount of sugar that can enter this country, to protect the sugar growers' special interest. Congress also sets the price that must be paid for domestic sugar to ensure profits to the 10,000 sugar growers. What is the bill that Congress hands the American people every year for sugar? A whopping $3 billion, by the time all the mark-ups of middlemen, soft drink companies, refiners, etc., are tacked on. Thanks to the members of Congress for making 10,000 sugar growers millionaires and handing us the bill. Think of this the next time you spend 75 cents in a pop machine for a couple of pennies worth of water, sugar, and flavorings on the world market. Congress' excuse for its behavior is that democracies are not efficient, as if it were the Founding Fathers who are responsible for their theft of our government.

If the foregoing is not preposterous enough, it becomes more amazing when we see what Congress receives in return for sticking us with an unnecessary $3 billion bill. Over the last decade the sugar lobby has contributed to congressional campaigns (bribed) a paltry total of $60,000! Congress over ten years has forced the American people to spend $30 billion for sugar in return for $60,000 in bribes. Does the reader recall the author stating that Congress is worse than prostitutes, because at least prostitutes sell what is theirs? We can amend that statement to read *cheap* prostitutes.

Why does Congress force us to spend $3 billion a year with special interests in return for a measly $60,000 a year in bribes? Because the highly organized sugar lobby made up of

10,000 millionaires will pay for the campaign costs to unseat the incumbent members of Congress if those incumbents do not deliver on the sugar quota and sugar price. I saw on television part of the debate in Congress over the sugar bill. The member of Congress who was the main proponent of high sugar prices stated that the sugar bill was "all about jobs, jobs, jobs." Whose jobs? Certainly not the handful of low-paid farm workers needed to operate a modern, machine-intensive agribusiness. The jobs he was referring to were the jobs of 10,000 millionaires and the members of Congress.

As an interesting aside to the Great Sugar Rip-off, let us perform an Einsteinian Thought Experiment. Let us view the situation from the perspective of a person from a third-world country like Jamaica or the Philippines. We look around us at the grinding poverty, starvation, and rampant poor health. We turn our gaze to the Great United States of America, the richest country in the world, where many of the major health problems are caused by overeating. A country that prides itself on leading the free world and helping less fortunate nations. A country that prides itself on being for free trade. However, the reality is that the fat Americans will not buy our three-cent-per-pound sugar, yet they expect us to import their expensive manufactured goods for which we have no way of paying. The rich Americans are selfish and only act in their own self-interest. When we show the slightest indignation at this treatment, the Americans think we are ungrateful.

Let us return to our American selves. The damage caused by programs like the Great Sugar Rip-off extend far beyond the money involved. The next time there is a vote in the United Nations in which we are opposed by a large number of third-world nations, perhaps we as Americans will more clearly understand why. Most Americans believe that the third-world countries oppose us because they are ungrateful and misunderstand us. The reality is more usually that they understand us very well.

In addition, even more damage is done by the Great Sugar Rip-Off in the state where the largest sugar crop is grown, Florida. In Florida, there is a large aquifer that, in normal times, flows southward from central Florida into Everglades National Park. The great demand for water to grow the unneeded sugar crop in central Florida has slowed the water entering the Everglades to a trickle. The water that does enter the Everglades is heavily contaminated by pesticides. The Everglades are in severe drought,[36] and if nothing is changed soon, the Everglades will be permanently lost as a habitable ecosystem.

Moreover, to increase profits for the sugar grower in Florida, the sugar cane is not even harvested by American workers. Jamaicans are flown in who, through special laws, are paid below minimum wage. More bad news is that in the last few years a particularly violent gang of drug dealers from Jamaica, known as the Jamaican Posse, has been expanding its operation into central Florida.

Furthermore, the sugar made from sugar cane in this country is not even of the highest quality. The highest quality is made in Fiji from unburnt cane. We burn our fields prior to harvest. The Fijian sugar is bought by Japan and other countries. We, the citizens, do not even receive the highest quality, although we pay the highest price.

One further point—an ethnocentric American may believe that despite the gross inequities caused by the Great Sugar Rip-Off, at least we keep the money in our own country. The truth, however, is that we end up giving the third-world countries foreign aid, which adds to our deficits, attempts to repair some of the damage done by our closed markets, and often has great difficulty finding its way out of the offices of corrupt third-world leaders.

---

36. As I write this, the Everglades, which used to be regarded (incorrectly) as a swamp, has just caught on fire.

Do things seem impossibly screwed up? Does America's way of doing things seem to be wasteful, inefficient, and counterproductive? They only make sense if you are a member of Congress desperate for re-election.

Additional Atrocities

The Dairy Industry also enjoys an unusually favorable position outside of the buffeting of the law of supply and demand. In this arrangement Congress sets an artificially high price on milk as if it were in high demand with a low supply. The reality is that it is in abundant supply. Such abundant supply that Congress buys, in the name of the people, hundreds of millions of dollars per year of dairy products that we do not want. We buy what we want from the stores, but the government buys us hundreds of millions of dollars more. It places these dairy products in warehouses in the form of cheese and powdered milk. Then, unbelievably, we pay many more millions per year in warehouse costs to store it.

I once saw on television a retiring U.S. senator from a dairy state bragging that in his last election, he had only spent $12 on his successful re-election campaign. Right, senator. Twelve dollars of your money and hundreds of millions of our money.

How can the relatively few members of Congress from the dairy states induce Congress to pass legislation so beneficial to them and harmful to the general interest? Because the dairy member of Congress has a deal with the sugar member of Congress. If the sugar member of Congress will vote for the dairy bill, then the dairy member of Congress will vote for the sugar bill. In fact, all the members of Congress from farm states vote for one another's farm bills. Together they pass what has become known as the Farm Bill. The Farm Bill provides special protections, as we have seen in sugar and milk, to a wide range of agricultural products, from peanuts to tobacco. The producers of these farm products have banded together to create the farm lobby. The farm lobby, composed of all the special interests that derive income from the Farm Bill, has so much money at its disposal that no farm-state senator or representative will stand up against it. For if the member of Congress did vote against the Farm Bill, in the very next election the member of Congress would be running against an extremely well-financed opponent instead of being guaranteed re-election like the senator who spent only $12. Does the reader remember the decadent Emperor Caligula who appointed his horse to the Senate of Rome? In effect, we have a dairy cow in our Senate.

The people of the United States of America are stuck with an unwise and inefficient farm program thanks to the corruption of Congress. It clearly appears that if any interest, no matter how opposed to the general interest, can either bribe a sufficient number of members of Congress or merely refrain from making the members of Congress' re-elections difficult, then Congress will reward that interest with unbelievable quantities of our money.

The stupidity of it all becomes even clearer when one realizes that not even the long-term interest of the farmer is being served. In America's present system of agriculture, based upon stressing the land to produce ever higher yields, we will inevitably witness the erosion of our topsoil and the poisoning of our ground water. One should realize that America has been farming in our agricultural heartland for only a little over 100 years, and already over half of our topsoil has been blown and washed away. In the few short decades of intensive pesticide, insecticide, and fertilizer use, ground water is beginning to become chemically polluted. What will the ground water be like at this rate in 30 years, 50 years, or 100 years? It is easy to see that in 100 years our ground water will be poisonous. But it will not matter because there will not be any topsoil to put it on. The topsoil will have eroded away by then.

The United States of America will have experienced many years of famine by then, under our present system of agriculture. If you thought the oil embargo was no fun, wait until we do not have enough food and need to buy it overseas. If the United States of America does not change its method of agricultural production, America will unquestionably collapse within 100 years from lack of food. Egyptian society was over 3,000 years old when Christ was born. The United States of America will not make it to 300, thanks to Congress.

On television, I once saw a picture of excited members of Congress congratulating one another at the passage of the Farm Bill. I shook my head and realized they had no idea at all what they were doing because the all-consuming desire to be re-elected had reduced all other considerations to insignificance. They had no idea as they were rejoicing that the Farm Bill they had just passed was part of an incremental death warrant for the United States of America.

It does not take a genius to see that what is in the farmers', and in America's, best interest is the introduction of a new system of agriculture based upon infinitely sustainable yields. To destroy the productivity of our farmland over the next 50 to 100 years is stupid. How long do we need our land to be productive? If we want the United States of America not to starve at some time in the future, then we need our land to produce our food until the sun goes out in 6 billion years. In other words, we need to develop and implement a new system of infinitely sustainable agriculture that closely links supply with demand and provides the farmer with stability, or we will end up like Haiti. To accomplish this will take a long-term project. We have already learned how ineffective Congress is at long-term projects.

Therefore, the problems caused by the members of Congress' stealing our democracy and selling it to the special interests go far beyond the free spending of the people's money in return for re-election, but actually distort the process of good government to the point of endangering the continued survival of our society.

Atrocities in Other Areas

Congress sells much more than the people's right to an intelligent and reasonable agricultural policy. Wherever government spends money, Congress has fertile ground to work its bribery scam. Does the reader recall during the mid-1980s the repeated votes in Congress on the MX missile? Here was a program that would have cost tens of billions of dollars over an extended period of time to replace our ageing intercontinental ballistic missiles with new, more accurate, and improved missiles. I can understand the reasoning if Congress voted not to buy the MX missile and save the tax-payers money. I can also understand the reasoning if Congress voted to buy the MX missile and provide the U.S. with additional security. However, I cannot understand the reasoning for spending the money for the MX and then holding votes every six months to potentially kill the program. Congress spends billions and billions to fund the program then risks killing it, so that the taxpayer would receive neither the savings from not buying the MX, nor the protection afforded from buying the MX. This is the worst possible method of buying weapons—or anything, for that matter. Why did Congress choose this worst of all possible methods? Congress needed a method to extort bribes from the contractor on a repetitive basis. The leaders in Congress came up with the idea of holding a series of votes on the MX missile so that the contractor and sub-contractors would have to come scurrying to Washington with briefcases full of money to bribe members of Congress to ensure passage of the MX at each vote.

Some defense contractors became so accustomed to bribing members of Congress that they actually attempted to include those bribes as tax-deductible costs of doing business with the government. However, do not think for a minute that the defense contractors do not raise their prices to cover the congressional bribes. They do. Therefore, the Congress is directly responsible for a significant portion of unnecessary defense spending.

By forcing the defense contractors to become involved in bribery, Congress has politicized the military procurement function. This causes enormous unnecessary costs to military spending programs. A further example is the B-1 bomber program.

In 1977, President Jimmy Carter made the decision not to purchase the B-1 bomber. Under President Reagan the program was revived and approved. Why did Congress approve the B-1? In the intervening years, North American Rockwell, the main contractor for the B-1, realized that it needed more congressional support to get the B-1 passed. It took the following incredible step to ensure passage. While under normal circumstances the aerospace industry is efficiently concentrated on the West Coast, North American Rockwell farmed out a sufficient number of the hundreds of thousands of parts that it takes to make a sophisticated, high-tech bomber so that, unbelievably, parts came from 37 different states. Can you imagine the enormous additional cost to coordinate, ensure quality control, and ensure on-time delivery? The additional and unnecessary expense to produce the B-1 in this manner was truly staggering. I invite the reader to imagine what the additional cost and frustration would be if the reader merely redecorated his own house with parts coming from 37 states to be assembled in Southern California. Do you think you would finish on time, on budget? Do you think all the wood grains and textiles would match? Redecorating a house is a piece of cake compared to building a sophisticated, high-tech bomber. Needless to say, the B-1 has been plagued by high cost ($300 million per plane) and unreliable performance. The B-1 was grounded during the Persian Gulf War. Therefore, the aged B-52, designed in 1948, was deployed against Iraq, and Congress wasted another $30 billion of our money.

Now isn't that special? Congress forces the defense contractors to build weapons systems inefficiently or Congress will not buy them. Then, when we need them in time of war, the weapons systems are too inefficient to be deployed. Do things seem screwed up? Does Congress' way of purchasing military hardware make no sense? It only makes sense if you are a member of Congress desperate for re-election.

Hence, Congress has distorted defense purchasing in the same way Congress distorts almost everything else that comes before it. When members of Congress meet an issue, they first ask of the issue, "How can this help or hurt my re-election?" Not, "How can I resolve this issue in the best interests of the people of the United States?" As Congressman Barney Frank, a Democrat from Massachusetts, has stated, "Do campaign contributions get traded for specific votes on specific legislation? Of course, they do." By this statement, a member of Congress openly admits to the bribery, corruption, and decadence in the Congress of the United States of America.

Still More Atrocities

It is clear from the foregoing examples that Congress perverts and distorts the legislative process in order to be re-elected. These examples are merely a small sample of Congress' abuse of the public trust. A detailed analysis of all of Congress' scams would fill many books this size. We have not even discussed a whole section of legislation called "private bills." Private bills are distinct from public laws, which apply to everyone. Private bills grant favors to individuals. An FBI agent posed as a Middle Eastern sheik in order to bribe members of Congress in return for citizenship, in the operation known as "Abscam." The citizenship would have been granted in a private bill. Do you realize that the two Congressmen convicted of the federal felony of selling their influence in the FBI Abscam affair continue to receive federal pensions of $50,000 to $60,000 per year as a reward for their fine service to their country? These people have made themselves untouchable and supreme. In a private bill, one member of Congress obtained an exemption from federal taxation for what was called a "family farm." The "family farm" turned out to be a 190,000-acre agribusiness in Montana. The abuses of private bills are outrageous, but I will not continue with them because presumably the reader is already outraged, or should be.

We also do not have the space to discuss the enormous waste and fraud in our social programs. The author has no special knowledge about them, and what the author knows would only be a repetition of what is already contained in the public record. The rampant abuses in these programs add up to hundreds of billions of dollars.

The author also will not delve into the sexual misconduct of Congress. As a famous New York madame once said, she thought she knew men until members of Congress became her clientele. She reported their sexual appetites as being eclectic and insatiable. Evidently Lord Acton was even wiser than we first thought when he said, "Power tends to corrupt and absolute power corrupts absolutely." Hence, we can understand members of Congress chasing strippers through tidal pools at dawn, members of Congress receiving oral sex from female lobbyists in the coat rooms of Washington restaurants, members of Congress' apartments being used as homosexual houses of prostitution, and the underage boy and girl pages of the House and Senate being used as both hetero- and homosexual sex slaves. Imagine the high hopes and pride felt by the proud parents of the fifteen-year-old boy when he was chosen to be a congressional page. Imagine the sadness and disgust felt by the parents when their son told them he lost his virginity to a homosexual member of Congress. Quite some statesmen and gentlemen, our members of Congress are!

In any normal institution, the adult pederast would have been thrown out and criminal charges filed. What happened in our wonderful Congress? Of course, the member of Congress still holds his seat (and presumably anyone else's seat he can get hold of). A few years ago, Congress actually investigated the "alleged" moral misconduct of its members. The results of a corrupt institution investigating itself for corruption were as one would expect. It was like reading an autobiography of Adolf Hitler. Both Congress and Adolf Hitler come off looking pretty good. It should be unnecessary to say (though I will say it anyway) that a corrupt institution cannot honestly investigate itself for corruption. However, as we have learned, Congress will not allow itself to be investigated by anyone else. I wonder why? Can the reader guess why?

Another example of the decadence of Congress is the abomination of the Judge Clarence Thomas confirmation hearings. Whether you were for or against Judge Thomas, those hearings were an insult to the American people as well as to everyone involved. We Americans were made eye-witnesses to how cheap, shabby, low, decadent, and inefficient the Senate of the United States is and how it can corrupt anything that comes under its control.

The Senate of the United States of America is so decadent that it is well beyond reforming itself. The senators are so used to corruption and stupidity and inefficiency that they can no longer view reality for what it is. Reality is that Congress is the problem. I understand some senators are making noises that the Senate should have more control over the selection of Supreme Court nominees. They believe that that will fix the problem. As we have already learned, Congress has removed the original system of checks upon itself by the Supreme Court, the president, the media, and the people. Now the Senate wants additional control over the

Supreme Court, which will further increase the already excessive power of Congress. I told you they are too corrupt and decadent to see reality for what it is. The Senate thinks it is a good idea to increase the power of an institution that is corrupt, is not needed, and should not even exist. It is demonstrably true that the Senate of the United States of America cannot even run a confirmation hearing in an appropriate, tasteful, and efficient manner. How, then, can members of Congress be entrusted with our future? They embarrass us in the eyes of the world. Can they be trusted to act in an efficient, businesslike, cohesive, and cooperative manner to plan our best possible future? Can they be trusted to ensure the long-term success of the plan? We need a plan for this country because the future that lies in wait for us down the path we are traveling is bitter and painful. The Japanese will have a very bright and happy future. The Japanese quality of life is continuing to rise.[37] Why cannot we have a future at least as good as theirs? Do we not share the same planet, and are we not therefore subject to the same external factors: oil-price hikes, international commercial competition, wars, etc? If the external factors are the same for the Japanese as for us, then the cause of our impending decline must be internal. The problem is amongst us. The government of the United States is that institution in our society which, as stated in the Preamble to the Constitution, is designed to promote the general welfare. Our government is charged with promoting the general welfare, but in fact our government is actively causing our demise by the budget deficits that Congress enacts every year. It is as if we were passengers in a car headed for a

---

37. As I write this, the Japanese economy is contracting and ours is expanding. This only reflects the short-term business cycle and is indicative of the Japanese's having saturated their available markets. In that sense, the Japanese contraction is almost a sign of victory because it demonstrates that they have achieved saturation in all currently available markets.

brick wall and the driver, instead of braking and changing course, stepped on the gas harder and harder. As we all must realize by now, America needs a comprehensive plan. Our government is so decadent that not only is it incapable of providing us with a good plan: it is incapable of providing us with any plan at all. Our governmental process, thanks to Congress, is so corrupt that if a plan were enacted, it could never be properly implemented. Congress is so corrupt that it does not even realize that America needs a plan. Congress is too busy playing power politics to honestly address the people's needs. Keep your eye on Congress, for it is so decadent that in the future it will do nothing but confirm what I have told you here.

The following example should be more than an ample demonstration of the decadence and blatant inability of the Congress of the United States to guide us into the future. In 1985 the United States became a debtor nation for the first time since 1914 because of the massive budget deficits that Congress so unwisely incurs. In December of 1985 the Congress of the United States passed the Gramm-Rudman-Hollings Act. This mandated congressional spending limits, which in turn would have caused the budget to be balanced by 1991. It should be redundant to inform the reader that in 1991 the national debt increased by $392 billion, and then by $404 billion in 1992. Having stolen from the president the right to spend our money, the Congress of the United States demonstrably has no ability to induce sacrifice in its members to uphold the very laws that Congress itself passes. Even when Congress itself passes a law against deficits, Congress itself cannot implement the law. I do not know of a greater example of decadence in an institution than this. The Congress of the United States cannot even follow the laws that Congress makes. Congress has no way, manner, or method of ever eliminating the deficit. It is far, far too decadent. Congress is like the sorcerer's apprentice who steals power from the sorcerer and, unable to control it, causes massive destruction. Congress has stolen the power to make the budget from the president and cannot control it and will therefore cause massive destruction. The Congress of the United States of America is out of control.

In rural Kentucky in 1991, many children were unable to attend school because their school districts could not afford to operate buses. The federal government must not have had any excess funds or this would not have been permitted to occur, right? Wrong. Are you ready for this? In 1991, Congress gave itself a 23 percent pay raise! While our children could not even afford to go to school, Congress rewarded itself for the great job of handling our affairs by giving itself a 23 percent pay raise. Incredible! My Chicago upbringing makes me want to call the members of Congress a string of vituperative expletives, but in deference to the sensibilities of the reader, I will merely refer to the members of Congress as crooks, for crooks they are.

The Killshot

From the seizure of power in the post-Watergate period, to the disastrous underfunding of the space shuttle and the Hubble Telescope, to the selling of our democracy to the special interest groups, to the absolute disregard of the general interest and wasteful spending of our hard-earned money, to politicizing our defense spending and thereby unnecessarily placing our country at risk, to its reprehensible personal behavior, Congress has made me angry and disgusted. As bad as all this is, the worst is yet to come. I ask the reader to remember what were proved to be the most important attributes of a government for the continued survival of a society. The Law of the Survival of the Efficient is being applied to our society just as it is to all things. With Congress as our most powerful and important institution, I ask the reader to predict what the future of America will be according to the Law of the Survival of the Efficient. I also ask the reader to recall the four important functions that a society requires to survive:

1) The ability of the government to *think in the future efficiently*.

2) The ability of the government to invent a *plan efficiently*.

3) An *efficient social organization* to implement the plan.

4) The ability of the people to *sacrifice* to carry out the plan *efficiently*.

I ask the reader to ask him or herself how well our government thinks in the future. My answer is that our government not only does not think in the future well, it does not think in the future at all. I ask the reader to ask him or herself how well our government plans for the future. My answer is the United States has no plan for the future. Does the reader know of a five-year plan? Ten-year plan? Twenty-year plan? No, because they do not exist. If we were to compare our society's ability to plan with that of the animals, we would rank below Cro-Magnon, below Neanderthal, below the lioness, because they all used planning. We would rank about even with the wildebeest, the stupid, "accept-whatever-happens-and-run-into-the-same-lion's-trap" wildebeest. As we have discovered, Congress cannot carry out long-term plans.

I ask the reader to ask him or herself whether we have the appropriate social structure to carry out plans. My answer is that Congress is incapable of either thinking in the future, planning, or sacrificing, and therefore America has an inappropriate social structure not only for carrying out plans but even for surviving in the modern world.

I ask the reader to ask him or herself if we have the necessary willingness to sacrifice needed to implement a plan.
My answer is that the people may still be able to sacrifice,
but that the crooks in Congress are so decadent that they will
not even sacrifice their jobs to improve America.

Congress clearly fails to provide us with any of the Four
Critical Abilities. Let us see how Congress rates in our three
tests for decadence. In the first test, derived from the Black
Box Technique, we place the Black Box over the institution
and determine if the actual results of the institution are similar to or divergent from the expected results of the institution.
In the case of Congress, since there is widespread public discontent with the actual results of Congress, we can conclude
that the actual results of Congress are widely divergent from
the expected results of Congress. Second, we judge if the
resources (money and people) consumed by the institution are
small, moderate, or great compared to the expected result. In
the case of Congress, they have the largest budget (money) in
the world to address a society's problems; in addition, by making laws, they direct the actions of the entire U.S. government
(people). Therefore, we can conclude that Congress has abundant resources in both money and people. Therefore, with

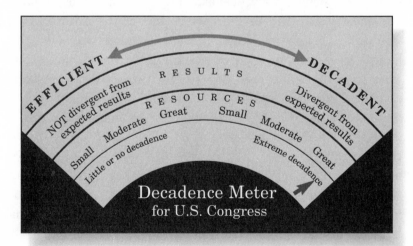

great resources but with widely divergent results between what is expected and what is delivered, the Congress of the United States is demonstrably the most decadent that test #1 can register.

Test #2 is to ask if the institution is capable of forgoing present benefits (sacrificing) for greater future benefits. With the massive budget deficits that Congress gives us every year, which will inescapably cause us great damage in the future, Congress shows absolutely *no* ability to make current sacrifices to achieve better tomorrows. Instead of a better tomorrow, Congress has set us on the path of destruction in the future. Therefore, test #2 shows Congress to be the most decadent that test #2 can register.

Test #3 for gross and extreme decadence is to see if the institution has the ability to induce its members to sacrifice their own goals for the achievement of the institution's goals? Should we ask representative Dan Rostenkowski? It is apparent from the theft of our democracy in the Campaign Reform Act of 1974 that members of Congress care more about their own re-election than about preserving the democracy of the people. Therefore, for runaway, galloping, gross, and extreme decadence, Congress is easily the most decadent that test #3 can register.

The Congress fails all three tests for decadence with the lowest possible scores. Congress has already failed to provide us with any of the Four Critical Abilities.

There we have it. Because of the decadence and inefficiency of our most powerful institution, Congress, the United States of America will collapse. We will not be able to meet the standard set by the Law of the Survival of the Efficient.

I invite the reader to join me in an Einsteinian Thought Experiment. Let us suppose that we exchange our Congress of the last twenty years for, let us say, a king or an emperor. In other words, let us imagine that a king has been the most powerful branch of our government since 1973, and that this single person, the king, acted in the identical way with the identical results as Congress has. Let us review a few of those actions: The theft of our democracy, the legalization of bribery, the setting up of an unfair election system, the stripping of the presidency of its traditional powers, the breaking of the system of checks and balances, the passage of the War Powers Act, the corrupt Farm Bill, underfunding long-term projects, the space shuttle, the politicization of the purchase of military equipment, the wasteful spending, the incredible budget deficits, the personal corruption, the bribery of the media, etc.

If the above acts had been the acts of a single person, a king, I believe that a clinical diagnosis of extreme mental illness (commonly referred to as "insanity") would be justified, not to mention the label "corrupt." At least it would be in my and the Black Box's clinic. In addition, we have already learned that since the 1930s our government has been acting unconstitutionally, and therefore illegally, by ignoring the 10th Amendment. Therefore, could not someone acquainted with these two facts make the valid statement: "Apparently, we are being governed by a government that is not only illegal, but also insane!" If we had been ruled by a king, would we have revolted by now? Is not the very purpose of a democracy to give us a government better than a monarchy? And have not the results been much worse? Our government is dysfunctional, even by comparison to that of an insane monarch.

CHAPTER ELEVEN

Step No. 2: Predict the Real Future

The Present to 2020

TO GIVE US AN IDEA OF THE DIFFICULTIES encountered in having a prediction for the future accepted by a contemporary audience, let us perform an Einsteinian Thought Experiment. Let us pretend that it is 1955, and that we will accurately predict what society will be like 35 years into the future, 1990, and then note what the 1955 society's reaction to the prediction probably would have been.

In 1955, President Eisenhower was in office. America was the wealthiest and most powerful country in the world. We had survived World War II without damage to our infrastructure. The economy was growing steadily. Americans were rich, proud, and confident. Two modern inventions were coming into widespread use: home air-conditioning and TV. Although the TV's were small and in black and white, Americans enjoyed such programs and performers as Ozzie and Harriet, *I Love Lucy*, Sid Caesar, Milton Berle, Jackie Gleason, Ed Sullivan, Eddie Cantor, Groucho Marx, and Phil Silvers. Magazines and newspapers predicted new inventions were just around the corner, such as jet planes, satellite communication, and nuclear power. We could not wait for the wonderful future that was in store for us.

Now, let us say that we had written a book in 1955 that accurately predicted the reality of 1990. We would have predicted powerful personal computers the size of notebooks, that men had already walked on the moon, and phones in our cars. To be accurate, we also would have predicted that every year new records would be set in the numbers of murders; that our jails would be so full of criminals that judges would order their early release; that dangerous, mind-damaging drugs would be available on almost every street corner of every city; that our schools would produce an increasingly high percentage of functional illiterates; that the neighborhoods in our cities would be fought over by gangs of youths with automatic assault rifles for control of the drug trade; that in middle-class families wives would have to work to maintain the standard of living, leaving the children to be raised by day-care centers; that the flow and use of illicit drugs into the country could not be stopped even with the active intervention of the military; that corruption would be pervasive in formerly trusted institutions such as savings and loans, banks, Wall Street, and Congress; that the people would lose confidence in the government's ability to solve their problems; and that the people would view the future with a sense of impending doom.

How would have the citizens of 1955 reacted to such a prediction? With disbelief, rejection, and ridicule. If the citizens of 1955 had voted on whether they would like the future or not, how would they have voted? In my opinion, they would have voted overwhelmingly against the future in which we currently live. It would have shocked and horrified them. I doubt that one person would have voluntarily traded the society of 1955 for the society of 1990 even with the technological improvements. We accept it because it has happened slowly and we do not have any choice but to live in this society. Or do we? Let us proceed, applying the Black Box Technique to predict the real future.

Step No. 2: The Real Future

Our next step in applying the Seven Steps of the Black Box Technique to the United States of America is to predict the real future. As we have learned, we accomplish this by viewing the accurate present events as causes, and thinking what the effects will be. We will have just predicted the future. To go farther into the future, we view the effects that we have just created as causes and think what their effects will be, and on and on until we have predicted the future as far as need be. The principle of Newtonian Trends requires us to predict that current trends will continue into the future unless we have a preponderance of evidence for a clear cause that will alter the trend.

Now that we can understand the past and the present, it becomes painfully easy to predict the future. The principle of Newtonian Trends requires us to predict that the corruption and decadence of Congress will continue, because there is no detectable cause that will alter or modify the behavior of the United States Congress. Or is there? Does the Republican victory in the 1994 congressional elections, wherein the Republicans gained control of both the House and Senate for the first time since our democracy was stolen, signal a change that will restore the proper functioning of our democracy, or will the Republicans merely be the beneficiaries of the stolen powers of Congress, attempt to wallpaper over the profound corruption and decadence of Congress, and attempt to use the supreme powers of Congress to perpetuate a Republican dynasty? The Republicans, of course, would like us to believe that they are white knights on trusty chargers who will save our democracy and that the Democrats are the bad guys responsible for the corruption and decadence of Congress. Amongst other actions, in order for the Republicans to restore our democracy, they will have to return powers stolen from the executive branch. This means that members of Congress will have to give up powers that they currently have and voluntarily return them to the executive branch. However, as we have already learned, neither dictators nor democratic institutions voluntarily give up power. They must be forced to do so if a change is to be made. No force has been applied to the Republican members of Congress. Due to the two-party system in this country, they are merely the beneficiaries of the anger and frustration that translated into the force of the ballot box used by the citizens against the Democrats. Therefore, no force has been applied to the Republicans in Congress, and therefore, were the author to predict the future with the Republicans in charge, the author would predict that the Republicans, instead of fundamentally and permanently restoring democracy to America, will merely make a great show of modest, inconsequential, and insubstantial changes to the powers of Congress.

Further evidence that points to the conclusion that the Republicans will not be our white knights is the following logic. The Republicans will be inheriting the power in an institution that is demonstrably corrupt. The structure is already in place for special interests to bribe whoever sits in the seats of power in Congress through campaign contributions that give them a much better chance of re-election. Therefore, it is in the best self-interest of the individual members of the Republican party in Congress to continue selling our democracy to the special interests. Therefore, if substantive change in the way campaigns are financed is not accomplished promptly upon assuming control of Congress, then the Republicans will have placed themselves under a waterfall of cash. Thousands of smiling, friendly lobbyists, who will treat the Republicans with great deference and respect, will be pushing checks at them, checks that will promptly total into the millions. The longer the checks are accepted, the more and more difficult it will be to end the acceptance of them. Until finally, like the heroin junkie, the members of Congress can no longer say no. And like the heroin junkie, their morals sink lower and lower until the special interests once again steal our democracy. Therefore, the Republicans, promptly upon assuming power in January of 1995, needed to pass substantive legislation to eliminate the ability to accept campaign donations lest the members of Congress be subject to a very efficient and powerful cause of corruption. A demonstration of the effectiveness of the power of the causes of cor-

ruption in this country is the depth and breadth of the anger
and frustration of us, the voters, as exhibited in the last election. We, the voters, may not all have understood that the
causes of the corruption date from the Watergate period, but
a majority of the voters recognized that our government is
not working properly.[38] It took a majority of us American voters to force the Democrats out of power in our corrupt government. However, the structure of the corruption and the causes of the corruption remain in place. If the causes remain the
same, the effect (corruption) will remain the same. Therefore,
if the Republicans do not act rapidly to end the legalized
bribery, then they will in turn be corrupted. If the
Republicans have not ended the bribery of Congress by, say,
the summer of 1995, then it is highly doubtful that they will
ever end it. Furthermore, this means that the force that will
cause the restoration of our democracy has yet to be applied
to our government. Then if democracy is to be returned to
America, the voters will have to repeat their manifestation of
frustration and anger at the ballot box at least one more
time, and probably more.

However, the realistic possibility remains that the
Republican leaders in Congress are, in fact, true statesmen.
The author's definition of a statesman is one who sacrifices
personal and party interest and power for the benefit of the

---

38. It is interesting to note that the overwhelming 1994 vote by the electorate against the way our government works was accomplished without
the benefit of the media's informing the people of the theft of our government, as they had done at the turn of the century. On election night, it
was amusing to watch many in the media report, with what appeared to
be quizzical surprise, that the exit polls showed the American people
were angry and frustrated. It was as if they were reporting that an
unruly child was throwing a temper tantrum. When explanations for
the anger were offered, it was usually attributed to dissatisfaction with
President Clinton's policies. Would someone please call the media and
inform them that our democracy has been stolen, and that as long as
special interests are permitted to bribe members of Congress, it will
remain so?

nation as a whole. What does the Black Box tell us to do when there are two realistically possible futures? As we learned in *Step No. 2: Predict the Real Future*, from the example of the young man awaiting a possible call to military service faced with two realistically possible futures, we should predict both futures and apply the other steps to both. We have two realistically possible futures, so we will apply the Black Box Technique to both. The first future will predict the real future if the Republicans do not take the appropriate steps to restore our democracy; the second future will predict the real future if the Republican leaders in Congress are true statesmen.

FUTURE ONE

We have learned that neither dictators nor democratic institutions give up power without being forced. No such force has been applied to the Republicans in Congress. Then we can confidently predict the continued corruption and decadence of the United States Congress.

Continuing corruption will cause the Congress to continue to be responsive to special interests, which in turn will cause the Congress to continue the budget deficits. However, before we can appreciate the enormous devastation to be caused by the budget deficits, we must appreciate the enormous size of the budget deficits. Our annual budget deficit is larger than the entire economies (Gross Domestic Product) of all but seven countries in the entire world (the G-7 plus Russia). The amount of money that the United States government was forced to borrow to cover the 1992 increase in the national debt (over $400 billion) was more than all the goods and all the services consumed by all the people in one year in the individual countries of: Australia ($288 billion, '91), or Brazil ($404 billion, '91) or China ($413 billion GNP '89), or India ($328 billion, '92), or Mexico ($276 billion, '91). Our massive budget deficits force us to borrow every year amounts equivalent to the entire economies of all but the largest and most industrialized of nations. Which means that in 1992 the United States took on an additional burden of debt roughly equal to the entire 1989 economy of China, the most populous country in the world!

Money must be borrowed to pay for expenses that Congress so unwisely incurs on our behalf. The United States government must sell IOUs (U.S. Treasury Bonds, Notes, and Bills) every year to raise the money. The IOU is a promise to pay the debt back in U.S. dollars in the future. In addition, every year a certain amount of IOUs issued in previous years comes due. In addition, the ever-increasing interest on the ever-increasing debt must also be paid. Therefore, it is easy to see that the total amount of money needed to be borrowed every year is a generous portion of all the money available for investment not only in the United States, but also throughout the rest of the world, and that it is growing larger every year. This gigantic and ever-increasing amount of the world's money must be borrowed by the United States government. For if we miss a payment, there will be no more money lent, which will result in the following devastation. The United States government will not be able to pay its bills. Some of these bills pay for the military, some for welfare, some for education, etc. They will all be drastically reduced or stopped virtually overnight. The economy will experience a massive dislocation resulting in economic depression as millions dependent on the government for income—government workers, welfare recipients, the retired, the military—all experience a large loss of income. The effects will immediately be felt throughout the entire economy as massive amounts of purchasing power are withdrawn from the marketplace. This, in turn, will cause massive lay-offs in the general economy. Needless to say, foreigners holding American dollars will try to get rid of them, causing the dollar's value to plummet. That will cause the cost of foreign goods—cars, stereos, etc.—to skyrocket and become luxury items not to be afforded by a society being driven into deepening depression. However, we will still need to import many items upon which we are dependent, such as oil. With the declining purchasing power of the dollar, the cost of energy will increase rapidly, causing runaway inflation to further batter down the economy. If history serves as a pattern, the burning cities will only serve as exclamation points to the misery felt throughout the society.

The above is what will occur if the United States government defaults on its debt payments. That is why the United States government scours the Earth vacuuming the cash equivalents of entire economies into a hose that sucks it back to the United States and, via the congressional budget process, distributes it throughout the country. The budget deficits of the Congress force the United States government into behaving like a heroin addict in search of ever-increasing amounts of dope, but since the government has no money with which to buy it, the government must give an IOU. As with the heroin addict, the day must come when no further credit will be extended and our world comes crashing down. With continuing massive budget deficits, the United States can only enjoy these prosperous times until the United States budget consumes all the available money (capital) in the world and there is no more to be had.

However, before that time is reached we will have probably already fallen victim to the equally disastrous consequences brought about by the $100 to $150 billion per year trade deficit. The U.S. dollar is found in ever-increasing abundance in foreign hands. The increasing surplus of U.S. currency (money) in international circulation is caused by the trade deficit. Currency (money), like all commodities, follows the law of supply and demand. As the supply of U.S. dollars increases overseas while the demand does not, the U.S. dollar must necessarily fall in value against other currencies. The foreign entities holding the IOUs will not like that, because when their IOUs are redeemed in the future, they will receive less purchasing power than when they lent the money to the United States. Therefore, IOUs of the United States government will be a bad investment. However, as we have discovered, the United States government must continue to borrow the money. Therefore, to entice lenders, the U.S. government will be forced to make the IOUs a better investment. The United States government will have to offer higher interest rates on the IOUs (Treasury Bonds). In turn, when the United States government lends money domestically (through the Federal Reserve) to U.S. banks, it must then charge a higher rate of interest. Charging a higher rate of interest to the banks, in turn, means the banks will have to charge higher interest rates to both consumers and businesses. It will cost more money to borrow. Borrowing will slow down. The economy will slow down. The declining dollar coupled with the recessionary economy will cause foreign entities not to want to invest in any more U.S. debt. To make U.S. debt attractive, we must raise interest rates more. This cycle repeats itself until the United States government will be faced with three options: 1) Raise our taxes, which will be insufficient to pay back the money and will in turn cause depression and the lowering of our standard of living. 2) Declare bankruptcy, which will cause the dollar to become worthless and in turn cause the lowering of our standard of living. 3) Print massive amounts of money, which will cause unbelievable inflation and in turn cause the lowering of our standard of living. All three options result in a rapid and severe decline in America's standard of living. A rapid and severe decline in standard of living is, by definition, a depression. The magnitude of the depression will be at least as devastating as the one of the 1930s. However, the American people, accustomed to a much higher standard of living than they were before the depression of the 1930s, and because of the instant-gratification society, will be shocked, angry, and frustrated, and much less able to cope.

Therefore, the effects of the coming depression will seem far more severe to us than the depression of the 1930s seemed to that generation.

A classical economist might suggest that after the collapse of the American economy, the American dollar will be so little valued that American goods will be extremely cheap, and we will then revive ourselves by massive exporting. Under past circumstances that would have been true, but because of the cheap dollar and the predatory nature of contemporary international business, virtually all of American businesses worth owning will have been purchased by foreigners, and therefore foreigners will benefit from a cheap U.S. dollar, not America.

Next, after briefly avoiding default, the government of the United States must finally default. Borrowings cease. The first scenario previously discussed will follow, wherein the burning cities will serve as exclamation points to the misery felt by all.

Even though the Black Box Technique easily permits us to reliably predict the above, the remarkable thing is that no matter what plausible future scenarios are predicted, as long as they include continuing, massive budget deficits they all end in the same destruction of our society. Therefore, without a change, the destruction of our society can be easily predicted because of the decadence of our most powerful institution, the Congress of the United States of America. Can anyone think up a set of cause-and-effect relationships that 1) can pass the Truth-Meter test and 2) starts from our current position in the present, 3) includes continuing massive budget deficits, 4) continues the current behavior of Congress, and 5) does not result in our devastation? The author cannot think up even one. If the reader can think up a future that contains the above elements but which does *not* contain tremendous economic suffering on the part of us, the people, then the author would like to hear about it by fax or at the Internet website listed at the end of this book.

Only one scenario can pass the author's Truth-Meter that does not result in our destruction. If Congress were to reduce spending, which would eliminate the deficit as soon as practicable (certainly no longer than five years), the above scenario *might* be avoided. However, that would in turn require the efficient implementation of a long-term plan, which in turn means that 1) our government (Congress) would have to make an efficient plan, and 2) the Congress, being the most powerful branch of our government, would have to oversee an efficient implementation of the plan, 3) the Congress would have to induce its members to sacrifice, and 4) the people would have to be willing and able to sacrifice to contain the budget deficit and reduce the national debt. We have already learned that Congress, unmodified, has absolutely no ability to efficiently create laws, to implement plans efficiently, to induce sacrifice in its members, and in fact, will actually be responsible, because of budget deficits, for causing our devastation and suffering. Therefore, the Black Box easily permits us to confidently predict that an unmodified Congress will destroy us. Prior to 1973, the massive deficits would have been stopped by the president's use of the right of impoundment (line-item veto). Therefore, as long as Congress retains its stolen powers we will be on the path to destruction.

Additionally, I would like to personally thank the members of Congress not only for the budget deficits themselves, but also for placing the future well-being of our country in the hands of foreigners by making it necessary to borrow. What incredibly shrewd and wise statesmen and stateswomen we have leading the country. I do not know how we could ever survive without them. The greatest of Americans, Thomas Jefferson, had this to say about budget deficits.

"I place economy among the first and most important virtues, and public debt as the greatest of dangers to be feared. To preserve our independence, we must not let our

rulers load us with perpetual debt. If we run into such debts, we must be taxed in our meat and drink, in our necessities and in our comforts, in our labor and in our amusements. If we can prevent the government from wasting the labor of the people, under the pretense of caring for them, they will be happy."

Awesome. What Thomas Jefferson wrote 200 years ago applies to us as if it had been written this morning. I wish he were here today.

Farther into the Future

The hopeless and unending economic depression in which we will find ourselves will in turn cause the American people to lose any expectations of achieving the American Dream. For better or for worse, American society is based upon the expectation of an improving economic situation. When Americans are convinced that it is no longer possible to achieve the American Dream, then the American society will rapidly begin to unravel. Why sacrifice, why be a good citizen, for a society that brings one only misery? The American society will unravel as it becomes everyone for him or herself. The glue that keeps this society together is the American Dream, the belief that if I work hard, some day I will be materially well off. I will have my house in the suburbs. The future will be better for my family and children. That is the American Dream. When it becomes readily apparent to the majority of Americans that no matter how hard one works, one becomes poorer and poorer, then the hard work will stop. It becomes everyone for him or herself. The society unravels.

Just as the modern Italians cannot be like the Romans of old, once a society loses its sense of sacrifice, it cannot be reconstituted. It is like a love affair between a man and a woman. When it is over, it is over. The man is the same man.

The woman is the same woman. But that glue that held them together is gone and nothing can bring it back. So it is with a society.

When a society falls from first place, it does not fall to second place. When virtually every important previous society fell, it fell very far—Haiti, Great Britain, Carthage, Bangladesh, Egypt, Greece, Rome, Mongolia, and most recently the Soviet Union. Even when the inhabitants of a country are the direct descendants of the people who ruled the world, the society that ruled the world is extinct. When a society falls from first place, it is as if the society begins a free fall down an elevator shaft. Once the fall begins, it is virtually impossible to stop. The current events in the Soviet Union are an excellent example. It is far, far better if the society were to accurately perceive the future and avoid stepping into the elevator shaft. Therefore, the society destined to survive must take action prior to the commencement of the fall.

What will happen next? We have only to turn to post–World War I Germany to see what occurs to a formerly successful, hard-working society experiencing economic disaster and hopelessness. After World War I, the victorious Allies caused the collapse of the German economy by burdening it with massive war reparation payments. This in turn caused the German people to seek a radical solution to their problems. A radical solution by the name of Adolf Hitler. The American people also will turn to radical political solutions. If a person the likes of a David Duke, the ex-member of the Ku Klux Klan, can achieve any political success in these relatively benign economic times, which will fondly be remembered as the "good old days," one can only shudder at the extremist political straws at which the impoverished and dispirited American society of the future will grasp. Not only can racism and anti-Semitism of the grossest kind be expected, but what will be the result when an extremist political party of the future gets its hands on the American nuclear arsenal? I believe I will stop predicting the future to which America is inexorably headed, because the foregoing should be more than sufficient evidence that this future should be avoided at all costs.

The predictions of disaster are virtually unanimous. Economists rarely agree on anything, but on the impending decline of America, if the budget deficits continue, there is almost universal agreement. They differ only as to when it will occur—five years or ten years. Budget deficits caused by the granting of favors to special interest groups so that the crooks in Congress can be re-elected and retain their power. The whole society will collapse and suffer because the crooks in Congress want to keep playing social King of the Mountain. How incredibly selfish! How incredibly decadent!

International Repercussions

An effect of the devastation to the United States economy will be a virtual stoppage of funds for the military. The military infrastructure will begin to decay. There will be no money for any type of military intervention overseas. The ability of the United States to project its power overseas will vanish. With our economy in ruins, our economic power will be lost. Foreign aid will be eliminated. The role of leader of the world will clearly shift to the Orient—Japan initially. Japan's groundwork for a claim to world leadership is being made in a current book, *Blueprint for a New Japan*, by Ichiro Ozawa, Japan's leading politician, and published by Kodansha America.

What type of leader will Japan be? The Black Box tells us that to accurately predict the future, we must accurately know the past and present. We have a right to ask how the Japanese have treated people from other societies who have come under Japanese control in recent years. I am reminded of the Bataan Death March of 1942, wherein the Japanese practiced inhuman cruelty upon American prisoners. The same can be said of what the Japanese did to the British and Australian prisoners of war from the fall of Singapore, as depicted in the film *The Bridge on the River Kwai*. Worse still were the Japanese atrocities committed in what is known as "the Rape of Nanking" upon poor Chinese civilians in 1937. Although I clearly do *not* predict any of the above types of behavior, it is a dramatic indication of the Japanese culture's attitude toward foreigners under their control. Additionally, a Japanese decision-maker who is 65 years old in 1995 was 15 years old at the end of the Second World War. The Japanese, as we have already learned, deplore the loss of honor more than death itself. The only time that the Japanese in their long, proud history have ever lost a war was to the Americans in World War II. The Japanese believe that the surprise attack on Pearl Harbor to initiate World War II was acceptable behavior, whereas our action of dropping the atom bomb to end the war was the immoral act of inhuman barbarians. The Japanese refuse to accept responsibility for starting World War II, but recently there has been discussion in Japan to request that the United States of America officially apologize for dropping the atomic bomb on Japan to end the war. The author will exercise all of his will power and refrain from comment.

Japan is a cohesive society renowned for its ritualized politeness. Following rituals of politeness helps prevent the all-important loss of face. When a superior levels criticism at someone, it invariably results in loss of face to that person. If the criticism is repeated over and over, that person is irrevocably humiliated and disgraced. The honorable thing, the proper thing to do is to commit suicide—*seppuku*. Therefore, in the Japanese mind, people who are repeatedly and directly criticized lose face, and the proper result for them should be extinction. Currently, respected, senior politicians of the Japanese government are directly and repeatedly criticizing the United States of America. On President Bush's state visit to Japan, the president became sick to his stomach and collapsed. Shortly thereafter in Japan, the owner of an animal act was staging a performance wherein the trainer would say "Bush-san" and a chimpanzee would spit liquid from its mouth and collapse. The act was widely reported. The Japanese people know what disgrace and loss of face and therefore insult is paid by such an act. I have never heard of a Japanese chimpanzee act imitating the Emperor of Japan in *any* way, let alone in an insulting way. Do you think that tells us something about the Japanese attitude toward us? In a recent poll, young Japanese were asked "With what country is Japan most likely to go to war?" The majority responded by saying the United States of America.

The present actions of the Japanese are those of an aggressive economic enemy that practices predatory "beggar-thy-neighbor" economic policies. And beggars are exactly what

Emperor Hirohito in the Imperial Garden

we will become. The average American does not travel overseas frequently, but as one who does, let me assure you that America is rapidly losing its position as the leading nation of the world. The change in America in the last ten years in the quality of life and standard of living in comparison to Asia and Europe is dramatic. Let me offer a striking example. The Emperor of Japan resides in a palace in central Tokyo. The palace is in a garden roughly one mile by one mile. Presumably, the garden is used by the figurehead Emperor for strolling, dallying, and amusing himself. The value of that small garden is more than the value of the entire United States of America. To put it another way, the approximately one-square-mile garden of the Emperor of Japan could be traded for the entire 3.5 million square miles of the United States of America and the Emperor would demand additional cash to boot![39]

People, we are in deep trouble. In five midwestern states that compose our industrial heartland, the Japanese own 1,200 small- and medium-size firms which employ 120,000 workers. For lack of an industrial policy, America has allowed foreign concerns to purchase the cream of our small and medium businesses. Our large businesses that have not already been driven out of business are under assault through a combination of unfair trade practices and suppliers who are foreign owned. I recently asked the CEO of an international pharmaceutical firm whether American business could still win the economic war with Japan. His wise response was, "No, you have already lost." Japan's purchase of our office buildings in our cities is well known. The Japanese have made substantial purchases of our farmland. It is being widely reported in the news media that family farms are disappearing, but what is not reported is who is buying them. Could it be the Japanese? If so, oh what a joy it will be when the world population inevitably outgrows the world's ability to feed itself. It will be so interesting to watch the Japanese sell food grown on our land to the highest international bidder while we starve because we will not be able to afford it. If you thought the oil embargo was no fun, wait until we do not have enough to eat. They also control significant portions of our ranches and produce beef for sale to Japan. The Japanese have purchased barge companies to transport our agricultural produce down the Mississippi River to be loaded on to Japanese ships in New Orleans. Meanwhile, the shrewd Japanese do not permit us to sell rice to Japan, let alone buy Japanese rice farms. Even if Japanese agricultural markets are opened, it will merely be a case of Japanese companies' raising grains and beef, transporting it on Japanese ships,

---

39. There has been a collapse of values in the Japanese real estate market. If we were really tough negotiators, we might be able to hang on to a state or two.

and selling it in Japan. There will be no profit to America—
only low-paying, menial jobs.

Therefore, it becomes easy to predict what type of future
world leadership we can expect from the Japanese. They will
attempt to manipulate the world to the greatest extent possible for the economic benefit of Japan. With the world economic levers indisputably in Japanese hands, the yen will become
the world's currency. With the Japanese ability to control
lending worldwide and to control the value of the Japanese
yen, the Japanese will have an enormous impact on whichever countries it chooses. Control over the economy is control
over the allocation of resources in a society. The allocation of
resources determines in the most profound sense what the
domestic policy of the United States will be; and it will be in
the hands of the Japanese. As we learned when we investigated ancient Egypt, when a foreign power rules a country,
decisions are made on the basis of the benefit to the foreign
power and not the benefit to the subject country. Therefore, it
is easy to predict that, after the economic devastation, our
future will continue to be most unpleasant with Japan as the
world's leader.

However, the international political situation becomes
even more bleak. Japan will unquestionably become the
world's leader, but, as we have learned, Japan is an economic
power, not a military one. Japan does not have the ability to
project conventional military power anywhere.[40] The
Europeans are, in general, hesitant to intervene militarily
anywhere, even in Bosnia. The Russians are no longer capable
of intervening intercontinentally. Thus, there will be no one to
prevent, say, an Iraqi invasion of Saudi Arabia that cuts off a

---

40. The Japanese have recently obtained a boatload of weapons-grade
plutonium, and I understand that Japan has cornered much of the world
market. The Japanese manufacture their own rockets to launch their
satellites. Therefore, the Japanese are capable of having world-class
nuclear armaments whenever they choose.

major portion of our oil supply, or any other trouble that occurs. The world will become profoundly more dangerous as dictators have a field day and old scores get settled. For example, it is highly improbable that Israel, having lost the support of the United States because of our economic difficulties, could withstand repeated and sustained battering without having to resort to the use of nuclear weapons sooner or later. With the small land area of Israel, the inevitable nuclear retaliation even by an inefficient attack only requires a small number of detonations to cause annihilation. Regional wars will proliferate with no one to stop them.

Then roughly ten to fifteen years after Japan assumes the leadership of the planet, a new factor will enter the equation. China will want to play a part in the world leadership role. It will not be possible for Japan to say no to China. China, by that time, will have the largest economy in the world. Its military will not only be the largest in the world, but it will be capable of projecting power world-wide. China is currently manufacturing its own nuclear weapons augmented by recent purchases of nuclear weapons from the ex-states of the Soviet Union. China manufactures its own rockets for launching its satellites and for intercontinental ballistic missiles. China already possesses a substantial, deliverable, nuclear arsenal. In addition, some Chinese believe that a nuclear war may not be without benefit to China. They believe that sufficient numbers of Chinese would survive, and that nuclear war would solve their population problem. China may not be reluctant to use nuclear warfare on the Japanese, especially if the Japanese remain high-handed in their dealings with the Chinese. Having traveled extensively in China and having visited their bomb shelters and remote areas, the author can vouch for the fact that some Chinese would survive. Therefore, it is possible that one of the rivals for future world leadership might not fear a nuclear war.

In addition, geographically in between the two rivals will be North Korea (with nuclear weapons) and South Korea (with nuclear weapons). North Korea will have continued its nuclear weapons program, and South Korea will have obtained nuclear weapons, because otherwise North Korea will be the only Korea left. Either way, there will be an uncooperative dictatorship with nuclear weapons in between the two rival titans vying for power.

Moreover, Russia, by this time in the future, will either have ameliorated its economic troubles and again be seeking to play a role in international affairs, or it will have failed to solve its economic troubles, and will have turned to an authoritarian and militaristic regime. Either way, Russia will have a panoply of nuclear weapons at its disposal and be desirous of exercising a strong international influence. Astoundingly, the above five countries—Japan, China, North Korea, South Korea, and Russia—are geographically so close that a circle with a radius of only slightly more than 200 miles would cross all their borders.

Additionally, nuclear weapons will be widespread. In fact, nuclear weapons will be the best chance a nation will have to survive in the future world, for there will be no one capable of intervening to prevent injustice on a global basis. Therefore, it can be reliably predicted that in the future there will be regional nuclear wars.

If we Black Box all the data in order to work the various possible cause-and-effect relationships that will be operative amongst the competing rivals, the probability of at least one major nuclear war is very high with these data alone. However, in addition, as we have learned, by this time in the future, the United States will have sought radical solutions to our problems, and an extremist political party will have its hands on America's nuclear arsenal.

What will happen after that? If the number of nuclear devices detonated in the wars is too large, then presumably "nuclear winter" will set in and we will all die. If the number of nuclear devices is small enough, then those of us who survive will live in a world of mutations. We can expect a wide variety of mutant life forms to appear, including human ones. Some mutations will be for the better, but the vast majority will not. You may continue to predict the real future if you wish.

Let me conclude by merely stating that the path that Congress currently has us on leads to our economic devastation, the loss of control over our own lives, our ability to plan, our ability to create a better future for us and our loved ones. In short, we lose the freedom for which our forefathers fought the British to be sold into an economic servitude we do not deserve by the Congress of the United States in order for the members of Congress to keep their jobs. Additionally, the only institution that has the power to intervene and prevent the above future from happening is the most corrupt and decadent institution in our society, the United States Congress.

As we learned when we studied the chapter on history, all societies are perpetually in a slow-motion struggle for survival as dictated by the Law of the Survival of the Efficient. It is crystal clear that we Americans are very rapidly headed toward the loss of our society. We are under economic assault from a very wealthy, very powerful, efficient, and well-managed Japanese society. For our defense we have the inefficient, corrupt, and incredibly decadent Congress, which is so decadent that it is too busy trading away our democracy and, hence, our future to even perceive the threat to our society. Does the reader recall the winner of the struggle between the Japanese and the American businessman? Who does the reader predict will win the struggle between the Japanese society and the American society? We are led by decadent, self-serving, corrupt politicians. America as we know it—an America with Americans in charge of our society—is about to become extinct in a short period of time. We are facing the same extinction that the Egyptians, Greeks, Romans, dinosaurs, dodo birds, and soft-bodies faced. The one difference is that our decline is in its early stages.

CHAPTER TWELVE

Step No. 3: Predict the Idealized Future

The Present to the End of Time

N OW THAT WE UNDERSTAND THE devastation that the
decadence of the U.S. Congress will cause, let us proceed with the Seven Steps of the Black Box Technique
(Step No. 3) and analyze what the future could be if we had a
properly functioning government, one that operated using the
Four Critical Abilities.

Warning: I must strictly caution the reader that to think
accurately in the future, we must use the pre-frontal lobes of
the brain, evolution's gift to humankind, that part of the
brain whose function it is to think in the future. Do not in
any case permit more ancient portions of your brain to enter
into the thinking process in any way. Never, for instance, permit emotion, which is processed by the limbic part of your
brain and which we inherited virtually intact from our reptil-
ian ancestors, to perform your thinking for you. Have you
ever watched a sad scene in a movie and cried? You did not
logically assess the situation and then order yourself to cry.
The portion of your brain that processes emotions ordered
your body to cry. This portion of your brain should not be
used for thinking, and particularly not for thinking in the
future.

Also do not let the smelling portion of your brain do your
thinking for you. Our ratlike ancestors 90 million years ago,
being warmblooded, could be active only at night, when the
coldblooded dinosaurs were dormant. As we all know, there is
not very much light at night and the ability to smell incredibly well became critical for survival. The limbic portion of the
brain also processed the signals from the nose very rapidly,
and because a quick reaction to what was smelled meant sur-

vival, this area of the brain did not send its information to other parts of the brain for further processing and decision-making but rather directly ordered action by the body. While this short-circuiting of the higher thinking portion of the brain sped up reaction time and no doubt saved innumerable rats' lives, this portion of the brain has come down to us modern humans also intact. And just as in the 90-million-year-old rats, that portion of the brain has the ability to circumvent the neocortex, the thinking part of the brain, and direct body function. Have you ever lowered your head to smell something disagreeable and at the first whiff, immediately jerked your head back up? You did not logically think about the situation and then order your head to jerk back up.

The smelling and emotional parts of the brain should be used for smelling and feeling emotion. The thinking part of the brain should be used for thinking. Using one part of your body to perform another body part's function will lead you to the same results that you will get if you attempt to unlock your front door by turning the key with your feet instead of your hands.

If you have ever seen children attend their first day of kindergarten you will no doubt recall the crying, screaming, and severe emotional response of the children to the disorientation of the new environment. College freshmen, the first day of class, experience the same disorientation as the kindergarten children, but the response is very different because the college students have learned not to permit their emotions to control their behavior. In the same way, we must not use our emotions for thinking. Keep your emotions for their appropriate use on family and friends, birthdays, weddings, bar mitzvahs, boyfriends and girlfriends. Do not use ancient portions of your brain for thinking or you will be using to think about the future the same part of your brain that dogs use to sniff one another's rear ends and then fight. I promise you the results will be equally unpleasant.

Advisory Note: In the first chapter it was stated that we must leave behind our preconceived notions from this society. The following future, based upon a perception of reality drawn from an understanding of the Fundamental Laws of the Universe, will cause disbelief in the reader, if the reader views the following based upon his or her current society's perception of reality. Just as Sir Isaac Newton's and Albert Einstein's new concepts of reality altered scientists' perception of reality to a new and more accurate one and thereby permitted the advances in science that followed, so the perspective of viewing all of reality accurately gained by knowing the Fundamental Laws of the Universe permits us to understand what the full reality and potential of humankind truly is. Humankind is far, far more powerful than previously believed. By taking control of the cause-and-effect relationships that, as we have already learned, control everything, we can create any future that we want bounded only by the constraint of being physically possible. In other words if our society arranges itself in conformance with the Four Critical Abilities so that it can actively and efficiently alter the cause-and-effect relationships that determine what a society will be, then *any future is possible and achievable as long as no physical law of the universe is broken!* Future generations will view this fact as being obvious. The only question that remains is whether the current generation will grasp it?

Step No. 3: The Idealized Future

To investigate our idealized future, we need to understand three principles. The first principle is that the time when events occur in the future is, to a great extent, controllable by actions we take in the present. Let us say that it would take, under normal conditions, three years to build a large cargo ship. However, if we want the cargo ship in fewer than three years, in effect we want the future to arrive sooner than it otherwise would. All we have to do is devote more labor to its construction. In fact, this is precisely what was done during World War II. The Kaiser shipyard was able to reduce the time it took to construct large cargo ships, called Liberty ships, to under 30 days by increasing the resources devoted to the task. In effect, they caused the future to occur sooner than it otherwise would have naturally occurred. The knowledge required to build a ship was well known. However, the future can also be caused to occur sooner under conditions wherein the knowledge required to complete the task is unknown. An example would be the Manhattan Project. Albert Einstein thought that it would be theoretically possible to create what we now call the atom bomb. The government was not certain that it would be technically possible to build the bomb. By assigning the highest priority to the project, it diverted a large amount of resources to its development and the bomb was created far, far sooner than it otherwise would have been. In effect, the government controlled when the future would arrive.

Likewise, President Kennedy did the same thing when in 1961 he assigned NASA the task of sending men to the moon by 1970. While in principle it was thought to be possible, the technical problems to be solved were enormous. In fact, the high-speed digital computer had to be perfected in order to calculate course corrections quickly and accurately. Since no other society has subsequently sent men to the moon and evidently will not for at least 10 or 15 more years, then it is clear that President Kennedy caused what would naturally not have occurred for 40 or 50 years in the future to occur in fewer than 10 years. Once again, by a mere shift in the allocation of money and the labor of scientists, the future was caused to occur decades before it otherwise would have. To put it in terms of our logic, the naturally occurring causes were changed into causes that would lead to the desired effect. Therefore, Principle No. 1 is: "That society which has the ability to allocate large quantities of resources has, within limits, the power to control when the future will arrive."

The first principle is fairly straightforward. The second principle involves a technological advance, or more precisely a group of technological advances. It is well known that the rate of technological progress is increasing rapidly. A familiar example is the computer. Twenty years ago, commercially available computers had a memory of 64,000 pieces of information (64K), filled a small room, and cost $35,000. To write this book, I recently bought a small chip the size of my fingernail that cost a couple of hundred dollars and had a memory of 4 million pieces of information (4 megabytes) and had it installed in my desktop computer. I could have used a computer the size of a notebook had I so chosen. Mosakazu Aono of the Japanese Institute for Physical and Chemical Research predicts that by the year 2010, Japan will be capable of producing a silicon chip containing 1 billion pieces of information (1 gigabyte). This chip may never be built outside of a laboratory. Why? It will have been supplanted by a technology that "will bring changes as profound as the industrial revolution, antibiotics, and nuclear weapons all in one," according to Dr. K. Eric Drexler. The new science is called *nanotechnology*. It involves manipulation of the physical world at the level of its basic components, individual atoms. In 1990, researchers used this technology to spell their company logo, IBM. The researchers manipulated and precisely placed 35 individual xenon atoms. Subsequently the Japanese have refined the technique and have individually arranged hundreds of atoms in precise locations in seconds. What does this new technology mean? It means that the entire Encyclopaedia Britannica can be written on the head of a pin. It means that all human knowledge and all the music ever written can be placed on a single 12-inch compact disc. It means that biomolecular factories can be created that take carbon dioxide out of the air and separate it into oxygen that can be released and carbon that can be reassembled with hydrogen to make fuel. Molecular machines can be made that can tour the human body and repair proteins gone bad or detect cancer. In his book *Unbounding the Future: The Nanotechnology Revolution*, Dr. K. Eric Drexler predicts molecular assemblers could begin with raw atoms and molecules and produce complex structures such as "super-strong tents complete with cooking facilities and air-conditioning, which future Red Cross workers might deliver to disaster areas."[41]

Research has already commenced that combines nanotechnology with biology. Known as *bionanotechnology,* it is attempting to harness the DNA molecule to produce not what the DNA wants, but the molecular assemblers. If bionanotechnology succeeds, then the factories that manufacture the molecular assemblers will be self-replicating. A Japanese group is attempting to fabricate a fully functioning human brain using bionanotechnology.

The human brain has at least 10 billion neurons in its cerebral cortex and therefore presumably has a memory of at least 10 billion pieces of information. Computers can already perform many operations at speeds far faster than the human brain and without tiring. Therefore, it is easy to reliably predict that in the near future, scientists will be able to create compact computers that will be able to mimic all but the highest order of human brain functions. We have already learned what the highest order of human brain function is— thinking in the future, which permits us to plan, invent, design, etc. Therefore, roughly speaking, computers in the near future will be able to function at least as well as reptile brains but with greater memory and the power to speak, read, and write.

It is also easy to predict that pairs of high-definition cameras could present digitized patterns to the computer, which it

41. *Science*, Vol. 254, 29 Nov., 1991.

could compare against patterns stored in its memory, thereby giving the computer intelligent binocular vision. Repetitive items that the computer needs to recognize could be bar-coded for fast, easy recognition. In addition, it is also easy to predict that scientists can construct an arm with a fully functioning, dexterous hand at the end of it. Moreover, mobility could be provided that would allow the computer to move itself, taking advantage of the curbs and ramps used by the handicapped. Therefore, considering all of the above, it becomes apparent that in the near future, science will be able to create a robot that can replace human labor in all jobs except those that require thinking about the future, which are typically those jobs held by scientists, engineers, artists, designers, planners, and decision-makers. The word "robot" is so over-used in our society that we will use the word "automaton." We have come upon Principle No. 2: "In the future, automatons will be able to replace human labor in all jobs except those few that require thinking in the future."

Principle No. 2 is also fairly easy to comprehend. It is Principle No. 3 that gives almost everyone a tough time. It is not a problem of intelligence. My father, whose I.Q., as he puts it, "has been tested as low as 139," took eight years to finally accept Principle No. 3 as the truth. It has to do with a person's ability to accept new ideas, particularly those that contradict ideas to which a person is emotionally attached. Principle No. 3 is actually a fundamental doctrine of classical economics. In fact, the founder of the study of economics, the Scotsman Adam Smith (1723–1790), not only enunciated the principle but also stated the lack of understanding of it. In the initial pages of his classic work, *The Wealth of Nations*, published in 1776, he states: "Though labour be the real measure of the exchangeable value of all commodities, it is not that by which their value is commonly estimated....Labour... is alone the ultimate and real standard by which the value of all commodities can at all times and places be estimated and compared. It is their real price; money is their nominal price only." "Labour, it must be remembered, is the ultimate price which is paid for every thing."

This concept was later echoed and expanded upon by the brilliant English economist David Ricardo (1772–1823) when he stated in his treatise, *On the Principles of Political Economy and Taxation*, "the value of a commodity, or the quantity of any other commodity for which it will exchange, depends on the relative quantity of labour which is necessary for its production." Ricardo adds the important modifier that human labor also includes the owner's labor, which we call profits.

In modern English the above two gentlemen mean to say, and this is Principle No. 3: "Human labor is the cost of all things." When we go to the store and purchase, let us say, an apple for 10 cents, we are, in fact, not purchasing the apple itself, we are merely paying for the sum total of all the human labor involved from the orchard to the grocery store. The truth of this principle can be verified by the fact that if we were walking in a forest and came upon an apple tree and picked and ate the apple, the apple would be free, because no human labor except our own was involved. We did not pay the tree for the apple. Only human beings (and their artificial substitutes, corporations, governments, banks, etc.) use money. Trees do not use money. Dogs do not use money. Mountains from which we extract minerals do not use money.

Therefore, when we go to a car dealer and think we are purchasing a new car, we are not, in fact, paying for the car itself, but merely the human labor that created the car. When the iron ore of which the car is made was extracted from a mountain, no one took dollar bills and pounded them back into the mountain to pay for the iron ore. The cost of the iron ore was only the cost of the human labor to extract it. The iron ore itself was actually free. All raw materials, even gold and diamonds, are free. The only cost to DeBeers Diamond Company for diamonds is the cost of the labor to extract them. If machinery is involved, the purchase price of the machinery is merely the sum total of the cost of the human labor to fashion it, transport it, and all other human labor all the way back to the extraction of the machine's raw materials.

I warned the reader that Principle No. 3 would be difficult to believe, but nonetheless it is true. I know that emotionally we want to believe when we purchase something in a store that we are paying for that physical object. In reality, we are merely swapping our money, which we received through our labor, for some other people's labor. The actual atoms and molecules that make up that object, and hence the object itself, is free. The same is true not only of all goods we buy, but also all services. The cost of all goods and services is merely the sum total of all the human labor involved. Perhaps the best way to understand this principle is to take a couple of products you buy and mentally track them from your purchase of them in a store backwards through all the steps it took to make them and get them there. Track all the costs associated with them back to their raw material state and you will see that the only costs in the final analysis are those of human labor.

Additionally, we can prove that labor is the cost of all things from our recently gained knowledge of the past. Prior to the division of labor in human ancestors, each creature provided his or her own goods and services. After the division of labor, say when two Cro-Magnon bands would meet, one person might exchange a shell necklace he had made for an ax that someone else had made. People collected raw material, used their labor to modify it, and then exchanged it for someone else's labor. They exchanged their labor. With the widespread introduction of money by the early Greek sailing traders, money became a more expedient medium of exchange than barter. Through the centuries we have lost the understanding that money merely represents a certain amount of labor.

Let me approach the same point in a different way. If you are ever standing in line at your bank or cash station, and there is something in line ahead of you other than a human being waiting to make a deposit or withdrawal, let me know immediately. Once you can overcome your emotional reaction to Principle No. 3, your logic will tell you that it is true.

For now, however, we must proceed with our logical analysis, and I am afraid our logical analysis will lead us to additional emotional disbelief. I advised the reader in the beginning of this book that it takes intellectual courage to seek fundamental truth. Here is where you will need all of it you have.

Let us review our three principles:

1. That society which has the ability to allocate large quantities of its resources has, within limits, the power to control when the future will arrive.

2. In the future, automatons will be able to replace human labor in all jobs except those few that require thinking in the future.

3. Human labor is the cost of all things.

Let us take Principle No. 3 and say it in another way: "Human labor equals all cost."

To express this in a simple mathematical formula:
Human Labor = All Cost

If we were to remove all human labor from the production and distribution of all goods and services, then the amount of human labor would be zero. If human labor equals 0, then substituting it in the formula we have:
0 = All Cost

All cost becomes equal to zero. If all costs are equal to
zero, then everything is free. Eureka! We have found the key
to our future society. If we remove all human labor from the
production and distribution of all goods and services, then all
goods and services become free.[42]

From Principle No. 2 we know that at some time in the
future, automatons will be able to replace virtually all human
labor except for a very few jobs that will require high-level
thinking. This means that, in reality, for a while some goods
and services will retain some modest cost. A car that currently costs $20,000 may cost $200. A 40″ TV that costs $2,000
may cost $20 when produced by automatons and human engi-
neers and designers.

The sociological, economic, and political implications, both
obvious and otherwise, of the above concept are vast. They
could easily fill several books of this length. The reader who
is probably still reeling in emotional disbelief would soon be
exhausted by even a superficial discussion of a society that
does not exist.

Few things exasperate the general reader as much as an
over-detailed plan of the future spelled out in incredible
minutiae by a proud author. On the other hand, the lack of a
precise, detailed plan leaves the work open to denunciation
by critics for incompleteness. If I err, I prefer it to be on the
side of the general reader. For if the general reader does not
appreciate this book, it is irrelevant if the critic does. If the
general reader does appreciate this book, the critic can be
satisfied in another forum at a future time.

The above notwithstanding, the author cannot refrain
from mentioning a few brief points. When the automatons
replace virtually all human labor, and all goods and services

---

42. $E=MC^2$ is the most famous formula in the world. It tells us that matter and energy are convertible and at what ratio. In terms of its potential
impact on human society, the formula Human Labor = All Cost is far, far
more important.

become virtually free, we will have achieved a state we shall call "Economic Freedom." However, the automaton factories will still be capable of turning out vast hordes of free automatons. What can we have the automatons do? If this is a democracy, then the correct answer is that we can have them do whatever we want. We are limited only by our imaginations. Does the reader recall our discussion of ancient Egypt, wherein the Pharaoh ordered his vast hordes of human workers to build the vainglorious pyramids and the question was posed to the reader, "What would he or she have commanded the people of ancient Egypt to do had they been Pharaoh?" The author will not even put forth any suggestions, so as not to pre-condition the imagination of the reader, but will merely offer advice: think big, really, really big. The possibilities are staggering! Whatever is physically possible both in the public sector (transportation systems, cities, amusement parks, etc.) and for individuals (homes, vehicles, Butler Automatons, personal possessions, etc.) can be made to occur, and it will all be free.

From the perspective of the consumer, the economy would function as if everyone were receiving Social Security. Every Friday, a certain sum of money (actually merely a number) would be electronically deposited into each person's account in a central computer. Then whenever the consumer wanted something, a car, a stereo, clothes, etc., the consumer would consult his or her talking Household Butler Automaton and through conversation determine whether the person wanted to design the product himself, choose between standard options, or just let the automaton choose based upon the best interests of the entire society. Routine household needs like food, soaps, bathroom tissue, etc., would automatically be reordered when needed by the Household Butler Automaton. Then the order would be directly transmitted to the factory staffed by automatons, which would make and assemble the product to the consumer's specifications and ship it overnight by the high-speed transportation system built by automatons. The following morning the product would be brought to your house by the Local Delivery Automaton. For recycling to work effectively, the consumer will be required to have the Household Butler Automaton return the used car, used stereo, used clothes, etc., to the Local Delivery Automaton for recycling. The consumer's Social Security account would be automatically debited while the factory's account would be credited. At the end of the week the computer would debit all the factories' accounts, as they do not need or use money (since no humans work there), and all the consumers' accounts would be re-credited. The "money" is, in fact, only a minute quantity of electricity stored in the memory of a computer, which shuttles it from the consumer's account to the factory's or seller's account and back again. The only purpose of the "money" is to regulate the flow of goods and services to prevent the inequities of hoarding and other abuses. *Poverty will cease to exist*. Pretty nice way to live, eh?

There are 8,760 hours in a year. The average human laborer is scheduled to work 2,000 hours per year (50 weeks x 40 hours). With sick days, tardiness, holidays, coffee breaks, etc., the average human laborer probably actually works fewer than 1,750 hours per year. Therefore, a tireless automaton could, on average, replace 5 human workers. There are 100 million workers in the U.S. labor force who could be replaced by 20 million automatons. However, in an automated economy far fewer than 100 million workers need be replaced. When one analyzes which jobs need replacement by our automatons and which jobs can be eliminated outright, it is remarkable the quantity of jobs that can be eliminated outright. For instance, banks, insurance companies, and all financial institutions become unnecessary. In fact, as a general rule of thumb with few exceptions, virtually all people employed in the private sector who work in offices need not be replaced. The primary exceptions are the previously mentioned scientists, engineers, artists, designers, planners, and decision-makers; in short, jobs that require creativity and thinking in the future.

In addition, virtually all people working in the retail sector need not be replaced. People involved in sales and advertising need not be replaced. We citizens can be made aware of product innovations by tuning to the product innovation channel of our television or by asking our Household Butler Automaton, "What's new?" All people employed in distribution will be replaced by an automated delivery system built by the automatons.

Inevitably, there will be some who are so thoroughly inculcated with the work ethic that they will feel ill at ease, nervous, and uncomfortable not having a job. Additionally, the author has been told that there are some people who actually enjoy going shopping and do not mind the inconvenience, crowds, and annoyance that shopping in contemporary society entails. For those people, we can keep the shopping malls open and permit those who want to work and those who want to shop to be inconvenienced, crowded, and annoyed to their mutual hearts' content.

Then who actually needs replacing by automatons? In the private sector, primarily those engaged directly in manufacturing and only those employed in rendering a direct service to consumers, for example car washes and dry cleaners. However, many consumer services could be eliminated by modifying them. For instance, the need for video movie rental stores could be eliminated by an interactive television system in which the consumers can order the desired video played directly over their televisions. If, for example, we want to eliminate dry cleaners and the need for the noxious chemicals they use, we consumers can choose to wear fabrics that our Household Butler Automaton can launder and press.

The author sometimes plays an interesting game that I invite the reader to try. While driving down the street, take note of the businesses one passes and imagine how the goods or services that the business provides would or could be provided in an automated society. The incredible conclusion is that the overwhelming majority could be easily replaced in the automated society described above, and almost all the rest would not be needed at all; very, very few would continue to require human labor. However, at the same time, the options available to us consumers would increase exponentially because of the customization possible through automated flexible manufacturing. It is not an overstatement to assert that through 1) advances in technology, 2) service provided by the Household Butler Automaton, and 3) choices in personal possessions created by customized automated manufacturing that every individual living under "Economic Freedom" would enjoy roughly the same level of comfort and service as is currently enjoyed by the queen of England, or in ancient times, an emperor of the Roman Empire or a pharaoh of Egypt.

Therefore, considering the above, far fewer than 20 million automatons would be needed. The number of people engaged in manufacturing in the private sector is 19,557,000, or roughly 20 percent of the 100 million labor force. If a tireless automaton can replace, on average, 5 people, then only slightly more than 4 million automatons could replace all of the manufacturing jobs in this country. In addition, manufactured products currently imported from overseas could be manufactured in this country free of charge, adding to the number of automatons needed. All in all, the author roughly estimates that 12 to 15 million automatons would be able to create "Economic Freedom" here in the United States, exclusive of personal Household Butler Automatons.[43]

---

43. The author, though not expert in the technical nuts and bolts of automation, was intimately involved with automation during his business career, and knows well its potentials and limits and credits it and the Black Box Technique with his being able to retire at the age of thirty-nine.

The ultimate real-world constraints are primarily: 1) Raw materials—where do we obtain them without destroying the environment; how do we recycle them so that we are not inundated by trash, and how do we process them non-pollutingly? 2) Energy—where does it come from? And 3) Population.

1) *Raw materials.* We will obtain the raw materials for all the manufactured products in two ways. First, if we mandate that the people who design how the products are going to be assembled also design how the products are going to be disassembled. Then when we are through with a given product, it can be returned to a fully automated disassembly factory, disassembled into its constituent parts, and recycled. We no longer have to trash the environment. Second, in the future, we can mine our garbage landfills. All we will need are atoms and molecules, and with the addition of energy we will be able to arrange them into whatever form we need. We can mine our own landfills and no longer need to mine in remote areas and pollute the environment. We can create a closed-loop, infinitely sustainable, fully-automated recycling environment.

We have an enormous waste of agricultural products in this country, particularly fruits and vegetables. What is needed is an infinitely sustainable closed-loop agricultural system. For instance, your Household Butler Automaton can project your farm product needs based upon what the automaton is going to cook for you based upon a history of what you like. Then, a central computer will gather all the information from everyone's automaton and know exactly what is required for the next growing season in food for the entire United States. The requirements can be allocated to the farms, which will be fully automated; the crops will be raised and the food distributed. We need to perfect ways to recycle our metabolic wastes to make them suitable to assist in the farming process again so that we do not end up like Haiti.

2) *Energy.* Energy will be one of the services that government will be required to provide free of charge. Just as the pro-

viding of police protection is one of the duties of government, energy will be a free public service. Since automatons will be building and operating the power plants and handling the distribution of the energy, there will be no cost to the government and hence no cost to us or the fully automated factories.

3) *Population.* A small, stable population can enjoy more freedom and more material wealth per person then can a large, expanding population, as we learned from Egypt. Does the reader recall the law we propounded earlier? When a creature develops even a modest advantage over its fellow creatures, not only it but its variants increase until the available resources are fully exploited, including its fellow creatures. Clearly this is the case with modern humankind. When I was born in 1945, the population of America was 140 million. In 1994 our population was 261 million. In terms of the time periods in which we have been thinking, the population of America is exploding. Our cities are overcrowded. Our expressways are jammed. Our quality of life is deteriorating.

The world population problem is even worse. In 1800, the world population was 1 billion. In 1925, it was 2 billion. In 1960 it was 2.9 billion. In 1990, it was 5.3 billion. By the year 2020, the world population will be 8.3 billion. Disaster is on the way. These ultimate constraints disappear if the society of the future is an infinitely sustainable, closed-loop one wherein all products, including agricultural ones, are recycled and the population remains stable and as small as possible.

Incredibly important side benefits accrue to having a closed-loop, infinitely sustainable society. The creation of a closed-loop, infinitely sustainable society will end economic competition between the citizens of that future society. If economic competition between the citizens is ended, then the cause for the overwhelming majority of crime is also ended. Except in instances involving domestic violence, substance abuse, and psychopaths, ***crime will disappear from the society***.

If the United States, after having achieved the closed-loop, infinitely sustainable society, shares the information with all the other societies on the planet of how to set up and operate fully automated factories and farms and how to recycle (close the loop), then economic competition between societies will end. If economic competition between societies is ended, then the cause for the overwhelming majority of wars is also ended. If in the interim period until a closed-loop, infinitely sustainable society is created, the world community could resolve the outstanding border disputes, then in an incredibly short time, all people could enjoy a planet virtually free of poverty, crime, and war that would survive indefinitely. If that occurs, then we will have repealed the Law of the Survival of the Efficient and its application to human societies. ***War will cease to exist***. Therefore, the planet will be a fundamentally stable, safe, and enduring "paradise" for its inhabitants!

The virtual elimination of crime caused by the ending of economic competition between citizens is caused by the society's ability to provide every citizen's material wants and needs free of charge, which is in turn caused by the freeing of the citizen from having to sell labor. The effects of these three causes on a society will be profound. People's social position will no longer be judged by their possessions. In the future society, individuals will be judged on their individual traits— their human-ness. Since individuals will no longer seek economic advantage over one another, humans will probably judge one another on the basis of friendliness, courtesy, and general likability. The freeing of one's time and the freeing of one's concern over material things mean that interpersonal relationships (family and friends) will take on greater significance.

In the future, no one will work, except, of course, those who want to work. One's time will be totally one's own. There will be no jobs that people will have to go to. If there are any required jobs at all, they will be few in number. The products for the society will be built by automatons working in fully automated factories. If you want a product, you will merely tell the computer you have with you at all times. One's time is free to do with as one wants. For the entire rest of one's life, there is no place you ever have to be and no time you ever have to be there. This would be freedom very few of us know, even in America, one of the freest of countries.

The freeing of one's time coupled with a safe, friendly, and secure society will permit individuals of that future society to exercise a maximum of creativity, from designing our own clothes, cars, video games, to works of art, sculpting, painting, writing, gardening. At our beck and call will be a computer of immense power. The computer will know every fact known to humankind. Whatever our interests are, we can pursue them. As long as they do not involve 1) hurting someone else or 2) hurting someone else's property, we will be totally free to create, to live our own lifestyles, and to enjoy ourselves. For the first time, *humankind will have the liberty to enjoy our lives in any way we choose virtually free of poverty, crime, and war*!

A s stated in the Declaration of Independence, "Governments are instituted among Men" for the purpose of securing "certain unalienable rights," amongst which are "Life, Liberty, and the Pursuit of Happiness." A society based on the concepts outlined in this chapter maximizes these rights to the highest extent possible and fulfills the dream of our Founding Fathers. It takes our society to a place beyond capitalism, far above socialism, very far above communism, to a place so high that the economy and the concomitant pursuit of money can be ignored as unimportant by the citizenry.

Incidentally, an additional benefit derived from "Economic Freedom" is that after it is achieved, it reduces any economic advantage gained by the Japanese to irrelevance. What difference does it make if Japanese banks are bulging with money? Our society will be supplying the material wants and needs of all of its members without cost. Money merely becomes a handy way to keep track of the transfer of goods and services, and is without value in and of itself. Therefore, regardless of the outcome of the economic struggle between the United States and Japan, any economic advantage gained by Japan will be as meaningless as if our neighbor came over to our house and won a game of Monopoly!

When will it be possible to achieve the above conditions? According to Principle No. 1, which is "That society which has the ability to allocate large quantities of its resources has, within limits, the power to control when the future will arrive," it merely depends upon the quantity of resources that are devoted to the task.

In actuality, it could occur surprisingly soon. Let us perform an Einsteinian Thought Experiment to see how fast we could make this occur. Let us say that our government makes this project its highest priority much as President Kennedy did with the moon mission. Then the government does two things. 1) It orders a large team of scientists to solve the technical problems and create one automaton. 2) It simultaneously begins to construct a factory that will not only assemble the automatons, but also manufacture all their parts from raw materials. The factory could be low-tech and therefore human-labor intensive. No doubt the factory could be completed first and be waiting for the scientists to create the first automaton. When the scientists create the first automaton, it would immediately go into production. Let us estimate that the factory would employ some 20,000 human beings. As the first automatons begin to roll off the assembly line, the first 20,000 produced would replace the 20,000 human laborers in the automaton factory. When the last human in the factory is replaced by the 20,000th automaton, a critical moment arrives because all human labor is then equal to zero, and therefore all subsequent automatons produced by the factory are free.

Then the next automatons produced could be sent to a new location to build a second automaton factory and, because no human labor is used, the second factory would be free. By the time the second factory is constructed, the first automaton factory would have created the 20,000 automatons required to staff it. Then there would be two factories with no human labor producing free automatons. The next group of automatons from the two factories plus the crew that built the second factory could build three new factories. By the time they are completed, the two already functioning factories would have completed a sufficient number of automatons to staff them. Then there would be five factories producing free automatons. The process could be repeated until we have the desired number of factories producing the desired number of free automatons.

A simple method of integrating the automatons with the minimum of distortion and disruption to the economy would be to withhold the automatons until we have the requisite number. Then the automatons could all be integrated into the economy over a relatively short period of time, a few months. Then no human beings would have to go to work and all goods and services would be free. Instead of merely stockpiling the automatons in warehouses until we have the required number, we can have them construct the automated high-speed transportation system that will be used to distribute the goods the automatons will later produce.

When could all goods and services become virtually free? We know from Principle No.1 that it depends on the resources devoted to it. A maximum effort by government on the scale of the moon mission would cause "Economic Freedom" to occur within perhaps 15 years, but certainly within this generation. The cost of the project, inasmuch as it becomes labor-free when the automatons replace the human workers of the first factory, would only entail three elements: 1) the scientific project to create the first automaton; 2) construction of the first factory; and 3) the cost of the first 20,000 automatons— perhaps $20 billion over 10 years, or $2 billion per year. This relatively small amount of money is less than Congress wastes every year in even one of its more modest bribery-re-election rip-off scams.

Interestingly enough, the objections to the above future that I have heard are social. Although young people who have read the foregoing have almost invariably been in favor of it, people over roughly 40 often times respond, "But what will I do?" I usually respond, "What do you do when you go on vacation?" We will only be limited by our imaginations. It seems that many older people have come to identify themselves by what their job is. What a shame. Remember the previously discussed nomads who would not come out of the Sahara Desert even though they faced extinction and adopt a new way of life, farming?

The second objection involves the point that if all people can have virtually whatever material possessions they want, then being envied for one's material possessions will cease. Incredibly, many people do not want that to occur. Evidently, they only want some of their material possessions in order for other people to envy them. The human being is truly an amazing creature.

In any event, if we expect politicians and bureaucrats to think up innovative futures for us, we are looking to the wrong segment of our society. People who can haggle endlessly with so little result are the least likely of us citizens to think up creative solutions to our problems. Expecting politicians to be creative is reminiscent of Samuel Johnson's remark about dogs walking on their hind legs—"It is not done well; but you are surprised to find it done at all."

The following portions of this chapter will be an exploration of the outer boundaries of the possible. In many readers, particularly older readers who have successfully passed their mid-life crisis and have come to accept the inevitability of their own death, the following may engender disbelief. However, both belief and disbelief, are merely opinions. We have already learned that opinion is not to be relied upon. Therefore, the reader who encounters disbelief in reading the following concepts is encouraged to analyze the logic and find flaws. If no flaws can be found, and the reader cannot think up logical reasoning of his own why the concept is impossible, then the reader's disbelief (opinion) is not valid and therefore probably in error. If the reader can find flaws or can think up logical reasons why any of the following concepts are impossible, then please do the author the favor of forwarding the reasoning to him at the fax or Internet website listed at the end of the book. For those of us who enjoy mental stimulation and an intellectual challenge, please feel free to wallow in the following.

Death Is Dead

While we are about the business of discussing the future, the author would like to discuss a persistent irritant that should be remedied—death. Death is a naturally occurring phenomenon that has outlived its usefulness. Like everything else, death operates by cause-and-effect relationships. To cure death all that is required is 1) for medical science to discover what the specific causes and effects are that cause death, and 2) that we interrupt the sequence of events that cause death at the most convenient point. *Voilà*, death is dead and human beings can live forever.

An article appeared on the front page of the December 8, 1991, *Chicago Tribune* stating how a 65-year-old Fred McCullough had been given weekly injections of a genetically engineered human growth hormone and his body reverted to that of a 45-year-old. The article went on to state: "Ageing is not programmed in us like a doomsday clock or an inescapable result of life's wear and tear. Rather it is a combination of related events governed by our genes. And, for the most part ageing is reversible . . . there may be no immutable biological law that decrees human beings have to get old and sick and die. . . . By design, the body should go on forever."

The amount of knowledge obtainable about the human body and its subset, the cause-and-effect relationships of death, is finite—extremely complex, but nonetheless finite. Any finite amount of matter must be controlled by a finite number of laws. For if a finite amount of matter were controlled by an infinite number of laws, the result would be chaos. Chaos is demonstrably not the case. A finite amount of matter may only be arranged and combined in a finite number of ways. Therefore, finite matter must be controlled by a finite number of laws. Or, to put it another way, the knowledge to be discovered about death must be finite. Therefore, medical science is searching for a finite number of cause-and-effect relationships (laws) about death.

Every human cell is controlled by a set of instructions that tells it what to do— instructions embodied in the DNA molecule. Therefore, the DNA molecule in a very profound way determines all physical characteristics of the human. It might be seriously interesting to apply our tools of logic to the evolution of the DNA molecule. At first, the instruction set of the DNA molecule would have been very, very simple. Only the minimal amount of instructions to sustain life would have been necessary. By using Occam's razor we can tentatively accept that one of the earliest strategies of survival would have been to multiply as much as possible. In fact, we find amongst primitive single-celled animals that as long as conditions are suitable each continues to divide into two identical organisms. This act is continued until conditions are no longer suitable. However, in more complex and therefore more highly evolved organisms like humans, we find that our cells do not act that way. The instruction set of our cells tells them to form a finite structure, then cease multiplying. Then our cells duplicate themselves only as needed to maintain the structure. This means cell division, in some instances, only once every seven or eight years. Then our cells cease dividing and maintaining our structure. Then we die. Clearly our instruction set is much more complex and sophisticated than that of the single-celled animals.

One of the most prevalent techniques used by our instruction set to evolve is to retain intact its currently successful form and to add an elaboration on to it. Evidence of this is that in our first few days of life the human embryo rapidly evolves through earlier life forms. At one point in our embryonic development we were all single-celled organisms, then we had gills and a tail. It is logical to conclude that our instruction set contains the blueprint for earlier life forms. Furthermore, it is obvious then that our more evolved instruction set contains an elaboration that permits it to control the blueprints for previous life forms and prevents them from being active. Then there is a high probability that our instruction set may contain the powerful survival strategy of the primitive single-celled organisms, which is to relentlessly divide and multiply as long as conditions are suitable. If the above is true, then if the elaboration in our instruction set that controls the primitive instruction to relentlessly multiply is interrupted, a condition of runaway cell growth would occur. We call this condition cancer.[44] What we know about the causes of cancer tends to support this conclusion.

If we further analyze the primitive single-cell organisms, their instruction set never orders them to die. They merely continue dividing. Then it follows that our instruction set may contain an elaboration that causes us to die. If the *Chicago Tribune* article is correct, then the condition that

---

44. The theory that cancer is caused by a primitive instruction for survival contained in our DNA is a discovery of this book, and is new knowledge in the field of medicine. If someone else has previously discovered this theory, the author apologizes and indeed welcomes it as further evidence of the correctness of the fact.

causes death may merely be an elaboration of our DNA code to control complex cell organization. There are three highly probable possibilities: 1) some gene, or more likely genes, switch *on* at some point in our lives and cause us to age and die, 2) some gene or genes switch *off* at some point in our lives and cause us to die, or 3) a combination of the two. Whichever it is, it should be possible in the future, through techniques of DNA manipulation and therapy, to control death. In fact, there is a program called the Human Genome Project which is in the process of mapping the human DNA molecule. The human DNA molecule contains approximately 100,000 genes, of which 5,480 have been mapped, 359 of them in 1990–91. If we increase the number of researchers, the DNA molecule will be mapped much, much faster, and death could be conquered much, much faster.

Practically speaking, the implementation could work like this: Initially, only relatively small sums of money would be required. The government would give grants to the best medical schools and biology departments to expand their facilities and create researchers specifically trained to investigate all of the human body in general and the cause-and-effect relationships of death specifically. As the number of researchers grows, laboratory complexes will have to be built. Laboratory buildings are relatively inexpensive in that once they are built, they can last a hundred years or more. The primary ongoing expense will therefore be in salaries to the researchers and their technicians. One researcher may have, say, four or five lower paid technicians working for him or her. Let us assume an average salary of $40,000 per year per person. If we also assume that a staff of 100,000 researchers and technicians will eventually be working on the project,[45] then the ongoing cost of the project will be $4 billion per year for salaries. Let us estimate another $500 million for admin-

45. There are currently only about 200 researchers working in the field of ageing.

istration, supplies, lab equipment, etc., for a total cost of $4.5 billion per year. Much less than this amount per year would be required during the start-up phase. This sum of money represents much less than four percent of the total national budget. It would also be the largest research project ever carried out anywhere at anytime.

While searching for the solution to death would be the goal of the project, the short-term results of this amount of labor applied to understanding the human body would be a dazzling array of new discoveries, resulting in new drugs and therapies to relieve the suffering of humankind in all fields, from genetic disorders, to cancers, to arthritis, and even the dreaded acne. After a few short years, the quality of life would show dramatic and inexorable improvement. New high-tech industries would result. Perhaps the fields of computers, miniaturization and bio-medicine would be combined in an industry that could create a miniature health monitor that would be painlessly implanted in the body to monitor health. It might be sensitive enough to, among other things, detect when the very first cell in our body becomes cancerous, pinpoint its location, and advise us to go to the neighborhood clinic to have that one cell painlessly removed, all in the same day.

However, back to the conquest of death. At first glance we might be tempted to say, "That is fine, but what good will all this do me? Even with this massive but relatively low-cost project, it will be a long time before they can find the causes of death and interrupt the process. I will be dead by then." Not necessarily. Follow this logic. Initially, as the project begins, there will be few results, but as more and more researchers are added, progress will begin to be made. In the first five years will death be conquered? No, but enough progress will be made to increase our average life expectancy by perhaps six months. In the next five years of research we can expect more progress to be made than in the first five years. Our average life expectancy will be increased as the incorrect avenues of research are canceled and the researchers and technicians are transferred to the correct avenues of research. We can expect progress at an even greater rate. Perhaps life expectancy will increase by, say, four years. Then, by perhaps the fourth five-year period, we may reach the critical point where it takes the researchers five years of research to give us an increase in life expectancy of five and one-half years. Bingo! The average person never dies as long as the researchers can keep the increase in our life expectancies greater than the amount of time to do the research! And they can.

As we have already learned from Principle No. 1, that society which has the ability to allocate large quantities of resources has, within limits, the power to control when the future will arrive. If, in our case, we want to speed up the rate of increase in our life expectancy, all we have to do is increase the number of researchers. Therefore, not only is death preventable, but the time it takes to reach the critical point of living forever is also controllable.

A further advantage can be gained from a program to cure death by dividing up the research and enlisting the support of the Europeans, the Japanese, and, since no security issues are involved, the Russians. The effect would be either that we could reduce our investment to perhaps $1 billion per year or that some 300,000 researchers might be involved, and results would come some three times faster. Either way, every person on the planet, from Moammar Gadhafi to pygmies of the Ituri Forest in Africa, dictators to politicians of every nation, would have a personal, vested interest in international peace and cooperation because that would be their only possibility of living indefinitely.

If society also begins a large-scale research project devoted to discovering all there is to know in the physical sciences of astronomy, physics, chemistry, biology, meteorology, geophysics, etc., then because the knowledge in these areas must also be finite, some day we will know all there is to know about how the real world operates. We will have the maximum ability possible to manipulate the atoms and molecules and energy that make up our world. In other words, we will have the maximum amount of power over the real world that it is possible to have.

If society does undertake these two research projects, then at some point in the future we will live as long as it is possible to live; we will know as much as it is possible to know; we will be as powerful as it is possible to be. In all the major religions of this world, God is defined as having three attributes: 1) living forever; 2) knowing everything; and 3) being all-powerful. Therefore, we will have become as god-like in these three areas that define God as it is possible for us to be. For those of us who are of a religious nature and believe that God created us in His own image, then we will have returned the compliment and become as much like God as it is possible for us to be. I am certainly *not* empowered to speak for God, but I would bet that that would please Him.

When will Economic Freedom, the conquest of death, and the discovery of all knowledge be achieved here in the United States? The answer to that question is easy. We learned it from Early Man. Since we have already thought in the future and made a plan, only three conditions must be satisfied. The plan must be implemented efficiently. The society must have an appropriate social structure capable of carrying out the task. (In our case, Congress must be reformed so that it is responsive to our needs and not to the needs of special interests). And the society must be willing to sacrifice in order to achieve the goal. In this case the sacrifice is merely a relatively small amount of money (compared to the national budget) spent over a long period of time. The more resources devoted to the project, the sooner the answers will arrive. The fewer resources devoted to the project, the longer the answers will take to arrive. Assuming that the above three conditions are met and assuming that the United States of America has a democracy in which the will of the people becomes the law of the land, then, according to Principle No. 1, it will be up to us, the citizens of the United States, to decide when death will be conquered. When we become as godlike as possible is in the hands of the citizens. In fact, if the United States is a democracy, then *when* we reach "Economic Freedom" is also a decision to be made by the people. Therefore, at what point in the future we attain "Economic Freedom," when death is conquered, when we achieve the maximum amount of knowledge and power that is possible to have, is a question better asked of the readers collectively than of the author. When do *you* want them to come?

If you answered, "As soon as possible," then I can give you a rather close approximation of the soonest we can achieve these states. Economic Freedom can be attained by the year 2010 or shortly thereafter. A closed-loop, infinitely sustainable society can be achieved with a rapid, maximum effort by 2015. That is 20 years. Death can be conquered at the earliest about 2050. That is 55 years. Total knowledge can be attained in perhaps 100 years, or roughly the year 2100. These times, 15, 20, 55, and 100 years, are really eye-blinks of time compared to the incredibly vast time scale upon which we have been thinking throughout this book. However, even if these time estimates are optimistic, the increase in life expectancy brought about by the conquest of death still makes most of these goals attainable by many who are fortyish and younger today. In addition, the amount of money required to achieve these goals is minimal. It is far less money than Congress wastes every year in its bribery-for-re-election scam. Therefore, it is accurate to state that a golden age for humankind is potentially just around the corner.

All that is required is that our government be reformed into an institution that can 1) think in the future, 2) plan in the future, and 3) ensure that we have the appropriate social organization (government) to implement the plan, and that 4) we, the citizens, be able to sacrifice to achieve the goals.

The More Distant Future

Presuming that we human beings of this planet are able to continue sustaining ourselves in the near term, we can look forward to a long bright future. The sun will continue to provide us with energy for the next six billion years, at which time it will have exhausted its supply of hydrogen and expand into a red giant. This rather rude and unneighborly act will end the conditions for life on Earth by consuming us in a fireball of plasma. We will have left the Earth by then to colonize an artificial satellite of our own design constructed in orbit around a neighboring young star chosen for its stability and long life.

The Far Distant Future

By the yet more distant future, we will have encountered other life forms from our own Milky Way galaxy. The reasoning goes like this: Within our own galaxy there are at least 200 billion stars. If the conditions conducive to the evolution of life (liquid water) are present in even an extremely low fraction of a percent of the star systems, then there are literally millions of planets with life forms on them that evolved in conformation to the environment of those planets. We can expect these life forms to be physically different from our own, but nonetheless caused by the Law of the Survival of the Efficient.

And finally, in the Grand Finale, humankind, all life forms, all matter, all energy, and all things that exist will face one of two futures. Remember the Big Bang? Remember some 15 billion years ago when everything in the universe was collected together in one spot and blew up? Then the debris cooled and formed galaxies? These galaxies, of which our

Milky Way is just one out of a hundred billion, are becoming farther and farther apart even as we speak. The first possible future is that everything just keeps getting farther and farther apart. Interactions among matter become fewer and fewer, until all heat and light are exhausted. The conditions necessary for life vanish. Small bits of matter adrift in a cold, dark, lifeless vacuum. END.

The second possible future is that the universe contains a sufficient density of mass to produce sufficient gravity to bring everything back together again. But do not start breathing easier yet, because the gravity will be so strong that everything will be smashed together again, ending the conditions for life. Then, with everything squeezed back together again under billions of tons of pressure per square inch and 100 billion degrees C of temperature, the Big Bang will occur again. Everything will expand again and galaxies will be formed again and life will begin again. This is known as the Oscillating Universe. It operates on a 100-billion-year cycle of expansion and contraction. It will continue to run forever and never needs lubricating. It has also already run forever. With the Oscillating Universe there was no beginning of time. There was no moment of creation of mass and energy. They have always been here and will always be here alternately expanding and contracting. If the Oscillating Universe is our future, then it has also been our past prior to the Big Bang. If the Oscillating Universe is our future, then we know what was occurring prior to the Big Bang 15 billion years ago—an infinite number of expansions and contractions of the universe.

The logical points brought up by our two alternate futures are far too tempting to overlook. Let us analyze the cold, bleak ending first. If the universe is a unique, one-time event and energy and matter were created some 15 billion years ago, we have the valid right to ask, "How was the energy for the Big Bang created, and what was occurring prior to the creation?" On these questions, science can offer us no ground upon which to stand. If we define God as the Creator of the universe, and if the universe was created 15 billion years ago as the ever-expanding-universe theory says it was, then if someone were to suggest that whatever force created the universe was, by definition, God, I would agree. Therefore, if the ever-expanding universe is our future, then, by definition, it is a certitude that God, in some form, exists.

In analyzing the second alternative future, the Oscillating Universe, the universe was never created but rather has been going through an infinite number of cycles of expansion and contraction and will continue doing so forever. The crunch comes when the next "Big Crunch" comes, followed by another "Big Bang." All that existed, all of humankind, all of our accomplishments and achievements and all of our knowledge and that of all other life forms, will vanish. None of it can withstand the "Crunch and Bang." All trace of us will end. Or will it? All that we need do is figure out how to repel the force of gravity long enough to hover at a safe distance while the rest of the universe smashes itself together and explodes. It may not be possible to rescind the law of gravity, but humankind has 85 billion years to attempt to find a solution. When conditions improve we could rejoin the rest of matter. We could rejoin the universe prior to the existence of life in the new universe. Then we could give the knowledge that we have accumulated to the newly emerging life forms if we choose. This act would presumably save them from the indignities of warfare, disease, poverty, crime, and death. Our other option would be not to interfere and let them develop naturally. Either way, if we make our presence known, from their perspective, we will appear to be all-knowing, all-powerful, and live forever. The difference in technology and knowledge between our culture at that time in the future and the newly emerging sapient beings of another future world will be far more vast than the difference in cultures was upon the first encounter between the Aztecs and Cortez and his men and horses. Upon their first encounter with our society of the future, do you think the newly intelligent beings will think the same as the Aztecs thought about Cortez? Do you suppose they will think we are gods?

Conclusion

Well, how did you do? Did you have trouble believing some parts? Almost everyone does. The difficulty probably lies in the author's inability to explain it well in the limited space available. As far as the contemporary society of the United States of America is concerned, what parts of the idealized future portrayed above are appropriate? Principle No. 1 informs us "that society which has *the ability to allocate large quantities of its resources* has, within limits, the power to control when the future will arrive." Sadly, due to our budget deficits, our society does *not* have the ability to allocate large quantities of our resources (if the economic devastation occurs that currently awaits us, then Economic Freedom may not be achievable at all). Therefore, the appropriate plan for the United States is merely to begin the research project by the team of scientists to solve the technical problems and create the first automaton. The first factory, instead of being constructed simultaneously, can merely be designed simultaneously. Then the factory could be built after the first automaton is created, adding approximately three to five years to the length of the project and reducing its yearly cost dramatically.

It is interesting to note that the ancient Egyptians had all the materials needed to invent hang-gliding. They had linen for a strong and light-weight airfoil, light structural members (sandalwood and rope), and the pyramids from which to launch. However, the ancient Egyptians failed to invent hang-gliding. Why? Because no one ever thought up the idea.

Why? No doubt, because the conventional wisdom of the time discarded the possibility of human flight. Therefore, no one "wasted" any time thinking about something that everyone thought to be impossible. The ancient Egyptians allowed their conventional wisdom to limit their imaginations. I hope we do not fail for the same reason.

In terms of our logic, there is definitely a lack of a preponderance of evidence upon which we can decide the appropriate future for the United States of America. Therefore, the foregoing chapter should serve merely as an example of the type of innovative future that our current government is not even capable of thinking up, let alone actually doing something about. It will be sufficient if the reader comes away from this chapter with the understanding that an efficiently managed country that employs the Four Critical Abilities extremely well can cause an undreamed of, fantastic, unbelievable, golden age for all of its citizens within this generation, whether it is the future described here or another one.

CHAPTER THIRTEEN

The Only Possible Solution

*Step No. 4: The Causes, Step No. 5: The Difference,
Step No. 6: The Plan, Step No. 7: The Sacrifice*

B Y APPLYING THE TOOL OF LOGIC known as the Black Box Technique, we have gained a profound understanding of the past and the present (Step No. 1 of applying the Black Box Technique). With that knowledge we were able to accurately predict the real future that awaits us if no change is made (Step No. 2). Then we predicted one possible idealized future that we could have (Step No. 3). The difference between the two futures is dramatic and obvious. It is crystal clear that the real future, our current course, will lead us to great pain and suffering and the loss of our society. The idealized future, either the one presented here or a better one (it would not be very wise to accept a future less beneficial than the one portrayed in the text) is far superior. It achieves many of the elements of a Utopia.

Step No.4: The Causes of the Idealized Future

Our next step is to determine the cause-and-effect relationships that will have to occur to achieve the idealized future. To accomplish this, we work the cause-and-effect relationships backwards. By knowing what the effect is (the idealized future), we can determine what must be the cause of that effect. If we view the just-discovered cause as an effect and determine what must have caused that effect and on and on until we arrive back at the present, then we will have determined the sequence of cause-and-effect relationships that must occur to result in the idealized future (Step No. 4).

In the last chapter, we learned the cause that will result in the idealized future. It was the implementation of the plan (the team of scientists and the first factory). To continue working backwards, what must be the cause of the plan to be implemented? The answer is a future government that is 1) desirous of fulfilling the people's goals as opposed to the special interests or the members own goals, and 2) capable of *efficiently* implementing a long-term plan. The first attribute required of our future government, being desirous of fulfilling the people's goals, is another way to say "being responsive to the people," which is another way of saying that what we need is the restoration of our democracy. The second attribute required of our future government is being able to efficiently implement long-term plans. Then the question becomes "What will cause our future government to be responsive to the people and to be able to efficiently implement long-term plans?" We have already learned how societies should efficiently implement long-term plans—by utilizing the Four Critical Abilities.

The Four Critical Abilities Applied to Our Future Government

1) *The government should be able to think about the future accurately and realistically.* Our future government must be actively and eternally vigilant in accurately perceiving reality both in the present and in the future. (This would entail a new branch of government to devote exclusive attention to so important a task.)

2) *The government should be able to make the best plan and be able to carry it out efficiently.* Our future government must be capable of producing excellent planning and plan-implementation. (The planning should be performed by that branch of government that perceives future reality the best—the aforementioned new branch

of government.) Plan-implementation and the laws required thereby should be handled by the president and Congress after restoration of the pre-1973 system of checks and balances.

3) *The government must have the appropriate social organization to efficiently carry out the above two principles.* In our case, we are lacking the appropriate form of government. Our future government must be capable of being responsive to the people. In short, we need our democracy restored. Therefore, the first attribute needed by our future government to be responsive to the people is included in the Four Critical Abilities.

4) *The people must be willing to sacrifice to carry out the plan.* In our case the people must also be willing to sacrifice to modify our government. The people must be willing to take the actions necessary to fulfill the plan. If people fail to sacrifice to save themselves from future assured destruction, then those people are decadent and deserve their destruction.

By having a future government that operates according to the Four Critical Abilities, we not only will have our democracy restored, but we will have a government that can address long-term solutions to our long-term problems and thereby have a realistic opportunity of solving the latter. Since our future government will be one of the first governments in the world to institutionalize the Four Critical Abilities,[46] we should investigate more thoroughly what changes will be required.

In reviewing the first theft of our democracy by the Senate in the 1880s, our democracy was restored by constitu-

---

46. Japan has a ministry-level planning institution (Ministry of International Trade and Industry).

tional amendment, which gave the people the right to elect the Senate. By amending the Constitution, the door was permanently slammed on that particular method of theft ever being used again. Amending the Constitution is the only certain and permanent way to ensure that our democracy will never be stolen again in the same way. For if only ordinary laws are passed, Congress can at any time change them. The historical precedent of amending the Constitution to correct the theft of our government is a very wise one. It would be silly for us to restore our democracy and leave Congress the power to steal it back at any time.

To continue to apply the Black Box Technique, we know that constitutional amendments will have to be the causes that result in an efficient future government that will be responsive to the people and utilize the Four Critical Abilities, which in turn will cause the plan (the team of scientists, etc.) to be implemented, which in turn will cause our idealized future to be achieved. The amendments will play an all-important role in shaping our future government and are worthy of more thorough investigation.

First Future Amendment

Our future government must have the appropriate social organization. The government must be responsive to the people. In our case, that means the return of our democracy. A constitutional amendment will have to be passed that not only repeals Section 4, Article 1 of the Constitution (the right of Congress to make its own election laws) but also places the power to make election laws with the Federal Election Commission. The Federal Election Commission will be charged with maintaining an election process that is fair to all participants, free from corruption, and equal to all contestants, and will be fully federally funded with no contributions from PACs or individuals for either congressional or presidential elections. Placing these responsibilities in the Constitution will cause the rulings of the Federal Election Commission to be subject to review by the Supreme Court for constitutionality in the normal way. Therefore, our electoral system will have the ability to evolve, but the Supreme Court will have the ability always to ensure its proper and correct functioning. If the Supreme Court performs its constitutional duty properly, then our democracy may never be stolen again!

Second, Third, and Fourth Future Amendments

Our future government must be able to promptly and efficiently implement long-term plans. This will necessitate cooperation between the president and Congress, which can be achieved by restoring the pre-1973 system of checks and balances. Specifically, we will need three amendments to the Constitution that 1) return to the president the Right of Impoundment (line-item veto), 2) return to the president his pre-1973 foreign policy powers, and 3) mandates a balanced federal budget within five years.

Fifth Future Amendment

We need an amendment that will institutionalize the Four Critical Abilities. An amendment will be passed to create a new, fourth branch of government consisting of experts, whose sole function is to think in the future and create a comprehensive plan for America that will take us into the future, solve our problems, and create the best possible future for us. Let us call this new branch of government the Council of Advanced Planning.

Do you recall when, earlier in this book, we discovered what differentiates humankind from the other animals? It was the human's ability to think in the future and make a plan. This is humankind's greatest weapon in the battle for survival. Our current government does not use the greatest and highest technique that it can possibly use to ensure a successful future for the United States of America. On the contrary, by not utilizing thinking in the future and the making of a plan, our current government dooms us to a bleak and impoverished future. By not having a government that can think in the future, we become easy prey for the future-oriented Japanese.

Amazingly enough in our present form of government, there is no provision for any branch of government to plan for the future. What is America's plan for the next five years? Ten years? Twenty-five years? Sadly, we do not have one. Even in the Constitution as originally designed, the government can have a plan only for the term of the sitting president—four years or possibly eight years at most. Not anywhere near long enough to solve our problems. We need a long-term plan that can be followed for at least thirty-five years. Our society is going into the future like people with their eyes shut, bumping into walls. Instead of managing our future, our government basically stumbles along without a plan and then reacts when it bumps into a crisis such as the Arab oil embargo or Saddam Hussein's invasion of Kuwait. Our government does not plan, but merely reacts when it finds itself in an intolerable situation. In business school, we learned that this is called "management by crisis" and is the lowest and worst form of management. Until America has a governmental institution that can view the future accurately, make plans, and have them efficiently carried out, America will be like a punch-drunk fighter standing in the ring of international competition with his arms at his side, taking a terrible beating.

As has been shown in this book many times, and as I am sure the reader believes by now, the society for which our governmental structure was created no longer exists. In the early history of our country, planning by the government was neither needed nor desired. Our government is inappropriate for the present situation.

The problems confronting America are mostly technical in nature. For example, the greenhouse effect, toxic wastes, education, the economy, the environment, energy, and agriculture are all problems that require experts to derive the best possible solutions. Experts, by definition, are the people most knowledgeable about the cause-and-effect relationships in their particular fields. Therefore, experts are the most capable of all of us citizens at predicting the future realistically in their particular fields. Therefore, a group of our best experts from a wide variety of fields would be the best at predicting the entire future realistically, and the best at making plans for that future. People like Nobel Prize winners, noted economists, experts from all disciplines of science and the social sciences. In short, people who have a proven record of perceiving reality well enough to advance the understanding of humankind. The members of the new branch of government should have lifetime appointments like the Supreme Court Justices to remove them from the possibility of political influence. Then we will have an institution made up of experts charged with creating a cohesive and all-encompassing plan for the future of America. A plan that not only solves our current problems and avoids future problems that we would otherwise encounter, but takes us to the best possible future in the shortest time possible. This comprehensive, all-encompassing plan would be voted upon by all citizens in a national referendum. If the plan is rejected, the Council of Advanced Planning would have to modify the plan until it is acceptable to us citizens.

In addition, being the fourth branch of government, the Council of Advanced Planning needs to be integrated into the system of checks and balances with the other branches with which it must cooperate, namely the president and the Congress. As we have already learned, if a leader is to lead (thinking and planning in the future is the quintessential act of leading), the leader must have the ability to reward and/or the ability to punish. In our case, what is to prevent the president and the Congress from treating the plans of the Council for Advanced Planning merely as a piece of paper that periodically is slipped under the door? In other words, what lever or mechanism of government will cause the Congress to want to pass required legislation and the president to want to efficiently execute the plan of the Council of Advanced Planning? After thinking of quite a few levers, the most effective appears to be placing in the hands of the Council of Advanced Planning the power to call for the election of both Congress and president. Politicians hate running for re-election because it carries the possibility of loss of power. Elections could not be called less than two years or more than five years apart. Given this punishment for failure, the president and Congress would attempt to efficiently and promptly implement the plan. Then there would be only two plausible reasons why the president and Congress would fail to efficiently implement the plan. First, the president and/or Congress could be guilty of not fulfilling their assigned roles due to their own incompetency, corruption, or inefficiency, in which case it is proper they be forced to run for re-election and be tossed out by the electorate for incompetence and inefficiency. Second, the president and Congress might disagree, for whatever reason, with the implementation of the plan. No matter how the people vote in the election, whether they return the president and/or Congress to office to continue blocking the plan, or throw the president and/or Congress out of office, the people will decide the issue. In short, the people will decide through their vote any unresolved issues among the Council of Advanced Planning and the president and Congress.

Additional Efficiencies

Furthermore, if we want to increase the efficiency of our future government, we have two clear options. The first is to reduce the Congress to a single house. With the election of the Senate by the people in 1913, our current government has the unnecessary complication of two houses of Congress representing the same electorate. By eliminating one, the government of the future will be more streamlined and therefore more efficient.

The second option to consider is a change to a parliamentary form of government with a single house. This is not the appropriate place for a discussion of the relative advantages and disadvantages of a parliamentary form over our current type of democracy. However, the following point should not be overlooked.

Our current governmental structure was the first prototype in a new wave of democratic governments that has been and still is sweeping the world. However, almost all the democracies that have followed ours have had the luxury of beginning with a clean sheet of paper. The modern parliamentary democracies that have followed us were already full-functioning, strong, central governments, usually monarchies, that switched to democracy. It typically was not a case of sovereign states' combining to form a union, as our nation did. The other democracies have adopted a more evolved form of representative democracy—the parliamentary system. The parliamentary system is more efficient. We have the archaic, original, compromised prototype democracy that has been stolen by Congress in addition. The fact is that no country in the entire world has a government older than the United States. I challenge the reader to think of a functioning government that is older than that of the United States. Amazingly, there is none. Even England has changed its governmental structure. Queen Elizabeth II does not play the same role in the modern English government that King George III played in 1776. We Americans consider ourselves to be a young country. In point of fact, we are over 200 years old. We have the most ancient government still functioning on the planet!

Recall what others have said, particularly Thomas Jefferson, who stated that each generation should rewrite the Constitution to decide what form of democracy it will live under. It is over 200 years later, eight generations, and Thomas Jefferson believed we should be on our eighth Constitution. Tench Cox, a member of the Continental Congress, stated in 1788: "The people, who are made and held supreme by the Constitution, will change and amend the Constitution when errors are found." The grand old dame, the ship of state, has weathered many storms in her 200 years of existence, and she is carrying a lot of excess baggage (for example, the facts that the 10th Amendment is being ignored and the Senate is redundant). It is time for a facelift to a more efficient means of coordination between the president and Congress. I suggest, after the return of our democracy, a valuable topic of national discussion would be the change to a parliamentary form of government.

If we do change to a parliamentary form of government with a branch devoted exclusively to planning our future, we will have the most advanced form of government on the planet. A government whose natural result will be the creation of plans that will solve our problems as we proceed into the future. A government that will be much more efficient than even the best of the parliamentary governments. The innovative American government of our revolution helped to skyrocket America to a place of leadership amongst all nations. As the noted historian Henry Steele Commager said, "Nothing in all history . . . ever succeeded like America." A new governmental structure that institutionalizes planning combined with a parliament will provide to America the same advantage over normal parliamentary forms of government that our prototype democracy had over monarchies. Thanks to the institutionalizing of planning in the future, our new governmental structure will be far superior to even the most recent parliamentary systems. It will be the best form of government on the planet.

By changing our form of government, we, the people, will re-invigorate ourselves. We will be more than capable of making whatever sacrifice is necessary. Currently, in many elections, less than 50 percent of *registered* voters actually vote,[47] not to mention those of us who do not even bother to register. We, the voters of this country, are apathetic because we realize that it really does not make any difference for whom we vote, Republican or Democrat. We know the result will remain the same abysmal abomination. Merely because we have a two-party system in this country, Republican and Democratic, why should the American people allow ourselves to be herded into the belief that there are only two possible types of solutions to our problems, conservative or liberal? What difference does it make if the solution to a problem comes from a body of thought titled "conservative" or "liberal," or from an entirely new perspective? I am sure that most Americans would agree with me that it is irrelevant from where the solutions to our problems come. The only matter of importance is that our problems are, in fact, solved. Neither Republicans nor Democrats, conservatives nor liberals have the answers to our problems. To believe that Republicans or Democrats, conservatives or liberals have the solutions to our problems is Neanderthal. Worse still is the fact that, given the corruption in Congress, no comprehensive solution to our problems, from any source, can be implemented.

---

47. In the 1994 elections, 37 percent of registered voters actually voted.

Let us summarize the way our new government would work. First, the Council of Advanced Planning would create a comprehensive plan complete with a timetable that would take us to an infinitely sustainable, closed-loop society as rapidly as possible. Next, the people would approve the plan in a nationwide referendum. If we disapprove of the plan, the Council of Advanced Planning would have to modify the plan until the people do approve it. Then the parliamentary Congress, working in cooperation with the president and the cabinet, would pass the laws necessary to implement the plan. The president as head of the executive branch would implement the plan. To ensure that the legislative and executive branches rapidly and effectively perform their functions in accordance with the plan, the Council of Advanced Planning could be empowered to call elections if a majority of the experts disapproved of the implementation. The president and Congress, not wanting to face a re-election in which they might lose, would do everything in their power to properly implement the plan. Elections could not be called more often than every two years or less often than every five years. The elections would be 100 percent federally funded and therefore fair and equal and free of corruption. In light of experience, the plan might need modification. The Council of Advanced Planning would modify the plan, the people would approve it and the Congress and the president would implement the changes.

The naturally occurring result of the above form of government would be an unbelievable golden age for all the citizens of America within this generation. If it were not for the unavoidable trouble caused by the budget deficits and lack of an industrial policy thanks to the decadence of the current Congress, the golden age could start even sooner.

Either way, the passage of these five amendments would not only restore our democracy, but moreover provide us with a government able to perceive the future and deftly guide us into it. Therefore, we know that the ratification of these five amendments is what will have to occur in order to cause our efficient future government, which, in turn, will cause the plan to be efficiently implemented—which, in turn, will cause the idealized future to occur. Then the question becomes, what causes the amendments to occur? The answer is by one of the two ways to amend the Constitution: 1) The first is by passage of a two-thirds majority in *both* houses of Congress and then ratification by three-fourths of the state legislatures, which is 38 states. 2) The second way is a convoluted, ill-defined method involving the use of state conventions; it has never been used and because of its vagueness may be unconstitutional. Since it is ill-advised to use method No. 2, method No. 1 must occur in order to cause the amendments to be ratified. Method No. 1 consists of two parts: first, a two-thirds majority in *both* houses of Congress must pass the amendments, and second, 38 state legislatures must ratify them. The approval of the 38 state legislatures should be fairly simple to attain. The states lose no power by ratifying the amendments, but do gain a more efficient partner with which to govern. Furthermore, if the amendments must already have been passed by two-thirds of both houses of Congress prior to their voting, the state legislatures will find no profit in thwarting the will of the people. Therefore, ratification by the state legislatures would probably be rather easy. Then the only difficult part of the question of what causes the amendments to be ratified is that a two-thirds majority in both houses of Congress must vote for the amendments.

Therefore, Congress will have to pass amendments that would take power away from itself. We have 5,500 years of recorded history that demonstrate that this will not happen without the use of force. Just as a corrupt institution is incapable of honestly investigating itself for corruption, so a corrupt institution is incapable of reforming its own corruption. Expecting a corrupt institution to correct its own corruption is like expecting a blind man to operate on himself to correct his own blindness. If the blind man could see well enough to operate, he would not need the operation.

Since we have 5,500 years of recorded history that tell us Congress will not voluntarily take power away from itself and distribute it back whence it came, then Congress must be forced to relinquish its stolen powers. As we have learned, neither dictators nor democratic institutions will ever voluntarily give up power no matter what cost the citizenry must pay. The question then becomes: "By whom and how will Congress be forced to pass the amendments and relinquish its stolen power?"

To whom can we turn for help? The president? The president cannot even get his own budget passed. How well do you think he can succeed in forcing Congress to restrict its own power? If the president were to publicly endorse the reform of Congress, his effectiveness in dealing with Congress would become nonexistent. He would be committing an act of political suicide. He would immediately become the least effective president in the history of the United States. President Millard Fillmore (1850–1853) would look like an executive dynamo in comparison. Therefore, we can expect no help from the president.

How about the Supreme Court? Although the Supreme Court can rule laws passed by Congress to be unconstitutional, none of the laws that Congress has passed that have created the corruption are in direct violation of the Constitution. The powers stolen from the president were never part of the Constitution, but were part of the system of checks and balances. Our Founding Fathers assumed that the least likely institution to become corrupt would be Congress. In reaction to the tyrannical rule of King George III, the Founding Fathers over-compensated in favor of the legislative branch, Congress. By not incorporating into the Constitution the presidential powers contained in the system of checks and balances, they left the presidency open to stripping of powers by a vengeful Congress. Power once taken will never be returned without the use of force. Our Founding Fathers could not have foreseen that the causes—special interests, money, and television—could lead to the effect— the theft of our democracy. In addition, the Supreme Court, particularly after its near brush with loss of power by Congress and President Roosevelt in the 1930s, is very wary of interfering with Congress. Therefore, the Supreme Court cannot be counted on to render any assistance.

How about the media, the so-called fourth estate and the "watchdog" and "guardian of the people's rights"? We have already seen how the media profit from our unfair campaign laws to the tune of one-half billion dollars every two years. A change to fair elections would deprive them of their windfall profits. We have already seen how, unreported by the media, Congress stole our democracy and sold it to the special interests. Can we rely on the integrity of the editors of newspapers and the producers of television news shows, who are accountable both for the stories they run and the profits of their organizations, to trumpet the theft of our democracy? I would not count on it. In fact, the media may actively oppose the reform of Congress in order to continue receiving its windfall profits.

How about our state governments? In the two hundred years of our history, our state governments have been reduced from sovereign states to lowly petitioners of the federal government. The Civil War marked the end of any pretensions to independent authority by the states. Our governors, our state legislators, and our mayors approach Congress on bent knee begging for increases in federal funds. Can you imagine what would happen to a state whose legislators began demanding reform from its superiors? Congress would cut off funds to that state in short order. The other states would quickly get the message. Also, before we turn to

our state legislatures looking for white knights, I am reminded of an incident that took place on the floor of the Texas
State Senate in 1988. While the Senate was in session, an
East Texas multimillionaire by the name of Lonnie "Bo"
Pilgrim walked down the aisles gratuitously distributing
checks for $10,000. He later admitted to exercising "poor
taste." The senators admitted to nothing. Can we expect help
from our state and local governments? Definitely not.

Who is left? Who can we turn to for help? There is only one
group more powerful than the Congress of the United States—
we, the people. The United States of America is our society,
not Congress'. This is a country of the people, by the people,
and for the people. *We* are the supreme authority in this *our*
own country. *We* elect members of Congress to carry out *our*
will. They have betrayed us by neglecting our welfare and promoting the welfare of special interests. It is our right—nay, it
is our duty—to take action in our own behalf. When a democratic government fails to carry out the will of the people,
then, by the very definition of a democratic government, the
burden falls on the citizens themselves to alter the situation.

Let me quote to you from the Declaration of Independence
written by the wisest of all the patriots, Thomas Jefferson.
He, of course, wrote it to apply to King George III of England.
In parentheses, I will make the appropriate references to
apply it to our current situation.

> *When in the course of human events, it becomes*
> *necessary for one people* (we, modern Americans) *to*
> *dissolve the political bands which have connected them*
> *with another* (Congress), *and to assume among the*
> *powers of the Earth, the separate and equal station to*
> *which the Laws of Nature and of Nature's God entitle*
> *them, a decent respect to the opinions of mankind*
> *requires that they should declare the causes which*
> *impel them to the separation.*

We hold these truths to be self-evident, that all men are created equal, that they are endowed by their Creator with certain unalienable Rights, that among these are Life, Liberty, and the pursuit of Happiness. That to secure these rights, Governments are instituted among Men, deriving their just powers from the consent of the governed. That whenever any Form of Government becomes destructive of these ends, it is the Right of the People to alter or to abolish it, and to institute new Government, laying its foundation on such principles and organizing its powers in such form, as to them shall seem most likely to effect their Safety and Happiness. Prudence, indeed, will dictate that Governments long established should not be changed for light and transient causes; and accordingly all experience hath shown, that mankind are more disposed to suffer, while evils are sufferable, than to right themselves by abolishing the forms to which they are accustomed. But when a long train of abuses and usurpations, pursuing invariably the same Object evinces a design to reduce them under absolute Despotism (Congress' theft of our democracy), *it is their right, it is their duty, to throw off such Government, and to provide new guards for their future security. Such has been the patient sufferance of these Colonies* (we, modern Americans); *and such is now the necessity which constrains them to alter their former System of Government. The history of the present King of Great Britain* (Congress) *is a history of repeated injuries and usurpation, all having in direct object the establishment of an absolute Tyranny over these States* (the people). *To prove this, let Facts be submitted to a candid world.*

It is amazing how slightly the Declaration of Independence need be altered to apply to our current situation. All we need do is change "us" for the colonists and "Congress" for King George III. Therefore, let us adopt it also as our Declaration of Independence in our struggle against the supreme Congress. I hope that it serves us and our just cause as it did our Founding Fathers.

The remaining paragraphs of the Declaration of Independence are a listing of the wrongs committed against the colonists by King George III. The wrongs committed by Congress have been partially listed earlier in this book. Then, the Declaration of Independence concludes with the signatures of 56 of our Founding Fathers—among them John Hancock, Benjamin Franklin, Samuel Adams, John Adams (second president of the United States), and of course, Thomas Jefferson (third president of the United States), Benjamin Harrison (father of the ninth president and great-grandfather of the twenty-third president), Richard Henry Lee (proposer of the Declaration of Independence), and Francis Lightfoot Lee. Coincidentally, another signer of the Declaration of Independence happened to be a merchant from Connecticut by the name of William Williams (1731–1811). The Declaration of Independence was not only signed by far more of the patriots who founded this country than the Constitution was,[48] but moreover it was unanimous. Therefore, the Declaration of Independence is the only document that unanimously expresses the thoughts of our Founding Fathers.

And therefore none other than our own Founding Fathers, speaking through the document that gave birth to our country, advise us that it is our right and our duty to alter or abolish Congress as we see fit.

Fortunately for us, we can alter our government in a different way from the method available to our Founding

---

48. As we learned, the Constitution was signed by only 39 delegates out of 65 certified to the constitutional convention.

Fathers. Upon exhausting the legal means available to them, they were forced to use armed revolution. Thousands of them gave up their lives in places from Boston Commons to remote fields like Cowpens, South Carolina. We do not have to lie mortally wounded on a field of battle waiting for our blood to drain out to regain our democracy. We can restore our democracy by simply voting. How do we do it?

First, we must *not* vote for any person currently serving in Congress. No matter to which party—Republican or Democrat—they belong, we must not re-elect them. No matter how powerful or well-known your senator or representative is, he or she must be defeated. In fact, the more powerful and well-known they are, the more important it is to defeat them, because they are precisely the members of Congress who continue to sell our democracy to the special interests. It may be tempting to think that the problem lies with the members of Congress from other states, and that our member of Congress is a good person. This is because members of Congress running for re-election only show their television ads depicting them as good people in their home states. Do not fall for this propaganda. Citizens from other states who have not been subjected to these television campaigns very likely consider others' members of Congress to be the crooks that they actually are. As we have already learned, these television ads are cunningly conceived to brainwash us into believing that our members of Congress are great statesmen. If they are great statesmen, why has not even one of them stepped forward and admitted that Congress is corrupt and has stolen our democracy? Also, we may think that it is wise to retain our members of Congress because they are effective in obtaining special privileges for our state, such as the sugar or dairy bills. What good will it do the sugar grower or dairy producer when the whole economy unravels? Selfish thinking like that is similar to being happy that one is on the top deck when the *Titanic* sinks and is thus the last to drown. Better that the ship not sink, and we all sail into port, and nobody drowns.

I have also heard the argument advanced that not all members of Congress are crooks and that there are some "good" members of Congress. If that is true, then why are not the supposed "good" members of Congress screaming their heads off attempting to notify the American people of the decadence and corruption of their crooked colleagues and the theft of our democracy? If any member of Congress were to draw attention to the decadence and corruption of their colleagues, that member of Congress would immediately become ostracized and lose all power and influence with fellow members of Congress. Not wanting to lose their power (after all, is not power the reason they ran for Congress in the first place?), they remain silent. In the American legal system, a person who knows of a crime and remains silent is known as a conspirator and is as guilty as the person who committed the crime. So, who are these supposedly "good" members of Congress? They do not exist.

Moreover, even if these supposedly "good" members of Congress actually did exist, what are we supposed to do? Not reform Congress and not despise Congress for what it has done, is doing, and will continue to do to the American people? Advocating not voting against all incumbent members of Congress because there are supposedly a few "good" members of Congress is analagous to advocating not attacking the German army during World War II because Hitler had a few generals who were decent men of integrity on the German general staff.

Not voting for your incumbent member of Congress will remove the current crop of crooks from Congress. It will also serve notice that we Americans want our democracy back. This will certainly be an improvement over the current situation, but for whom *do* we vote? Since we have basically a two-party system in this country, it means that we will have to vote for the candidate from the other party. This means that we will merely be exchanging Republicans for Democrats, and Democrats for Republicans. Or to put it another way, we will merely be exchanging crooks for thieves, and thieves for crooks. I repeat, "For whom do we vote?"

Both the Republicans and the Democrats are responsible for selling our democracy to the special interest groups. Both the Republicans and Democrats prostitute themselves to the special interests in order to assure themselves of re-election. Both the Republicans and Democrats forsake what is best for us the people. Both parties are equally corrupt and incapable of honest reform. I repeat, "For whom *do* we vote?"

The answer to the question, "For whom *do* we vote?" is particularly vexing because there are no congressional candidates running on the platform of the reduction of the power of Congress, and the passage of the aforementioned amendments to the Constitution. These people do not currently exist in our contemporary political environment. There are only two possibilities. 1) One of the two current parties will change platforms and endorse the above (of which I would be very suspicious), or 2) a new party or parties will be formed (of which I will also be very suspicious) that endorses these amendments. Either way, until at least one of the above is done, we are left with no option other than to continually cast our vote for the challenger in all congressional elections in order to continually demonstrate our disapproval of the theft of our democracy, even if this means voting against the member of Congress for whom we just voted two years before. For if after we have understood that Congress has stolen our democracy we continue to vote for the incumbent member of Congress, then we are validating that theft. We are, in effect, saying, "Go ahead. Take my democracy. It is OK with me. I do not mind. Keep up the good work."

We will know we are winning when the re-election rate of incumbents trends downward toward 33$\frac{1}{3}$ percent in both the

House and Senate. By that time, one or both of the two political parties will have modified its platform and a number of third parties will have sprung up to appeal to the increasing number of citizens who are not being represented. The problem will have become not a lack of parties but rather too many parties desiring to represent us. We will have created a political vacuum, which a variety of new and existing political parties will come rushing to fill. They will come from all corners of our society begging to represent us. The prize will be the running of the most powerful government on Earth. I am reminded of the movie *Field of Dreams*, in which Kevin Costner hears a mysterious voice telling him that if he builds a baseball diamond, Shoeless Joe Jackson will arrive: "If you build it, he will come." I guarantee you that when an ever-increasing percentage of incumbent members of Congress are defeated, new political parties will come. If you vote against incumbents, they will come.

We must be careful not to accept any party to represent us that attempts to go beyond the scope of the aforementioned amendments. Imagine what would happen if other issues were brought into play, such as the abortion issue. It would divide us and cause us to become powerless. Therefore, we cannot support a party that has a larger agenda than the aforementioned amendments even if we agree with the agenda. Other issues must be resolved in another forum at a later time. Also, we clearly cannot accept anything less than the aforementioned amendments. In addition, after the party or parties control two-thirds of both houses, it will take less than two years to ratify the aforementioned amendments. If the amendments are not ratified within two years, then in the next election we will have to vote against the new incumbent and vote in others. How will we be able to tell who wants to honestly represent us and who has another agenda? There is no certain way to judge a person or an institution that has not acted and only promises to act.

However, I can state how we will be able to judge when our democracy will have been restored to us. Only when the following amendments are ratified and made a part of the Constitution will we know that at least this method of stealing our democracy is permanently closed.

1) A constitutional amendment that will remove from Congress the power to regulate its own elections and place it in the hands of a commission to ensure fair elections. In addition, the commission will be empowered to determine acceptable levels of outside income and to what benefits members of Congress are entitled. The regulations of the commission will then be subject to review for constitutionality by the Supreme Court in the normal way. Therefore, in effect, the Supreme Court will be able to order the correction of any inequities found in the election process, and our democracy will be far more securely safeguarded in the future. Both congressional and presidential elections will be 100 percent federally funded. No PAC money or private contributions will be allowed.

2) A constitutional amendment that will return the right of impoundment (line-item veto) to the president.

3) A constitutional amendment that will return pre-1973 foreign policy powers to the president.

4) A constitutional amendment that mandates a balanced federal budget within three to five years.[49]

5) A constitutional amendment that creates the Council of Advanced Planning.

---

49. Ending the budget deficits in fewer than three years would withdraw such a substantial amount of purchasing power from the economy so rapidly that a major recession would result. Ending the budget deficits in more than five years would be to flirt needlessly with disaster.

The ratification of these amendments will restore our democracy and permit our future government to efficiently implement long-term plans and thereby cause the idealized future to actually occur. Therefore, a majority of voters continually voting for the challenger for both the House and Senate in every congressional election until the above five amendments have been ratified will cause new and/or existing political parties to offer us candidates for Congress who, upon election, will pass the five amendments, which in turn will create our efficient future government, which in turn will cause a plan to be created and efficiently implemented, which in turn will cause our idealized future to occur. The author is not aware of any course of action other than the passage of these five amendments that would be anywhere near as beneficial to the American people.

The reader will note that there is no provision for an amendment to limit the terms of members of Congress. Although I support any action that lessens the influence of the current members of Congress, I question if merely limiting the terms of members of Congress will achieve the desired effect for the following reasons. 1) The institution of Congress itself is corrupt. It is not a case of just certain individuals being corrupt. 2) Limiting terms will have no effect upon the causes of the corruption. The causes of the corruption—the special interest groups, the campaign laws, and the supremacy of the congressional powers—will all remain. Therefore, if the causes remain, the effect—the corruption— also will remain. 3) What happens when we send presumably uncorrupt people to serve in a corrupt institution? Do the uncorrupt people cause the corrupt institution to become uncorrupt, or does the corrupt institution cause the uncorrupt people to become corrupt? I fear it will at best be some of both. 4) If it is some of both, then how long will it be before the newly arriving uncorrupt members of Congress see that corrupt departing members of Congress are departing with 20 million dollars and that uncorrupt departing members of Congress are departing empty handed? However, they are both departing. We know that people will always act in their own best self-interest as they perceive it. Limiting the terms of Congress may, in the longer term, only intensify the corruption in Congress by creating the perception that "I am only here for a short time, I better get all I can while I can." 5) And most important, by limiting the terms of Congress we trade crooks for, at best, inexperience. Inexperience will not sufficiently improve the efficiency of our government to permit us to survive, let alone to plan, to enact, and to implement the long-term plan that America so desperately needs. In addition, 6) the typically suggested amount of time that terms in Congress would be limited to is usually 12 years. There is no conceivable way that Congress would make term limits retroactive. In other words, the 12 years would only begin to run when the amendment is passed. Therefore, it will be at least 12 years before the first member of Congress is forced from office by this amendment. The future of the United States of America will have already been decided by then. At most, term limits will make the American people feel good, but term limits will be too late to have a substantive impact on our future. Congress has broken our system of government. It is as if we were driving a car with a flat tire. In effect, term limits would merely require that we periodically replace the flat tire with a new flat tire. If we make the sacrifice required to impose our will on Congress in the form of term limits, why do we not correct the entire problem by reforming Congress so that it *can* solve our problems? We need to change the cause-and-effect relationships that cause members of Congress to act in the corrupt manner they do, not change how long individual members of Congress are exposed to the causes that corrupt them. Term limits, I am afraid, will be an ineffectual bandage on a terminally ill patient.

What will cause the majority of voters to vote for the challenger in all congressional elections until the five amendments are ratified? The cause will be understanding the concepts presented in this book.

What will cause the voter to understand the concepts presented in this book? The forms of communicating concepts, thoughts, and ideas (information) to our society at large are television, radio, newspapers, magazines, movies, conversation, books, and audio cassettes. Except for books and audio cassettes, all are inappropriate for the transmittal of a long chain of causes and effects. As the reader who has read this far knows, it takes many hours of intense concentration to understand the concepts presented in this book, and we moved right along. It is inconceivable that these concepts could be accurately relayed to the voter by television, even with the cooperation of the media, not to mention the distortion that can be created by a Congress with virtually unlimited access to television and desperate to stay in power. In addition, the very powerful special interests will no doubt assist their friends in Congress. Does the reader think that a citizen who has not read this book will be able to piece together from eight-second sound bites what is really going on? Radio, not even an entire talk show, can inform listeners of what they must know. Even a lengthy newspaper article is insufficient, as are magazines. Movies are also inappropriate. Conversation, even an in-depth discussion, is also insufficient. The only methods that can possibly convey the information in this book are this book and audio cassettes. Of the two, the book is superior because readers, by the speed at which they read, can control the rate of incoming information, easily re-read portions, and refer back to earlier sections. For some, however, the audio cassette would be the most effective means of understanding the contents of this book. Therefore, the answer to "What will cause the voter to understand the concepts presented in this book?" is for the voter to read a copy of this book or listen to an audio cassette of this book

What will cause a majority of voters to read this book or listen to an audio cassette of this book? Since the cooperation of the media is, at best, questionable and Congress and special interests can be counted on to distort and spread disinformation, the only sure cause of inducing a majority of voters to read this book or listen to a cassette of this book is by word of mouth from citizen to citizen. Therefore, the only certain way of restoring our democracy and achieving our idealized future is for citizens who have read or listened to this book to convince their friends, relatives, neighbors, fellow students, acquaintances, fellow workers, and business associates to read this book or listen to an audio cassette of this book.

By working the cause-and-effect relationships backwards from our idealized future to the present, we now know what must be the sequence of events that will result in our achieving the restoration of our democracy and our idealized future.

They are:

1) Readers of this book must convince others to read or listen to this book.

2) Those new readers of this book will convince others to read this book, and so on.

3) The readers of this book will then understand the concepts presented in this book. This will cause an ever-increasing number of voters to vote against the incumbent members of Congress and to vote for the challenger in every congressional election.

4) When an ever-increasing number of incumbents are turned out of office, new political parties will form and/or

present ones will change to adopting the platform of ratification of the five amendments.

5) The challengers running on a platform of voting for the five amendments will be elected, thereby forming a two-thirds majority in the House and Senate.

6) This will cause the five amendments to be passed by Congress and ratified by the states.

7) This will cause the return of our democracy and the creation of an efficient government.

8) The efficient, democratic government will create and implement plans at least as beneficial as the ones described in this book.

9) This will, in turn, cause our idealized future actually to occur.

10) Sharing these plans with other countries will cause the planet to become fundamentally safe, stable, and secure; virtually free from war, poverty, and crime.

These ten events are the set of cause-and-effect relationships that will result in the idealized future (Step No. 4 of applying the Black Box Technique).

Step No. 5: Determine the Difference Between the Two Sets of Causes and Effects

Next we compare the above set of cause-and-effect relationships with the set of cause-and-effect relationships that will result in the real future and note where the differences are (Step No. 5). The set of cause-and-effect relationships that result in our real future has the current Congress remain in power and continue its corrupt and decadent practices, which in turn results in the destruction of our society for failure to meet the standard set by the Law of the Survival of the Efficient. Therefore, the two sets of cause-and-effect relationships are mutually exclusive, which means that the differences between the two are total and complete.

Step No. 6: The Plan

Therefore, our plan becomes the action necessary to substitute the above ten cause-and-effect relationships for the cause-and-effect relationships that will result in the real future (Step No. 6). In reviewing the above ten cause-and-effect relationships, it is apparent that the plan requires us citizens to perform only two actions to bring about our idealized future:

1) Convince others to read this book and/or listen to the audio cassette of this book.

2) Vote *against* all incumbent members of Congress and vote only *for* challengers until the five amendments have been ratified.

Step No. 7: The Sacrifice

Therefore in order actually to achieve our idealized future, all we citizens must do is pay the sacrifice to cause the above two actions to actually occur.

Hallelujah! Just think of the great news. If we had used the Black Box Technique back in 1776, the sacrifice we would have been forced to pay would have been a large number of us being killed in a field by the British army. We lucky modern Americans merely have to vote and persuade. However, we are patriots just the same. The difference is only in weaponry. Instead of muskets and bayonets, we can read and vote ourselves to our better future. How do we do it?

1) Make sure you are registered to vote. Learn the names of three people (your incumbent two U.S. senators and one U.S. representative). Go to the polling place on election day and vote for any challenger other than those three names. If you know of a candidate other than the incumbent who promises to pass the five amendments, vote for that person. Repeat every two years until the five amendments have been ratified. That is our prescription for the idealized future. Progress toward achieving our plan can be objectively verified by noting a downward trend in the percent of incumbents re-elected to both the House and Senate.

2) Convince your fellow citizens to read and understand this book or audio cassette of this book. This will necessitate four acts on the part of one who has not read this book: 1. obtaining a copy of this book or audio cassette of this book; 2. reading or listening to this book; 3. understanding this book; and 4. acting according to the plan in this book.

To fulfill the plan, our second action is to induce our fellow citizens to do the four things listed above. This will be a great humanitarian deed—not only for the idealized future, but moreover for the personal favor of enlightening your fellow citizen. The reader who has read this far in this book is greatly more knowledgeable than before the reading of this book. Your fellow citizen who has not read this book no doubt does not have a clue as to what is really going on around here. Therefore, in my book, you will be doing us all a great service.

1) How does a citizen who has not read this book obtain a copy of this book or cassette? Although it would be a magnanimous gesture of great patriotism for the reader to purchase several books or cassettes and induce other citizens to read them (needless to say, the author would be eternally grateful), there is a more effective way. Psychology tells us that if a person incurs a sacrifice, however small, to obtain something, then that person is much more likely to value that object, or in our case, read this book. Therefore, in our case, it is preferable if the reader were to induce fellow citizens to obtain their own copies, either by going to the local bookstore or local library. In some circumstances, the reader may lend his or her copy of this book or cassette, but the reader may find it difficult to secure its return. It is only advisable to do this with a person with whom you come in contact on a regular basis.

2) Reading this book—Check periodically with people whom you convince to obtain this book or cassette to make sure they actually read it. Since this book, to be understood, must be read over the course of a few days, it should not take the new reader very long from the time of obtaining this book to finish it. Also, it would be wise to advise the new reader not to skim this book. The author is sure that the reader can now appreciate the proviso at the beginning of this book warning against skimming. The author has no idea what a person would understand who skimmed this book.

3) Understanding this book—After the person has read this book, discuss it with him or her to make sure he or she understands it. As a suggestion, perhaps start by discussing the idealized future.

4) Acting according to the plan—During your discussion, ask the person if he or she intends to implement the plan, i.e. vote against all incumbent members of Congress and con-

vince other citizens to read this book one way or another. If
the answer is yes, then you have fulfilled your duties of sacrifice as a patriot.

I f everyone who reads this book votes against all incumbent
members of Congress and, *within one month,* convinces at
least *two* other persons to obtain a copy of this book, read this
book, understand this book, and act according to plan, then
without fail, 100 percent guaranteed, we will restore our
democracy, achieve the idealized future, and live in a world
virtually free of poverty, crime, and war! If the reader would
like the future to arrive faster than it normally would, then
the reader need only increase the number of people whom the
reader convinces to read this book.

The author is aware that most of us in this society are
very busy and stressed out attempting to achieve our next
goal in life. The last thing any of us need is another duty or
responsibility that impinges upon our time. However, if we do
not sacrifice our time to fulfill the plan, then I can virtually
guarantee you that whatever economic goal you are currently
working so hard to achieve will be swept away in the coming
economic devastation. If the readers of this book, for whatever
reason, fail to act, fail to sacrifice, then Congress will remain
corrupt, and the future of this society will be one of devastation, economic collapse, and social disintegration. In effect, it
is as if we are dinosaurs who must become aware of our
impending doom and must consciously make the decision to
change into birds! As we have learned, if people fail to sacrifice to save themselves from future assured destruction, then
they are decadent and deserve the destruction.

In comparison to the restoration of our democracy, there
is no other issue in America. Without the resolution of this
issue, the resolution of other issues becomes unimportant.
The misery that is coming if the current corrupt Congress
remains in power will far outweigh any advantage obtained

from the resolution of any other issue. No matter what other issue may seem important, it is overshadowed by the immensity of the problem of the corruption of Congress. Prior to the resolution of the problem of the corruption in Congress, no other issue that Congress addresses can be expected to be resolved without the influence of those known sources of corruption. It would be as if Congress fixed the headlight in a car and then drove the car over a cliff. Therefore, Congress' moral right to formulate the laws by which we live is seriously in question. By all that is fair, all that is just, all that is decent, Congress no longer has the right to rule in this land of ours.

In addition, Congress must be reformed soon. We are running out of time. As I write this in 1994, even if a change in Congress could be made immediately, because of our already massive national debt, we, the American people, will still have our ability to sacrifice tested. One other point is absolutely clear: the sooner our democracy is restored, the sooner the budget deficits can be stopped, the less pain will come to the American people. It is in our own best self-interest to reform Congress as soon as possible. The last time our democracy was stolen, it took 24 years to win it back (1889–1913), even with the help of the media. If it takes us 24 years to achieve the return of our democracy this time, it will be far, far too late.[50]

---

50. It took Congress 100 years to steal our democracy the first time (1789–1889). The second time Congress stole our democracy, it took only 60 years (1913–1973). If this trend continues, we can expect Congress to attempt to steal our democracy again 36 years after its next restoration.

FUTURE TWO

Now let us predict the future if the Republicans are, in fact, our white knights and actually intend to restore our democracy. To determine what they actually intend to do, let us analyze the Republican Contract with America. Perhaps the best way to do this is in the form of an open letter to Newt Gingrich.

Open Letter to Newt Gingrich

Dear Mr. Gingrich:

Congratulations on your recent election victory. Since Congress is the most powerful branch of our government and since the United States of America is the only remaining superpower, the case can be made that you and your colleague in the Senate, Mr. Dole, are the two most powerful people in the world. It is an awesome responsibility, and I am sure, the American people wish you well in tackling the daunting problems you face.

Prior to the election you and your fellow Republicans offered the American people a contract. A contract that contains your solutions to the problems of America. In university, I was taught to read all contracts very carefully before agreeing to them. As one of my business law professors advised me, "Read all contracts very critically because all that any court will ever require of the other party is exactly what is stated in the contract, not what you assume is meant." Therefore, I would like to critically analyze what is stated in the contract as faxed to me by Congressman Richard Armey before giving my response. (The contract will be in italics; the author's comments will be in roman type.)

Contract with America

As Republican Members of the House of Representatives and as citizens seeking to join that body we propose not just to change its policies, but even more important, to restore the bonds of trust between the people and their elected representatives. That is why, in this era of official evasion and posturing, we offer instead a detailed agenda for national renewal, a written commitment with no fine print.

This year's election offers the chance, after four decades of one-party control, to bring the House a new majority that will transform the way Congress works. That historic change would be the end of government that is too big, too intrusive, and too easy with the public's money. It can be the beginning of a Congress that respects the values and shares the faith of the American family.

Like Lincoln, our first Republican president, we intend to act "with firmness in the right, as God gives us to see the right." To restore accountability to Congress. To end its cycle of scandal and disgrace. To make us all proud again of the way free people govern themselves.

This preamble contains your statement of intent and understandably contains no specific action on the part of Congress. Concerning the basis upon which you intend to act, though admirably employed by Lincoln, it was also the same basis for action used by the Ayatollah Khomeini and Torquemada, the Inquisitor-General of the Spanish Inquisition, not to mention the Roman Empire in the final years before its fall. If you would like a more rational basis upon which to act, may I refer you to Chapter One on logic in this book.

On the first day of the 104th Congress, the new Republican majority will immediately pass the following major reforms, aimed at restoring the faith and trust of the American people in their government:

First, require all laws that apply to the rest of the country also apply equally to Congress;

This provision will cause the Congress to be subject to such laws as the Equal Employment Opportunity Act and laws against sexual harassment. Although this is clearly laudable and will, no doubt, save innumerable secretaries the indignity of being chased around desks by sex-crazed and power-hungry Congressmen, I fail to see how this provision will have a profound impact on the future of America, but it is a positive step.

Second, select a major, independent auditing firm to conduct a comprehensive audit of Congress for waste, fraud, or abuse;

Selecting a major auditing firm should not prove to be a very difficult task, as I am sure that all of their phone numbers can be found in the Washington, D.C., phone book. The difficult part seems to be what will be done with their recommendations. On this point, the provision makes no comment.

Third, cut the number of House committees, and cut committee staff by one-third;

Fourth, limit the terms of committee chairs;

Fifth, ban the casting of proxy votes in committee;

Sixth, require committee meetings to be open to the public;

These four provisions alter the rules under which congressional committees will work. Although this may seem like a major change to those inside the Washington Beltway, to those of us outside the inner circles of power, it is far too arcane. I doubt that most Americans are aware of how the committee system in Congress works. I also doubt that these changes are what most Americans have in mind when promises to "transform how Congress works" are made. The committee system did not cause the corruption and decadence of Congress, and procedural changes to *Roberts' Rules of Order* will not restore it. At most, it seems that the above four provisions may cause confusion for a few weeks concerning to whom the special interests should write checks. If you would truly like to transform how Congress works, see the earlier section of this chapter on institutionalizing the Four Critical Abilities.

Seventh, require a three-fifths majority vote to pass a tax increase;

A three-fifths majority is 60 percent. It currently requires 50 percent plus 1 to pass tax increases. The net result being a 9+ percent increase in the number required to pass a tax increase. That is nice; unimportant, but nice.

Eighth, guarantee an honest accounting of our federal budget by implementing zero base-line budgeting;

It is difficult to understand what is meant in this provision, if anything. The method that an institution uses to determine its budget does not have any effect upon, let alone guarantee, honest accounting. Perhaps when you hire the above-mentioned major accounting firm, you can discuss this with them. It seems you have a tendency to link nouns that are buzz words, like "honest accounting" and "zero base-line budgeting," with verbs that only serve to diffuse and obfuscate meaning. It seems very odd that an obviously well-spoken, ex-college history professor should have difficulty writing clearly.

Thereafter, within the first hundred days of the 104th Congress, we shall bring to the House Floor the following bills, each to be given full and open debate, each to be given a clear and fair vote, and each to be immediately available this day for public inspection and scrutiny.

You refer us here to a number of bills, which seems to derogate your previous promise of no fine print.

1. The Fiscal Responsibility Act

A balanced budget / tax limitation amendment and a legislative line-item veto to restore fiscal responsibility to an out-of-control Congress, requiring them to live under the same budget constraints as families and businesses.

My previous comment about obscurity in meaning applies even more poignantly in this provision. Since you are discussing merely a law to be passed by Congress, a balanced budget/tax limitation amendment (whatever that may be) only refers to an amendment to a normal law and not a constitutional amendment. If you mean a constitutional amendment, why do you not state it? As far as your reference to a *legislative* line-item veto is concerned, inherent in the power of Congress to create a budget is the ability to delete items, which is, in effect, a *legislative* line-item veto. The line-item veto that should be under discussion is the one taken from the president in the 1974 Congressional Budget and Impoundment Control Act. It is not possible to determine from the above whether you favor amendments to the

Constitution to require a balanced budget and to return the line-item veto to the president.

2. *The Taking Back of Our Streets Act*

An anti-crime package including stronger truth-in-sentencing, "good faith" exclusionary rule exemption, effective death penalty provisions, and cuts in social spending from this summer's crime bill to fund prison construction and additional law enforcement to keep people secure in their neighborhoods and kids safe in their schools.

3. *The Personal Responsibility Act*

Discourage illegitimacy and teen pregnancy by prohibiting welfare to minor mothers and denying increased AFDC for additional children while on welfare, cut spending for welfare programs, and enact a tough two-years-and-out provision with work requirements to promote individual responsibility.

4. *The Family Reinforcement Act*

Child support enforcement, tax incentives for adoption, strengthening rights of parents in their children's education, stronger child pornography laws, and an elderly dependent care tax credit to reinforce the central role of families in American society.

5. *The American Dream Restoration Act*

A $500 per child tax credit, begin repeal of the marriage tax penalty, and creation of American Dream Savings Accounts to provide middle-class tax relief.

6. The National Security Restoration Act

No U.S. troops under U.N. command and restoration of the essential parts of our national security funding to strengthen our national defense and maintain our credibility around the world.

7. The Senior Citizens Fairness Act

Raise the Social Security earnings limit, which currently forces seniors out of the work force, repeal the 1993 tax hikes on Social Security benefits, and provide tax incentives for private long-term care insurance to let older Americans keep more of what they have earned over the years.

8. The Job Creation and Wage Enhancement Act

Small business incentives, capital gains cut and indexation, neutral cost recovery, risk assessment / cost benefit analysis, strengthening the Regulatory Flexibility Act and unfunded mandate reform to create jobs and raise worker wages.

The above eight bills address some of the social problems of America with answers derived from a conservative ideology rather than the liberal ideology previously employed by Congress. The names of the bills seem to promise far more than the bills will deliver, but the previous solutions did not work, therefore why not give these a try?

9. The Common Sense Legal Reforms Act

"Loser pays" laws, reasonable limits on punitive damages, and reform of product liability laws to stem the endless tide of litigation.

Long overdue. With so many lawyers in Congress, it will be interesting to see if you can deliver on this one. Lots of luck.

10. The Citizen Legislative Act

A first-ever vote on term limits to replace career politicians with citizen legislators.

From the way this is phrased, "a first-ever vote," it does not seem that you intend to pass this legislation, let alone make it a constitutional amendment, but merely to vote on it. Once again, this is merely an ordinary law and not a constitutional amendment. What I believe the American people clearly desire is a roll-call vote for a constitutional amendment rather than merely a promise for a first-ever vote. What we would like is a last-ever vote.

Further, we will instruct the House Budget Committee to report to the floor and we will work to enact additional budget savings, beyond the budget cuts specifically included in the legislation described above, to ensure that the federal budget deficit will be less than it would have been without the enactment of these bills.

This seems to be further evidence that you do not intend to pass a constitutional amendment requiring a balanced budget in the near future.

Respecting the judgment of our fellow citizens as we seek their mandate for reform, we hereby pledge our names to this Contract with America.

Mr. Gingrich, based upon a close analysis of your Contract with America, it is apparent that the only actions of substance are a shift from liberal to conservative approaches, which may have a modest impact on some of our social problems. You fail to address in any substantive way the most critical problem in America: the fact that Congress has stolen our democracy by permitting special interests (PACs) to give members of Congress money (bribes or, as they are known in Congress, campaign contributions), which then gives the incumbent member of Congress an unfair advantage in re-elections.

The problem is that Congress is the problem. Until the corruption and decadence of Congress is solved, no other problem that Congress addresses can be solved in the best interests of the American people. The tendency is to throw the American people some bones and window dressing, while Congress' real business is the agenda of special interests. The special favors given to the special interests in exchange for money will far outweigh any real or alleged benefits gained by conservative approaches to our social problems. By the very definition of the word "democracy," only a majority of the American people have a right to influence our government. The above proposed changes to the committee system in Congress are equivalent to recommending dusting and washing the windows of a house that is on fire. Our government is broken and nothing proposed above fixes it. Congress has demonstrated that it cannot be trusted to make its own laws concerning its own election. Therefore, an independent commission must be created in order to ensure fair elections.

In addition, Congress has destroyed the delicate system of checks and balances by usurping powers from the president. The president's traditional right of impoundment or, as it is commonly known, the line-item veto, was stolen from the president in the 1974 Congressional Budget and Impoundment Control Act. Up until 1974, the budgets of the United States were roughly balanced. Since 1974 we have had incredible budget deficits—$4,000,000,000,000 in unnecessary deficits. This one law, which removed the line-item veto from the president, has caused our national debt to skyrocket. You merely propose a *legislative* line-item veto. Since Congress is the institution that passed the deficits in the first place, a *legislative* line-item veto is meaningless. Returning the line-item veto to the president will restore the responsibility for balanced budgets to where it has historically resided.

Budget deficits are so dangerous to the continued survival of our society that a constitutional amendment should be immediately passed outlawing them within a five-year period. However, in an article in USA Today (November 17, 1994), I have read that you plan a constitutional amendment to take effect in 2002 that permits continued deficits beyond that time if approved by 60 percent of Congress. If you intend to restore the faith of the American people in our government, proposals like this one will not achieve your intended results.

In addition, America has changed from a rural, frontier society whose citizens neither needed nor desired interference from their government into the only remaining superpower on an urban, complex interdependent planet. Whether or not Brazil, for instance, chops down its rain forest has profound implications for the whole planet. Whether North Korea produces nuclear weapons or not has profound implications for the whole planet. To suggest that a return to some idealized 19th-century laissez-faire government that never existed is the appropriate course for us, Americans, and for the planet, is to ignore the obvious. To have the future of a very complex interdependent society decided by 535 legislators who are mostly lawyers, who are always faced with an election within two years, and who accept bribes from special interests will result in disaster. We can no longer lurch from crisis to crisis. We Americans need our future planned for us by experts who are not pressured by elections. We need the previously described Council of Advanced Planning, and we need the foreign policy powers that pre-date 1973 to be returned to the president.

Therefore, Mr. Gingrich, let me propose a contract to you. I propose adding to your Contract with America the five following amendments to the Constitution:

1) A constitutional amendment that will remove from Congress the power to regulate its own elections and place it in the hands of a commission to ensure fair elections. In addition, the commission will be empowered to determine acceptable levels of outside income and to determine to what benefits the members of Congress are entitled. The regulations of the commission will then be subject to review for constitutionality by the Supreme Court in the normal way. Therefore, in effect, the Supreme Court will be able to order the correction of any inequities found in the election process, and our democracy will be far more securely safeguarded in the future. Both congressional and presidential elections will be 100 percent federally funded. No PAC money or private contributions will be allowed.

2) A constitutional amendment that will return the right of impoundment (line-item veto) to the president.

3) A constitutional amendment that will return pre-1973 foreign policy powers to the president.

4) A constitutional amendment that mandates a balanced federal budget within three to five years.

5) A constitutional amendment that creates the Council of Advanced Planning.

Amendments to the Constitution, as opposed to ordinary laws, will prevent our government from being corrupted and stolen in the same manner again. These five amendments can be put to a roll-call vote by both the House and Senate in a few short months. Although I do not speak for the American people, I would bet that anyone standing in the way of the ratification of these constitutional amendments would not be elected to any public office ever again. Which means that the amendments in question will be ratified at the latest after the next election. What will you get out of this new contract? Other than the knowledge that you did the right thing and the undying gratitude of one author and the citizens who have read this book and think like the author, maybe not much. But I can tell you what the people of the United States did for the last person who returned our stolen democracy, Teddy Roosevelt. We had his face carved on a mountain called Mount Rushmore, alongside carvings of George Washington, Thomas Jefferson, and Abraham Lincoln. All four of these men did what was right. All four of these men sacrificed for us. None of them would have permitted political action committees to bribe our Congress, and therefore steal our democracy. I know that Mount Rushmore is a long, long way from Washington, D.C. I know that in Washington, D.C., you are surrounded by innumerable people wanting a few minutes of your time and that it must be very exciting being famous, powerful, and on television all of the time, as Tom Foley knows. Mr. Foley has no chance of ever being on Mount Rushmore, except as a visitor. Very few of us have the strength of character, the sense of sacrifice for our fellow citizens, and the vision required to be the kind of statesmen who deserve to be on Mount Rushmore. That is why there are only four people carved on that rock. Furthermore, the type of people whose faces are carved on that rock are exactly the type of people who do not care if their faces are carved on that rock. A person is either that quality of person or not. It is not something learned at 51 years of age and certainly not taught by a letter. I fervently hope you are indeed that type of person. For if you are not, by the time the American people realize that their government is still corrupt and still sold to the special

interest groups, it may well be too late to take further corrective action. You are probably our last hope to avoid the bitterly painful future that lies in wait for us.

Thank you for taking the time to read my letter.

Sincerely,
Citizen Williams

Well, what does the reader think? After our analysis of
the Contract with America, do you think the Republicans will rescue us or will they merely take advantage of the
usurpation of presidential powers and the advantage that
incumbents have in elections to attempt to perpetuate a
Republican dynasty? A good gauge of the intent of the
Republican leadership in Congress is if Mr. Gingrich and Mr.
Dole have accepted a substantial increase, say, more than a
20 percent increase, in campaign contributions (bribes) from
special interests (PACs) in the period from the 1994 elections
until the spring of 1995 versus the amount of campaign contributions received for the same period of the previous year. If
they have accepted more than a 20 percent increase, then
this would be an excellent indication that they intend to continue the theft of our democracy. In any event, if this book
makes it to any of the bestseller lists, then we can be sure
that the Republicans will be aware of the need for the five
amendments, and if the Republicans fail to bring them to the
floor of both the House and the Senate for roll call votes by
the election of 1996, then we can be sure that the
Republicans are only conservative crooks who have replaced
the liberal crooks. In that case, the only course of action open
to the American people that will avert disaster will be to vote
against all incumbents until the five amendments are ratified. In other words, the Republicans will have proven themselves not to be our white knights, and we will have to revert
to the strategy in the first future for the next election.

Of course, the best possible result would be if the Republicans are in fact true statesmen and pass the five amendments by the next election. Then we can avoid disaster and have the opportunity for a bright future. Therefore, if the five amendments are passed, I suggest we put Mr. Gingrich and Mr. Dole on Mount Rushmore. They will have earned it.

The reader can predict which of the two futures will occur, but the author has no plans to rush out and buy chisels.

The real danger in the Republican victory is that they will not restore our democracy, but will institute a modest improvement in the efficiency of our government (it will be impossible not to improve on the past performance). However, the modest improvement will be insufficient to avoid the disaster awaiting us and will only waste the time we have remaining to take effective steps that would save us from the impending disaster.

Therefore, if the Republicans do not restore our democracy by passing the five amendments to the Constitution before the 1996 elections, then the wisest course of action will be to vote against all incumbents until the five amendments are ratified. The reader should realize that the only constitutionally provided role in our government, the only part we play, the only ability to cause change in our government by the citizenry, comes every two years when we vote. Because of our two-party system, the American people have been herded into voting for either a liberal or a conservative, Democrat or Republican. It is analogous to having to choose between two mathematicians. One mathematician, regardless of the problem, will derive only even numbered solutions to our problems, and the other mathematician will derive only odd numbered solutions to our problems. It is obvious that both mathematicians are closed-minded and that neither can be relied upon to derive correct answers. In a like manner, it is equally ridiculous to choose between two politicians who will derive solutions to our problems from one set of answers, one narrow philosophy only, while disregarding all other possible correct answers. Not only is it closed-minded, but the priority is inaccurate. Is it not far more important to derive correct solutions than to follow an ideology? When a person tells the author "I am a conservative" or "I am a liberal" or "I am a Republican" or "I am a Democrat," the author thinks to himself that the person really means "I am a closed-minded ideologue."

It would be far, far better for the future of this society if we citizens cast our votes, not on the basis of some loyalty to an ideology, but rather as a signal of approval or disapproval of the way our government is functioning. If we approve of what is going on, then we should vote for the incumbent. If we disapprove of what is going on, then we should vote for the challenger. Casting one's vote on this basis will stimulate a fundamental change in our politicians. They will be forced to become responsive to the citizenry rather than adhere to an ideology that virtually automatically brings them the votes of certain segments of the populace.

As far as our current situation is concerned, it means that Republicans have until the elections of 1996 to bring to a vote the five constitutional amendments. Failure to do so should result in the disapproval of us citizens, and we should therefore vote for the challenger. We should continue to vote for the challenger (display disapproval) until the five constitutional amendments are ratified and our democracy is restored. The "good" guys are the members of Congress who will restore our democracy by ending the ability of special interests (PACs) to give money to members of Congress, which gives them an unfair advantage in elections. By the very definition of the word "democracy," only a majority of the American people have a right to influence our government. Until our democracy is restored, all other issues are a side show. Only when our democracy is restored will our government pay full attention to us, the people. The "bad" guys are the members of Congress of whatever ideology who continue to sell our democracy to the special interests. Therefore, our wisest and indeed our only action that can force the return of our democracy is to vote against all incumbents until the five constitutional amendments are ratified. To someone who has not read this book and is locked in the conservative versus liberal mind-set, it will seem bizarre to advocate voting against the Republican majority and giving control back to the Democrats, but if the Republicans are not statesmen enough to restore our democracy, it is our only hope. Then the Democrats will have two years to ratify the five amendments. If they fail to do so, then we will have to vote against the Democrats in the election of 1998. By that time, at least one viable third party will have presented itself. One or both of the two current political parties will wither and die.

Although the above scenario may seem inefficient and slow, it is the *only* method we citizens have that can force the return of our democracy. Let us summarize the unbreakable chain of logic that brings us to the only possible solution to our problem.

1) Our democracy was stolen by post-Watergate Congresses and remains so today. Only a majority of American voters has the right to affect the outcome of elections, not special interests.

2) History tells us that neither dictators nor democratic institutions have a tendency to give up power without being forced or without a credible threat of force, unless there are one or more statesmen involved. The odds are against us that our democracy will be returned without the application of force.

3) If our properly functioning democracy is not returned to us by statesmen in Congress, then who will force the Congress to return our democracy? The other branches of government and the other institutions in our society do not

have the power to create change, except one. The media has the power to apply the force required to cause change, but for reasons of self-interest, the media may not force the change. In addition, when the author questioned a print media editor concerning the role of the news media, he stated that the role of the news media is not to force change in governments, but rather to report the news. Clearly, the odds are against us that the media will apply the force required to restore our democracy, and may indeed oppose us.

4) Therefore, the only force that can definitely and positively guarantee the restoration of our democracy is that force held by the people, by us, the citizenry. What specifically is that force? The only constitutionally provided force that we, the citizens, have is when we vote every two years. Voting is the *only* role we have under the Constitution. Furthermore, because of the two-party system, we have only two choices when we vote. As we have discussed, if after we have realized that our democracy has been stolen we still vote for the incumbent, our vote for the incumbent validates the theft. In effect, we are saying that it is okay to steal my democracy, that I like it that way, and I do not desire change in the course of government. When we vote for an incumbent, we are in fact rewarding with another term in office the very person who profits from the theft of our government. It is as if we were saying to a mugger, "Please, stay in the neighborhood and be sure to beat me up and steal my money over and over again in the future." Only in our case, the theft is of something far more valuable than our pocket change: the theft is of our entire democracy and our future with it. Therefore, since voting for the incumbent continues the theft by rewarding the very crooks who are stealing the democracy, the ***only possible solution*** that guarantees the return of our democracy is for a majority of us to vote for the challenger in every congressional election until our democracy is restored.

History tells us that our only other option is the one used by our Founding Fathers, revolution. This option is unsatisfactory, not only for the resultant turmoil and bloodshed but because history also informs us that there is a great likelihood that after the revolution we would very probably be ruled by a Napoleon or Stalin. The author does not advocate, nor would he take part in revolution, not when we can accomplish a better result by voting. Voting is the only constitutionally provided role in our democracy for us citizens. If we fail to use the constitutionally provided force of the ballot box to cause the change required to save ourselves, then we are to blame. We will prove to be as decadent and corrupt as the Congress. We will deserve the fate that will destroy us.

CHAPTER FOURTEEN

Conclusions

IN REVIEWING THE VAST SCOPE of the information that we have covered so far, the author cannot help appreciating the assistance rendered us by the Black Box Technique. For a simple technique of logic, it is awesomely powerful. It has permitted us to rapidly and provably discover truths that have eluded humankind since, at least, the invention of writing. The Black Box Technique gives us the power to solve extremely complex problems with no more difficulty than it takes to section a grapefruit. The author hopes the reader will consciously begin applying the Black Box Technique to the world at large. The reader now has the power to find out virtually whatever is desired to be known in the past, present, or future. In applying the Seven Steps of the Black Box Technique, it should be apparent that the overwhelming amount of our time was spent learning the past. Of the fourteen chapters of this book, ten chapters were spent on learning the Black Box Technique and the past. Only three chapters were used to apply the rest of the Seven Steps of the Black Box Technique even to the extremely large and complex topic of the United States government. Those ten chapters are now in the memory of the reader and do not need to be learned again. Therefore, were the author to write another book about an equally complex topic, for the reader who has read this book, the new book would only have to be three chapters long. However, for a person who has not read this book, it would take thirteen chapters to achieve the same level of understanding. The reader and the author now share a common database consisting of the Black Box Technique and an accurate outline of the past, which do not have to be restated for us to communicate.

Imagine in an Einsteinian Thought Experiment that the reader and the author bump into each other on the street and decide to have a 20-minute discussion over a cup of coffee. We could have a wide-ranging discussion over the length and breadth of topics covered in this book. Now let us change the experiment and say that the reader bumps into someone who has not read this book and decides to have a 20-minute discussion over a cup of coffee. It would be frustrating to attempt to discuss in any depth the topics covered in this book because the person who has not read this book does not share a common database with the reader. Most of the 20 minutes would probably elapse with the reader's explaining bits and pieces of the past, which would probably not make much of an impact on the one who had not read this book. By reading this book, the reader has acquired a fundamentally important database that can be of great value throughout the reader's life. It also means that for the reader to conduct another Black Boxing, 80 percent of the work has already been done. The general past does not have to be relearned. It becomes far faster and easier to Black Box from now on. All other Black Boxings are a subset of this one. All other Black Boxings can use this Black Boxing as the general past, present, future, and idealized future. Therefore, the reader only needs to Black Box the subset of information relevant to the topic desired to be known. The reader is far more knowledgeable than when we started. Let us give this body of knowledge a name, "Mega-Knowledge." It should be realized that Mega-Knowledge as presented in this book is merely an outline. The reader is invited and encouraged to learn more about any part of Mega-Knowledge that aroused the reader's curiosity. The Bibliography at the back of this book is a good place to start. Let us analyze our newly acquired Mega-Knowledge.

The past (Mega-Knowledge) has been shown to be a verifiable series of causes and effects resulting in us, the present. In looking back over the past, one event caused the next in a

logical, straightforward, easy-to-understand manner. Even if
we allow for the small discrepancies that may have crept into
the story when we used Occam's razor to Black Box the portions of the story unknown to science, the past, as briefly outlined here and which can be found in parts in other works,[51]
clearly surpasses the amount of evidence required to pass our
preponderance-of-evidence test. Does the reader recall the
story of the computer that failed in analyzing the flight characteristics of the bumblebee? From our analysis of the past
there are no inexplicable events or anomalies. In short, there
are no flightless bumblebees. Therefore, we can accept as the
truth the story of the past as outlined in this book. If anyone
is to seriously challenge the foregoing explanation of the past,
then he must offer a larger preponderance of evidence or be
rejected by the Truth-Meter.

Our generation can now see for the first time the entire
history of the universe. It is displayed for us in an unbroken process from 15 billion years ago to the present. Each
frame of our theoretical strip of movie film was caused by the
frame that came before it and in turn caused the frame that
came after it. The cause-and-effect relationships that caused
the past to happen also caused the current frame in which we
are living—the present—to happen and will, in turn, cause
the next frame, the future. The cause-and-effect relationships
that we have observed are the fundamental laws of the universe by which everything operates. Any individual can discover on his own those fundamental laws of the universe that
pertain to anything in which he is interested.

Humankind is the result of a 15-billion-year process of
cause-and-effect relationships. We have learned that the Law
of the Survival of the Efficient not only applies to all living
things, but that it also caused life to form on Earth. We have

---

51. See the Bibliography at the back of the book.

also learned that every second of every day of every year since the beginning of life on Earth, the Law of the Survival of the Efficient has unrelentingly determined which species lives and which species dies. The Darwinian Law of the Survival of the Efficient operates on human beings, not on an individual basis, but on a larger scale. Entire societies are in competition with one another for survival. The life and death cycle of the typical human society is played out over much longer time periods—hundreds and thousands of years—than those of which we are accustomed to thinking. Just as the number of extinct animal species is far larger than the number of surviving animal species, the number of extinct societies is far larger than the number of surviving societies. In the contemporary world our societies are organized into nations. The study of history in the largest sense is the study of the Law of the Survival of the Efficient as applied on an international basis over time.

We discovered that what makes humankind unique among the animals is the ability to think about the future, which permits humankind to plan. We have also learned that humankind's and individual human societies' greatest weapons for causing the Law of the Survival of the Efficient to operate in our behalf are the Four Critical Abilities. Therefore, every society's best weapons in the struggle for survival are the Four Critical Abilities:

1. To accurately think in the future.

2. To plan for the future.

3. The appropriate social structure necessary to implement the plan.

4. To have the necessary sense of sacrifice in the members of the society to carry out the plan.

The societies, or in our case the countries, that can utilize the Four Critical Abilities the most efficiently will prosper and flourish. Those countries that cannot perform the Four Critical Abilities very efficiently will falter and fall victim to the Law of the Survival of the Efficient. No other past society and hence no other individual from a past society could have profoundly and provably understood these facts.

The Four Critical Abilities are so important that all societies past and present can be evaluated on the basis of the most efficient utilization of the Four Critical Abilities. The critical nature of these abilities, which permit a society to look into the future, to foresee problems that could end that civilization, to form the best plan to solve the problem before it becomes a crisis, and then to implement the plan, is demonstrated by the great number of extinct societies. The highest form of problem-solving is identifying problems in the future and then making a corrective plan of action so that not only does the problem never threaten the society, but it never even materializes. The best way of dealing with a problem already present in a society is to identify the problem, choose the best plan to solve the problem, and implement the plan. Then, as the future unfolds, the society sheds its problems as a snake sheds its skin. Therefore, the society cures its current problems and does not take on any new ones. The society that can solve its present problems and avoid future problems then becomes problem-free. A society without problems is by definition Utopia.

Since the Four Critical Abilities have been for the first time disclosed in this book, then amazingly enough no society past or present has ever been consciously aware of them. Which means that no society has ever acted on the basis of this knowledge, and, just as important, no society's form of government has ever been designed with these principles in mind. Not even Thomas Jefferson or James Madison could have been aware of the Four Critical Abilities.

Moreover, wise application of the Seven Steps of the Black Box Technique gives us three of the Four Critical Abilities:

1. to accurately think in the future

2. to plan for the future

3. the appropriate social structure necessary to implement the plans

4. to have the necessary sense of sacrifice in the members of the society to carry out the plan

Therefore, since in this book we have applied the Seven Steps of the Black Box Technique to the United States of America, then we can only fail as a nation if we do not have the necessary sense of sacrifice to implement the plan.

Why has the body of fundamental knowledge never been recognized before? Because humankind has only recently discovered the knowledge. The Theory of Evolution was first published by Darwin in 1859. Understanding how life on Earth roughly formed and the discovery of the structure of DNA occurred in the early 1950s. The Big Bang was verified in 1965. The knowledge of tectonic plate movement was also verified in the mid-1960s. It was only by the middle 1970s that a sufficient amount of fossil evidence was discovered to reconstruct human evolution in detail. In short, the broad outline of the history of the universe or Mega-Knowledge has only been known for some fifteen years. Science continues to fill in more of the history of the universe. Every few months, a major discovery is announced that increases our knowledge of some aspect of Mega-Knowledge. Therefore, this generation is the first one to have the possibility of incorporating it into a common perception of reality. Therefore, the people who are currently living in the present are the first people who can derive the benefits of knowing what is really going on around here. Incidentally, none of the leading colleges and universities teaches the body of fundamental knowledge as a sequential whole.

Contained on the time line is everything that has ever been known to have happened. The history of every particle of matter and every quantum of energy in the universe is on that time line. Therefore, all reality is on that time line. All reality and therefore all knowledge is on that time line. The body of fundamental knowledge is that time line, and that time line is the body of fundamental knowledge.

When one also realizes that the time line is a series of cause-and-effect relationships, then the time line contains all the cause-and-effect relationships that have ever existed. This means that by analyzing the cause-and-effect relationships on the time line, we can discover the fundamental laws of the universe. By learning the story of that time line in chronological order, an individual can obtain an understanding of the entire body of fundamental knowledge, which is to say all knowledge. The individual is in a position to determine the fundamental laws of the universe for him- or herself. It is not possible to give more important knowledge than this to anyone, for all other knowledge is merely a subset of the story from the beginning of the universe until the present. It conveys to the individual not a mere world view, but a universe view. Everything has a context and a history within this view. Everything becomes understandable and fits and has a place. If the individual has a curiosity about any aspect of the story, then the individual should consider delving into it in more detail. From the individual's perspective all knowledge learned subsequent to learning the story of the universe can intellectually merely be dropped into the appropriate mental file folder. The overview of knowledge and reality gained by this perspective is quite literally the most fundamental and therefore the most important a person can know.

The subjects needed to be studied to understand the history of the universe and therefore the body of fundamental knowledge are included on the time line. Upon inspection of these courses, it becomes apparent that only two disciplines are involved—science and history. Therefore, all knowledge is fundamentally made up of science and history only. All other knowledge is merely a subset of these two subjects. If we analyze science and history more closely, it becomes apparent that recorded history is merely a subset of cultural anthropology, which occurred after the invention of writing. Therefore, from this perspective, all fundamental knowledge is only science in chronological order, or to look at it from the other side of the coin, all fundamental knowledge is the history of what has occurred in chronological order as discovered by science. From either perspective, the body of fundamental knowledge remains the same.

The power granted to us by understanding the body of fundamental knowledge (Mega-Knowledge) is awesome. For the first time in the history of the human race we humans can perceive the broad sweep of reality factually and accurately. The value of receiving this knowledge is inestimable. What the potential benefits to the individual and society will be from a coherent and in-depth chronological understanding of reality can only be estimated because no society in the history of the planet has ever before achieved this level of comprehension. The perspective from which we can not only view, but analyze, all things is provably correct. The amount of new thinking in fields ranging from anthropology, history, and biology to political science and economics contained in this book demonstrates the incredible power of this perspective. It is understandable that a genius like Leonardo da Vinci (1452–1519), working in the early Renaissance in a society primarily composed of illiterate peasants, could produce a wide range of new ideas and new thoughts, but to do so at the end of the 20th century, when half of all scientists who have ever lived are still working, validates the fact that we have finally come upon the body of fundamental knowledge. It is not the intelligence of the author, but rather the power of the techniques of logic in conjunction with the fundamental body of knowledge that permits us to solve virtually whatever problems we want. It is merely a case of, "What do you want to know?" It is as if all knowledge is a very complex jigsaw puzzle. Up until now the scientists and researchers have been, with great struggle and with great difficulty, fitting individual pieces of the jigsaw puzzle together. However, by knowing the body of fundamental knowledge we can now for the first time discern what the whole picture actually is that the jigsaw puzzle is making, and filling in the missing pieces is relatively easy. Anyone can do it. It merely requires the use of the Black Box Technique.

From our newly achieved perspective, a general understanding of the Fundamental Knowledge of the Universe, our relative position has shifted from one of hopeless puzzlement at how we can ever be able to understand what is fundamentally going on around here, to one of simply being able to ask "What would you like to know?" The problem changes from an inability to solve a question to one of being a keen enough observer of the world around us to be curious enough to ask the question in the first place. There is no fundamental law of the universe that states that an individual cannot know what, in the most profound sense, is going on around here. The only constraints to our perspective are those that we have culturally learned from previous generations, who demonstrably did not understand the Fundamental Knowledge of the Universe (Mega-Knowledge).[52]

The ease with which we can uncover new truths virtually wherever we focus our attention attests to the power and correctness of the fundamental body of knowledge and the Black Box. The new perspective from which we can view reality permits the reader to unlock truths that currently stump our experts. If everyone in our society shared this common perspective of reality, what a wonderful society America could be.

The dictionary definition of the word "ignorance" is "lack of knowledge." It is demonstrably true that all individuals from past societies lacked the knowledge and therefore were, by definition, ignorant of the profound forces governing their societies. Therefore, it is accurate to state that all individuals from past societies were profoundly ignorant. The author does not in any sense mean to imply that we are somehow better or smarter than those humans who came before us. On

52. The identification of the Fundamental Knowledge of the Universe is a discovery of this book, and is new knowledge in the field of epistemology (the study of knowledge).

the contrary, there is absolutely no evidence that indicates we are the least bit smarter than previous generations. The author merely desires to emphasize the qualitative advantage that understanding what is going on around here in a fundamental sense imparts to our generation over the generation of even a John Stuart Mill or a Thomas Jefferson.

The importance of this statement is not only the advantage it gives to our generation—the profound understanding of reality for the first time—but moreover, for the first time, we have the potential to control the cause-and-effect relationships that control us. The human species is very, very powerful. The sad news is that individuals in our society who, like individuals in past societies, lack this profound knowledge are also, by definition, profoundly ignorant. A democratic society wherein all individuals profoundly understand reality will have a significantly improved opportunity for cohesion and cooperative action by those individuals. Improved cohesion fosters more efficient sacrifice and therefore greatly improves the efficiency of a society to implement plans. An increase in the efficiency of plan implementation and in the citizens' ability to sacrifice means an increase in the chances of survival of that society, according to the Four Critical Abilities. Just as decision-making in the game of Monopoly mentioned in the Introduction became very easy when the rule book was read, decision-making in a democracy would become far easier if all the citizens shared a profound understanding of factual reality.

The Empowerment

The author is aware that most Americans feel powerless and insignificant compared to the events occurring around us. However, that feeling is incorrect. Let me explain why. America is the only remaining superpower.

That means we are the most powerful society on the planet. The sheer size of our economy causes us to have enormous impact on global markets. The impact of our economy is profound. For instance, a decision on from where or where not to import items without applying tariffs can literally cause the industrial revolution to come to a country. In the all-important arena of economics, the actions of the United States can determine, within limits, which countries can become economic successes and which cannot. It must be remembered we are very, very large and very, very powerful when compared to 95 percent of the other countries. In addition, we are relatively isolated from the rest of the world. We, in effect, have only two neighbors, Canada and Mexico, with whom we enjoy good to comfortable relations. In addition, we have a relatively short history. In an interesting paradox, we have one of the world's shortest histories but we have the world's oldest government. In short, the United States, by definition, does not have long-standing irreconcilable feuds with our neighbors or any other countries, such as do Bosnia and many, many other countries. Therefore, we are in the best position of any modern nation to be the fair and impartial leader of the world.

The difficulty is that the United States has been forced by the do-or-die nature of the Cold War to view its entire foreign policy through the lens of "How does this affect our relationship with the Soviet Union?" This, in turn, from the viewpoint of most of the other nations other than NATO members, causes them to judge us as a fairly poor leader insofar as achieving their goals is concerned. The leader, correctly, was concerned about the leader's survival and could not pay much attention to other matters. However, the situation has changed. The Soviet Union is no longer a military threat to our existence. The government of the United States has an opportunity, at least until the budget deficits catch up with us, to lead the entire world. Where are we, in fact, leading the

world? Who knows? Does the reader know of any foreign policy goals of the United States government? If we Americans do
not know, then who does? It is embarrassing to watch the
United States stumble around in search of a policy as we confront each crisis situation as if we had no idea that the country or countries involved had previously actually been on the
map. America has no foreign policy goals. If one has no goals,
no destination, one cannot be lost. We are not lost because we
are not going anywhere. We merely react when something
outrageous occurs on the international scene, without consis-
tency, scrambling for a policy, which usually leaves observing
nations with, at best, mixed signals as to our intentions.
Furthermore, because we have no goals, our intentions are
subject to change. Observing the post Cold War foreign policy
of the United States is reminiscent of watching a sultan of
the Ottoman Empire reclining on his cushions. The observer
does not know which fly will sufficiently irritate the sultan
enough to cause the sultan to halfheartedly wave his silk
handkerchief in the fly's general direction in hopes that the
fly will assume some less irritating position.

Historically, America has practiced an isolationist foreign
policy. When we have actually acted as the leader to the rest
of the world it was in reaction to a specific external cause for
a well-defined goal (World War I, World War II, the Cold
War). The United States has never led the world for the purpose of achieving global goals. We do not know how to lead.
However, leading is very easy. It becomes a much simpler
task when one leads to where the followers want to go! And
guess what? All the other nations, particularly the impoverished third-world nations, want a world free of war, free of
poverty, a society virtually free of crime in which all of their
material economic needs and wants will be supplied. The
world political scene would be very different from what it is
now if every nation knew and believed that the most powerful
and leading nation on Earth was implementing a plan whose

natural result would be, within this generation and getting closer every day, a world of peace, infinite wealth, virtual freedom from crime, state-of-the-art medical care to all citizens of the planet—and it will all be free.

Except for a handful of large nations, the world is composed of nations that are mostly the size of our states. It would be highly inefficient to attempt to jam into each country all the automated factories required to supply a fully self-contained economy. In some cases the number of factories required would almost outnumber the people. Therefore, the implementation would only be practical if the nations of the world were grouped into rather large economic regions, as Europe is currently attempting. Of course, those countries that are unstable, uncooperative dictatorships would have to be excluded because the other nations in the region would not want to rely upon a factory located in an uncooperative nation subject to disruption of supply. Therefore, rogue nations that do not cooperate with the international community, e.g. North Korea, Cuba, Bosnia, would be isolated. They could continue to exist for a while, but their days would be numbered. How long do you think the leaders of those nations will survive in office after the other nations of the world are enjoying "Economic Freedom"? The people of those nations will be driving donkeys and working very hard in the sun and/or cold while the rest of us only have to verbally make our wishes known to receive whatever we want. How long will it be before they beg to join the regional economy? How long will it be before the people of those nations tear their uncooperative leaders apart?

The only nation on Earth that can both lead the cooperative nations to "Economic Freedom" and defend the cooperative nations is the United States of America. However, the United States will forfeit the ability to lead if we experience the economic devastation that currently awaits us. Therefore, we have a relatively short window of opportunity to lead the world to a safe paradise. No other nation has the combination of attributes required to bring about this change. However, our current decadent, corrupt, and inefficient government also has no ability to bring about the change either.

Therefore, we, the voters of this country, have a small window of opportunity to vote and thereby cause the reform of our government, which in turn will create an efficient, properly functioning government, which in turn will be able to lead the almost six billion people of this planet to a wonderful future. As we have learned from the very meaning of the word "democracy," the people have the strength. The people have the ultimate responsibility for ensuring the proper functioning of a democracy. No form of democratic government, no piece of paper can protect a democracy if the citizens of that democracy become decadent and fail to take the steps necessary to elect representatives who will act in accord with majority wishes.

Roughly 65 million voters voted in the 1994 election. Then roughly 33 million voters could replace all the members of Congress. However, we only need 67 percent replaced. Therefore, roughly 22 million American voters or roughly 8 percent of the population of the United States hold the key to the future of planet Earth. Less than one half of one percent of the almost six billion people on this planet have it within their power to save the planet, and if you are a voter in this country, you are one of those people. Sadly, citizens who have not read this book have no clue to what is really going on around here. They do not even know which came first, the chicken or the egg. We are not powerless and insignificant. We are the world's only hope. We are the only people who can save the planet. Therefore, each of us citizens who has read this book knows that we are the most powerful people on this planet because only those of us who have read this book know we are the only ones who can act to save the planet. You, the reader of this book, have just become greatly empowered.

Thank you for taking the time to read my book. As you are by now painfully aware, my profession is not writing books. I am only a citizen like yourself. Goodbye and all the best in the future.

P.S. The reader is encouraged to re-read this book. Reading this book for the second time, already knowing what follows, will permit the reader to deploy the Black Box Technique and discover whatever the reader is interested in discovering. As we progressed on our journey in chronological order through this book, the first-time reader was continually placed in the position of knowing only one of the two periods of time required to Black Box (the past). The second-time reader, armed with Mega-Knowledge, now has an understanding of the second period of time, the future, which will occur after any unknown event. The reader is now in a position to effectively utilize the Black Box Technique. You can now fundamentally take control of your life and control the cause-and-effect relationships around you. It will become apparent to you that those people around you who are not deploying the Black Box Technique and not utilizing the Seven Steps are relatively unarmed and ill-prepared to deal successfully with life.

ABOUT THE AUTHOR

WILLIAM B. WILLIAMS was born in Chicago, Illinois, in 1945. After earning a B.S.B.A. from the University of Denver in 1969, he continued his post-graduate studies in business at two universities. The author taught at a Jesuit college when he was 24 years old. After a career that permitted him to retire from active participation in business at 39, Mr. Williams has traveled extensively throughout the world. His insatiable curiosity has led him to such varied activities as living with ex-headhunters in Borneo, tracking musk oxen in the Arctic, scuba diving in the Red Sea, hang-gliding, running afoul of the KGB, white-water rafting in New Zealand, talking his way into the top-secret Chinese Space Center, trekking in the Golden Triangle, being involved in a whip-duel with Mangarai natives in Indonesia, flying in a Russian MiG-25 to the edge of space at Mach 2.35, driving race cars, descending in deep-diving research submarines, and hot air ballooning over the Serengeti. Mr. Williams is a bachelor. As he puts it, "I eat when I am hungry, I sleep when I am tired, I go wherever I want, whenever I want, for as long as I want. There is no place I ever have to be, and no time I ever have to be anywhere, ever again. In short, I am free." Mr. Williams believes if society were properly managed, within this generation we would all be free.

The author can be contacted for comment by writing to:

Patriot's Publishing Company
P. O. Box 4307
Lisle, Illinois 60532

Fax: 708 663-9668
Internet: http://www.futureprfct.com

Additional books can be charged to a credit card for $29.95 per book or 4 books for $100, or 10 books for $200, by calling 1-800-209-9442. Operators are on duty now and orders will be shipped within 24 hours.

ANNOTATED BIBLIOGRAPHY

The following books are easily understandable by the general reader with no special knowledge base. The author strongly encourages the reader to pursue any subject in which the reader develops an interest. If the reader would like to go even deeper into an area of Mega-Knowledge, the author will share a technique he has found most valuable in learning the current state of the database in any particular field. The author calls the bookstore of our best colleges and universities and has them send their current course catalogue (the author recommends Harvard, Yale, Princeton, Stanford, MIT, CalTech, and Duke). After reading the course catalogues, the author determines which courses from which schools address the subject area(s) in which the author is interested. Then, the author calls the bookstore(s) back and orders the textbook(s) for those classes. The textbook(s) for a given class can usually be read in a week or two and normally cost under $100. Though it is not exactly equivalent to actually attending the class at the university, it also does not cost $3,000 per class, or take 18 weeks, nor do you ever receive a bad grade. This is a cost- and time-effective technique for determining whatever society knows that the reader wants to know. To go beyond what is currently known only requires using the Black Box Technique.

Many of the following books contain bibliographies that can lead the reader to other books that have bibliographies and so on until the reader is satisfied. Books are in order of relevance to the text.

Chapter Two—Take No Prisoners

Jastrow, Robert. *Red Giants and White Dwarfs.*
New York: Norton, 1990.
   This book is the recommended starting point for the general reader. It covers the period from the Big Bang to the arrival of humans on Earth. It is easy to read and to understand. For the reader without a background in science, this is a superb introduction to Mega-Knowledge.

Weinberg, Steven. *The First Three Minutes.*
New York: HarperCollins, 1993.
   Dr. Weinberg worked out the mathematics of the first three minutes after the Big Bang. Incidentally, this is part of the mathematical evidence we rejected in Chapter Two. However, do not be put off by this statement as the book itself is a fascinating narrative of the first three minutes of time and highly readable by the general reader.

Gribbin, John. *In Search of the Big Bang.*
New York: Bantam, 1986.
   This book is a more in-depth discussion of the Big Bang. It is easily read by those without a background in science and is very well written. Excellent for those interested in science's explanation of the early universe. If the reader's curiosity is still unquenched after the above three books, then it is time for the textbook approach described above.

Sagan, Carl. *Cosmos.*
New York: Random House, 1983.
   Of more general interest is an intellectual journey conducted by Carl Sagan. It touches upon many interesting topics of astronomy and displays the wide knowledge-base of its author. An intellectual tour-de-force.

Chapter Three—...in Some Warm Pond

Watson, James D. *Double Helix.*
New York: Penguin, 1976.
   This is a short, non-technical book about the discovery of the structure of DNA by one of its discoverers. It is interesting on several levels, one of which is the way scientific discoveries are made.

Darwin, Charles. *Voyage of the Beagle.*
New York: Penguin, 1989.
   If the reader has an interest in Darwin's theory of evolution, this is the book to read. Darwin's more famous *The Origin of Species* and *Descent of Man* were written primarily to answer the scientific debates at the time and are not easy reads. It is interesting to realize that at the start of the voyage, which was to take Darwin to so many places to study natural history, Darwin believed in Creationism. It was several years after the voyage that Darwin pieced together the evidence that led him to believe the theory of evolution. This is an edited version of Darwin's journal of the voyage.

Norman, David. *Prehistoric Life.*
New York: Macmillan, 1994.
   An excellent starting point for the general reader who is interested in the period from the inception of life on Earth through the development of humans. Easy to read, profusely illustrated, and highly recommended. If the reader were to read only one book on the evolution of life on Earth, this would be the one.

Curtis, Helena and Barnes, Sue N. *Biology*, 5th Ed.
New York: Worth, 1989.
   This is used as a textbook in college introductory biology classes and in advanced-placement high school biology classes. It is a thorough, well-written, and well-illustrated introduction to all areas of biology. However, for the general reader, its greatest value is probably in investigating a given area of biology rather than being read front to back. There seems to be a shortage of books written for the general reader explaining biology.

Chapter Four—Bye, Bye Bronty; Hello, Bonzo

Goodall, Jane. *In the Shadow of Man*.
Boston: Houghton Mifflin, 1988.
   This book is a fascinating account of Ms. Goodall's research with wild chimpanzees, humankind's closest relatives. I think it will surprise the general reader to find out how close we really are. Highly recommended.

Jurmain, Robert, and Nelson, Harry .
Introduction to Physical Anthropology,6th Ed.
St. Paul: West, 1994.
   This is a college textbook used for introductory classes in anthropology. It is extremely interesting and gives a good overview of the history of human ancestors. It would be an excellent introduction to anthropology for the serious general reader.

Chapter Five—From Caves to Cowsheds

Trinkaus, Erik and Shipman, Pat. *The Neandertals*.
New York: Vintage, 1994.
   Dr. Trinkaus is a recognized authority on Neanderthals and therefore is entitled to use the alternate spelling for them. The book is a complete and thorough history of the scientific investigation of Neanderthal. If the reader has an interest in the Neanderthals, this should satisfy it.

Burenhult, Goran, ed. *The First Humans*.
New York: HarperCollins, 1993.
   This is a superb overview of the current state of knowledge about the development of modern humans. It is wide-ranging, very informative, easy to read, and well-illustrated. This is also the book in which Paul Bahn and the reindeer-herding hypothesis are discussed. Published under the auspices of the American Museum of Natural History, it is the recommended starting point for the general reader interested in learning more about the history of modern humans.

White, Randall. *Dark Caves, Bright Visions*.
New York: W.W. Norton & Co., 1986.
   A lavishly illustrated book that gives the general reader a photographic introduction to the cave art of Cro-Magnon man.

Hicks, David and Gwynne, Margaret A.. *Cultural Anthropology*.
New York: HarperCollins, 1994.
This enlightening book is an excellent introductory college textbook for exploring the field of cultural anthropology. The author is aware of no better textbook for the subject.

Oates, David and Oates, Joan. *The Rise of Civilization*.
New York: E.P. Dutton, 1976.
A book for the general reader on the beginnings of the civilizations of the Middle East. Very easy to understand, well photographed, and brief at only 136 pages.

Time-Life Books (eds.). *Mind and Brain*.
New York: Simon & Schuster, 1993.
An excellent introduction to the current state of understanding of human brain function for the general reader.

Chapter Six—The Rise and Fall of Human Societies

Kramer, Samuel Noah. *History Begins at Sumer*.
Philadelphia: University of Pennsylvania, 1990.
An interesting and informative look at the first literate society. In addition, the book is useful if the reader would like to read the world's first love poems.

Gardiner, Sir Alan. *Egypt of the Pharaohs*.
Oxford: Oxford University, 1988.
This is a classic history of Egypt down to the conquest by Alexander the Great. It is clear, concise, and well written. The general reader who is interested in the history of ancient Egypt can do no better than this work.

Kees, Hermann. *Ancient Egypt*.
Chicago: University of Chicago, 1978.
This is the classic work on what life was like in ancient Egypt. A reading of this book and the Gardiner book above will give the general reader an understanding and knowledge of ancient Egypt exceeded only by that of Egyptologists.

Grosvenor, Gilbert M., ed. *Ancient Egypt*.
Washington: National Geographic Society, 1978.
An excellent, coffee table, photographic survey of ancient Egypt as only *National Geographic* can do it.

Lattimore, Richmond, trans. *The Iliad*.
Chicago: University of Chicago, 1951.
The author is not aware of another translation of *The Iliad* that can transport the reader's imagination to ancient Troy as this one can.

Hamilton, Edith. *The Greek Way.*
New York: Norton, 1983.
The classic work that gives an understanding of the importance and contribution of the Greek civilization. The method used is analyzing the society through the perspectives of its important authors. An easy, quick read that gives much food for thought.

Hamilton, Edith. *The Roman Way.*
New York: Norton, 1984.
The same is true of this work as *The Greek Way.*

Mattingly, Hugh, trans. *Tacitus: The Agricola and the Germania.*
New York: Penguin, 1970.
This book contains "de Germania," a short, easy read, and very interesting.

Gibbon, Edward. *The Decline and Fall of the Roman Empire.*
New York: Penguin, 1984.
The classic work on the Roman Empire. The original runs to over 3,000 pages, but this edited version is only 700 pages. This book is for the serious reader who has an intense interest in the story and causes of the collapse of the Roman Empire.

Holmes, George, ed. *The Oxford History of Medieval Europe.*
Oxford: Oxford University Press, 1992.
The recommended work for the general reader interested in the Middle Ages.

Durant, Will. *The Age of Faith.*
New York: MJF, 1950.
One of eleven volumes in the author's favorite survey of history. The length of the work permits the in-depth analysis required for making history come alive. Shorter works have a tendency to become a numbing blur of names, dates, and battles. It is nice to have a set of these books around so that the reader can dive in and out of them when the interest or need arises.

Durant, Will and Durant, Ariel. *The Lessons of History.*
New York: MJF, 1968.
This book uncovers many truths which from our new perspective we view as the fundamental laws of the universe.

Garraty, John A. and Peter Gay, eds. *The Columbia History of the World.*
New York: Marboro, 1981.
This is a concise history of the world. It is handy for checking dates and reading a different viewpoint on a given event. I suppose some overachiever could read the book front to back, but I am not sure what would be understood of world history.

Kennedy, Paul. *The Rise and Fall of the Great Powers*.
New York: Random House, 1987.
A well-documented and -researched account of the leading world powers from 1500 to the present. It pays particular attention to one of the most important areas most often neglected by not employing the Four Critical Abilities: economics. The book wisely admonishes the United States to be concerned with its economic future lest it fall victim as the other powers did.

Chapter Seven—Democracy Triumphant

Randall, Willard Sterne. *Thomas Jefferson*.
New York: Henry Holt, 1993.
A highly readable account of the life of Thomas Jefferson. The reader will learn much of interest about the great genius. For instance, the wisdom of Mr. Jefferson was not in the least bit diminished by his studying for up to 15 hours per day for more than a decade, wherein he read a sizable percentage of all the books extant at the time in the colony of Virginia.

Sinclair, Upton. *The Jungle*.
New York: Penguin, 1985.
A classic novel that exposed the corruption in the meat-packing industry and caused its reform. On a larger scale it showed the corruption of the U.S. Senate.

Nevins, Allan, and Commager, Henry Steele. *A Pocket History of the United States*.
New York: Pocket Books, 1992.
This is a short but nonetheless superb history of the United States.

Brinkley, Alan, and Current, Richard N., and Freidel, Frank and Williams, T. Harry. *American History*.
New York: McGraw-Hill, 1991.
A college textbook and high school advanced placement textbook that gives an excellent account of American history.

Chapter Ten—The Results of the Theft

Jackley, John L. *Hill Rat*.
Washington: Regnery Gateway, 1992.
This is an eye-popping, first-hand account by the press secretary to a U.S. Congressman. The sloth, decadence, and deal-cutting will make the reader boil.

Gross, Martin L. *The Government Racket*.
New York: Bantam, 1992.
This book is an excellent accounting of the waste and decadence of the American government.

Chapter Eleven—The Present to 2020

Fallows, James. *Looking at the Sun*.
New York: Random House, 1994.
   The highly regarded author gives an impressive analysis of Japan's threat to our society.

Ozawa, Ichiro. *Blueprint for a New Japan*.
New York: Kodansha America, 1994.
   Japan's leading politician lays the groundwork for Japan's emergent supremacy.

Cleary, Thomas. *The Japanese Art of War*.
Boston: Shambhala Publications, 1991.
   This book is must reading if the general reader is to understand the way Japanese view foreigners.

Thurow, Lester C. *Head to Head*.
New York: Warner, 1993.
   The noted MIT economist details the flaws in the American economy and offers appropriate solutions.

Chapter Twelve—The Present to the End of Time

Heilbroner, Robert L. *The Worldly Philosophers*.
New York: Simon & Schuster, 1992.
   For the general reader this book is the most interesting approach to the study of economics. It traces the evolution of economics by introducing the reader to those who made major contributions to economic thought, such as Adam Smith, David Ricardo, Reverend Thomas Malthus, John Stuart Mill, and John Maynard Keynes. Extremely well written and easy to understand by the general reader.

Smith, Adam. *The Wealth of Nations*.
Chicago: University of Chicago, 1976.
   The study of economics (or political economy, as it was called) was initiated by the publication of this classic in 1776 by the Scotsman Adam Smith. The remarkable thing is that it is still useful for learning the cause-and-effect relationships of economics.

Baumol, William J., and Blinder, Alan S. *Economics: Principles and Policy*.
Orlando: Harcourt Brace, 1994.
   This is a college textbook for introductory classes in economics. The author is aware of no more interesting introductory textbook to the study of economics. The amazing thing about economics is that once one understands it, economics is pretty straightforward and functions by relatively simple cause-and-effect relationships. It works much as the reader's personal economic situation does, only made much more complex by

the number of institutions involved. However, it probably takes a couple of years of study to appreciate the fundamental simplicity of economics. Unless the reader has a special reason to study economics, he will generally be on safe ground if he applies the same cause-and-effect relationships that apply to his personal economic condition to larger-scale systems such as businesses and governments.

Drexler, K. Eric, and Peterson, Chris. *Unbounding the Future*.
New York: William Morrow, 1991.
   Dr. Drexler is the guru for nanotechnology. An interesting vision of the future, which the reader is recommended to investigate.

O'Neill, Gerard K. *The High Frontier*.
New York: Bantam, 1978.
   This most interesting vision of the future is currently out of print and may be most easily accessed via the library.

Toffler, Alvin. *Future Shock*.
New York: Bantam, 1971.
   The dean of futurists is must reading. Mr. Toffler sees very well into the future.

PICTURE CREDITS

Index

Note: Page numbers followed by n
indicate footnotes.

THE TEXT of this book
was set in New Century Schoolbook
using QuarkXPress 3.3 and printed on 55 lb.
Quebecor Liberty Antique Cream/white paper.
The cover material consists of Teclar
Kid Skiver on .088 binder boards.
The end sheets are Antique
Blue Slate Permalin.